DATA CABLING

DATA CABLING

BY

NASIR ALI
TIM BROWN

KNOWLEDGE
BAKERS

KNOWLEDGE BAKERS

Cataloging in Publication Data--DK

Courtesy: D.K. Agencies (P) Ltd. <docinfo@dkagencies.com>

Nasir, Ali (*Writer on data cabling*), author.

Data cabling / by Nasir Ali, Tim Brown.

pages cm

Includes bibliographical references.

ISBN 9789391502454

1. Telecommunication wiring. I. Brown, Tim (Writer on data cabling), author. II. Title.

LCC TK5103.12.N37 2023 | DDC 621.382 23

ISBN: 978-93-91502-45-4

Published by : **Knowledge Bakers**
Pune, India
Email: knowledgebakers2019@gmail.com

Digitally Printed at : **Replika Press Pvt. Ltd.**

ACKNOWLEDGEMENT

Special thanks to my first supervisor, Professor Alistair P. Duffy, for his advice, guidance, support, criticisms, and comments during my regular meetings with him that made this PhD research and thesis possible. My thanks also go to my second supervisor, Dr Chris Oxley for his support and suggestions during this period with the University before retirement. I also acknowledge Dr Ammar Ghazal who stepped in as my second supervisor for his inputs to this work.

My appreciation also goes to Dr Hugh Sasse, Mrs Virpal Kang and Ms Florence Akinnuoye of the Electronic and Communications Laboratory, De Montfort University, Leicester, the United Kingdom for their technical assistance. I will also like to acknowledge the efforts of Paul Cave from Mayflex and James Withey of Fluke Instruments for their support in the measurements.

Finally, my special thanks to my wife, Mrs Ngozi Hope Arihilam and my children Charles Chigaemezu, Stephen Chibugo and Doris Chidalu for their incredible support, love, and encouragement throughout the period of study.

Tim Brown

PREFACE

Nonuniformity in transmission lines is known to be one of the causes of electromagnetic compatibility (EMC) and signal integrity (SI) issues, especially at high frequencies. This may include unpredictability in the manufacturing process, design constraints, tolerances in the values of terminal components, pigtail effects, etc., that can generate, common mode currents – with resultant degradation of signal performance of transmission lines with respect to ground. All these phenomena are capable of converting the desired differential mode (DM) signal into the unwanted common mode (CM) signal and vice versa. This study looks at cable nonuniformity resulting from irregular cable twists in twisted pair cabling, using the Category 6 UTP as an example, and considers this phenomenon responsible for signal mode conversion. Although twisted pair cables are generally often regarded as balanced transmission lines, the study shows that signal mode conversion is capable in twisted pair cables, and that makes twisted pair cabling a non-ideal balanced transmission line.

However, it is difficult to analyse nonuniformity using differential equations because of the changing per-unit-length (p.u.l) parameters throughout an entire line length. Because of this, experimental measurements based on mixed-mode s-parameters analysis are designed and used to show that twisted pair cables can convert a differential mode signal to common mode signal and thus cause radiated emissions to the circuit environment. A vital contribution of this study is in the measurement techniques used. Similarly, a common mode signal (represented by an externally generated noise signal) can couple onto the transmission line, and because of the physical structure of the line, the line could become susceptible to external noise. These phenomena are not associated with ideal balanced transmission lines. In either case, if the mode conversion is not minimized, it has the potential to affect the performance of the twisted pair transmission line in terms of bit error rate. Bit error rate, BER, is basically the average rate at which transmitted errors occur in a communication system due to noise and is defined as the number of bits in error divided by the total number of bits transmitted. Therefore, reducing mode conversion in a transmission line helps to reduce the bit error rate and indeed minimise crosstalk in the communication channel.

The experiments were conducted using a 4-Port Vector Network Analyser. The significance of using the 4-port VNA is that it has a general application in cable parameter measurement in the absence of specialized/customized measuring instruments.

Nonetheless, with some transmission line assumptions based on the Telegrapher's equation and applying the concept of modal decomposition, the mechanisms of signal mode conversion could be recognised. Consequently, an approximate first step symbolic solution to identifying EM radiation and hence DM-to-CM conversion and vice versa in data cable were proposed.

Dr Nasir Ali

Dr Tim Brown

CONTENTS

LIST OF SYMBOLS AND ABBREVIATIONS

3D	Three Dimensional
AC	Anechoic Chamber
BCI	Bulk current injection
BLA	Best Linear Approximation
BNC	Bayonel Neill-Concelman Connector
CUT	Cable Under Test
CE	Conducted Emission
CI	Conducted Immunity
CISPR	International Special Committee on Radio Interference
CM	Common Mode
CMRR	Common Mode Rejection Ratio
CST-MWS	Computer Simulated Technology-Microwave Studio
DM	Differenetial Mode
DPI	Direct Power Injection
DUT	Device under Test
EM	Electromagnetic
EMC	Electromagnetic Compatibility
EMI	Electromagnetic Interference
EMR	Electromagnetic Radiation
GSM	Global Systems for Mobile communications
GTEM	Gigahertz Transverse Electromagnetic cell
HBC	Human Body Communication
HPMP	High Power Microwave Pulses
IEMI	Intentional Electromagnetic Interference
IoT	Internet of Things
M2M	Machine -to- Machine
MAX	Maximum
MoM	Method of Moments

MSRC	Mode Stirred Reverberation Chamber
MTRC	Mode Tuned Reverberation Chamber
OATs	Open Area Test Site
PCB	Printed Circuit Board
RC	Reverberation Chamber
RE	Radiated emission
RF	Radio Frequency
RFID	Radio Frequency Identity
RI	Radiated Immunity (susceptibility)
RP	Reception Pair
SA	Spectrum Analyser
SE	Shielding Effectiveness
SVM	Support Vector Mechanism
TEMPEST	Transient Electromagnetic Pulse Emanation Standard
TL	Transmission Line
UWB	Ultra-Wide Band
Wi-Fi	Wireless Networking (Trade mark)
WNoT	Wireless Net of Things
WUR	Wake-Up Receiver
VNA	Vector Network Analyse

LIST OF FIGURES

LIST OF TABLES

CHAPTER 1

INTRODUCTION

1.1 Introduction

The concept of the Internet of Things, IoT [1], is used to refer to a variety of information sensing equipment and other short-range wireless and wired networks connected through a combination of a variety of access networks such as Wi-Fi, cellular phone networks, blue-tooth and the internet to form a vast intelligence network. Besides the use of wireless technology, the IoT infrastructure also needs wired channels including optic fibre for backbone systems. However, due to growing network needs and higher bandwidth requirements within the IoT applications, copper-based cabling (Ethernet) has become dominant technology. Ethernet which represents a global system of wires and cables that can be connected to multiple devices and machines began as a single cable. Today, Ethernet network can be expanded to devices as may be needed and is the most popularly used network technology around [2].

Moreover, Ethernet has the promise of growth with the coming of smart technologies in energy distribution, transportation and automotive applications. However, in the industrial environment, wired Ethernet has the disadvantage of crosstalk and environmental noise coupling to adjacent wire pairs [3].

Ethernet cabling (the twisted 4-wire pair) are arranged in pairs to propagate electrical signals down the transmission line for the following reasons:

1. Signals are propagated down an individual twisted pair, rather than using various signal wires plus a single common ground. This generates less distortion, at higher frequencies than the single common ground connection.
2. The twists minimise cross-talk and other forms of interference between signals in the same cable and between cables. On the other hand, twisting can also lead to severe reduction of the TWP immunity to outside fields.

Twisted pair cables can be either shielded (STP) or unshielded twisted pair (UTP). In STP, a conductive layer (typically aluminium metal foil), surround each pair and in some cases the entire cable. This shielding method helps reduce interference from either coupling to the cable or radiating away from it. Crosstalk is also reduced when individual pairs are shielded. The unshielded twisted pair, UTP, lacks shielding. It is less expensive, more flexible and much more commonly used, especially in new installations than the STP. However, the STP has a superior interference rejection ability, particularly when the shield sheath of the STP cable is adequately grounded [4].

Twisted pair cables are inexpensive and have application in structured cabling for data transmission (e.g. digital subscriber line (DSL), in wide area networks, (WAN) as well as in local area networks (LAN), responsible for delivering telecommunication, wireless and internet signals. TWP cables are also used for differential dc buses for power delivery in avionics where the TWP cables are meant to run above a metallic ground plane [5].

The TWP cable has as well become popular in many emerging applications like video transportation and can be expected to play a critical role in the emerging IoT. According to [6], the most fundamental role will come from machine-to-machine (M2M) connections which will boost manufacturing, agriculture, healthcare, industrial processing, and other professional services.

However, wires generally act like antennas and can send and receive electromagnetic waves. The conductors of twisted pairs cables are typically driven in differential mode, i.e., the signal at any point along the circuit is equal in magnitude and opposite in phase to that on the other point to ground. Therefore, outside electromagnetic fields (noise) coupling into the cable can induce the same interference voltage (magnitude and phase) into it – common mode coupling. Overall, noise coupling to the wires of a cable has the potential to interfere with data borne by the cable and thus make the cable behave more like unintentional radiator/antenna.

In typical network environments, terminal equipment and components at each end of the cable are designed to respond to differential mode signals only (by connecting the twisted pair through transformers (baluns and filters, etc.). As a result, the network is specifically designed to reject common mode signals and propagate the desired differential mode signal. Hence, though the twisted pair can pick up noise through signal coupling, throughout the transmission line length, this is done in such a manner that the terminal network circuitry rejects the unwanted common mode signal.

Moreover, the desired differential mode signal in wiring channels can convert to the undesired common mode and cause electromagnetic interference to other circuits within the environment. Both differential-to-common and common-to-differential mode conversion phenomena are known to be caused by some factors namely: imbalance due to line terminations and line cross sections, as well as nonuniformity in differential, interconnects.

Therefore the central research question in this study is: what effect does the twist nonuniformity have on the twisted pair cable in terms of signal mode conversion? The sub-questions seek answers to the following:

- Does the resulting mode conversion in TWP cable affect the immunity of the TWP to external noise?
- What level of signal emissions result from the TWP cable as a result of mode conversion? And how does it impact on adjacent circuits and the environment?

This work started with the measurement of mixed-mode s-parameters of fabricated symmetric (balanced) and asymmetric (unbalanced) test transmission line fixtures using a four-port vector network analyser. Knowledge from these test fixtures was considered for practical Ethernet (Cat 6 UTP cable) application where coupling can occur along a representative 10-meter length. The mixed-mode s-parameter analysis of the cable provided an understanding of the contributions of the differential and the common mode circuit characterization of the CUT at each stage in terms of return loss, RL, and insertion loss, IL, crosstalk and sensitivity of the s-parameter matrix to external noise sources, etc., as though the device functioned in its intended environment. Since single-ended scattering parameters do not rightly designate any DUT operational mode, differential devices are meant to function in differential mode.

Thus, this suggests investigating mode conversion in "long" cables where coupling can occur from the environment, adjacent cables or adjacent pairs. To do this, the current probe method of noise injection was used to represent localised noise and a noisy representative environment. It was expected that the investigation of these noise scenarios will help unravel the mechanism of noise coupling or whether the methods are related. A good way to do this was using the reverberation test method. However, comparison with localised coupling was useful to see whether a reverberation chamber was needed or whether the tests can be done on the bench using the current probe approach.

Furthermore, in implementing the current probe method, a measure of both emission and immunity of the twisted pair cabling (coupling attenuation) was investigated. This helped in verifying that the noise emitted by the UTP cable and the noise induced into the cable was within specified limits.

Hence, this research work investigates Measurement of Electromagnetic Noise Coupling and Signal Mode Conversion in Data Cabling and establishes the context, background and statement of the problem of the research topic. It also introduces the aims and objectives, contribution to knowledge and provides an overview of the report structure.

1.2 SE Performance Measurement of Protective bags

Although not documented in this thesis, one of the positive contributions of this research was the work done by the author on shielding performance tests of shielding and protective bags. During the period of this research work, the IEEE Standards project P 2710 ("shielding performance of enclosures for portable electronic devices") was approved, and input was advertised. The contribution on the shielding performance of protective bags proposed a test method to provide shielding information for protective bags and pouches of virtually any size. The test method was based on the use of a comb generator, and the reverberation chamber which operated in mode tuned. This contribution has been accepted and is due for publication in The Philosophical Proceedings of the Royal Society Part A, Vol. 1, with April 2018 re-submission deadline after minor amendments.

1.3 Research Background and Statement of Problem

Feedback from conversations between my research group and the cable industry showed an increased interest by the industry on how much of environmental noise is coupled to Ethernet cables. The issue of environmental noise coupling to ethernet cable and how much of noise can radiate from the cable has grown in importance in the light of increased speed of data transmission in recent times. As a result, high-speed data cables are showing evidence of increasingly becoming unintentional radiators owing to imbalances and manufacturing processes. Significantly, there has been no detailed investigation into how twist nonuniformity can contribute to imbalance in TWP cabling that could lead to EMI in data cables.

Differential signalling which is associated with balanced transmission lines can be described as a technique of transmitting signal in differential pairs, each on a different conductor, and has been identified by system designers [7] as a proper design priority to make differential circuits immune to interfering signals. Optimum design practice, therefore, requires that differential signals transmitted either by twisted pair cabling or traces on circuit boards minimise noise at their output ends.

Conceptually, the twisted pair cable (TWP) is regarded as a balanced transmission line. As the name implies, twisted pair cables have twists which are uneven all through the line length. These twists are useful in the minimization of coupled noise onto the cable from the external source. However, it has been predicted [8] that twist-pitch nonuniformity of a TWP running above ground and illuminated by a plane wave field plays a fundamental role in reducing the immunity of the TWP cable.

Mode conversion in transmission lines is known to give rise to interference and electromagnetic emissions to adjacent circuits. Hence, part of the aim of this study is to investigate the mixed-mode s-parameter cross-mode conversion in a Cat 6 UTP, as an example of a balanced line, and to determine if nonuniformity in cable twist could give rise to EMC or Signal Integrity effects.

The behaviour of transmission line structures to differential signals had been described in the past using parameter circuits. The application of computational electromagnetics (CEM) in modern engineering is now a popular design method. However, the mastery of the underlying mathematics and physics behind the numerical formulations still pose a challenge.

One of the most significant challenges of characterising the behaviour of differential structures using the impedance, admittance, hybrid and the chaining ABCD parameter matrix is that in using these parameters, circuits or devices must be in either open or short circuit conditions. With these circuit parameters, when circuits (DUTs) are tested in the open or short circuit at high frequency, they oscillate, that is, the device or circuit becomes unstable. Hence, in this work, the s-(scattering) parameters which are based on the functions of power waves, is used.

Describing networks with their scattering waves is essential, especially with an increased frequency of operation, so that the circuit elements are made a significant fraction of a wavelength (i.e., one-tenth of a wavelength). S-parameters are easy to measure with network ports terminated in its characteristic impedance.

1.4 Identification of Research gap in this Study

Central in this research is the analysis of noise coupling to network cables and systems in differential and common modes. Although the characteristics of differential and common mode noise coupling and its cross-conversion consequences to differential structures are established, researchers are still making contributions into new test methods to investigate cross-conversion of noise into ethernet cables. Manufacturers of most twisted pair Ethernet cables have tended to characterise the parameters of their cables using specialised equipment. This study aims at characterising these cable parameters using the mixed-mode s-parameter analysis for measurements made with a 4-port VNA.

It has been presented using computational method that cable twist nonuniformity is among the factors responsible for the imbalance in network cables pairs [9]. However, it is not certain whether an analytical approach to the same problem could yield that twist nonuniformity may have any role in twisted pair, (TWP), radiated immunity (i.e., TWP cable can operate satisfactorily when subjected to strong EM field). This indicates a need to understand the various perceptions of mixed-mode s-parameter cross conversion that exist, especially in network pair cables. Although some studies have characterised the behaviour of different differential structures, e.g., microstrip lines, at high-frequency using the impedance and admittance parameters [10], few studies have investigated the use of s-parameters to determine the performance of network cable.

However, it is not clear whether the twist property of a TWP cable could give rise to unintentional EMI, thus leading to radiation (EMC) and susceptibility (Signal Integrity) issues. Therefore, the goal of this research is to investigate the mixed-mode s-parameters of a UTP cabling and to find out if nonuniformity in the cable twist could contribute to mode conversion, and hence unintentional radiation and cable vulnerability issues.

1.5 Research Aim

I. This study is focused explicitly at investigating the characteristics of s-parameter mixed-mode noise conversion in balanced transmission lines, using Cat 6 UTP cable as an example, and to identify if nonuniformity in twist could contribute to making the TWP cable an unintentional radiator.

II. The narrow aim is to propose an approximate circuit model, valid for electrically short wiring structure, to explain the mechanism of mode conversion due to transmission line nonuniformity.

1.6 Objective

Unintentional noise coupling is a critical problem in high compactness circuits, and it is a proper design priority to make differential circuits immune to such interfering signals. For effective differential circuit designs, the aim of this research is to be achieved through the following objectives:

I. By designing, verifying the performance of and implementing reverberation chamber-based tests to investigate the performance of network cables at high frequencies.

II. By the design, fabrication, and stimulation of symmetric and asymmetric network components - transmission lines - using numerical modelling and by assessing their mixed-mode s-parameter performances using a 4-port network analyser.

III. Data sets will be extracted from the s-parameter performance of the test pieces to interpret the cable data.

IV. Data sets will be extracted from the current probe method and plotted to establish the conducted DM disturbance on TWP cable due to external noise.

V. Both data sets will be synthesised to find out if there is any relationship in the mixed-mode transmission behaviour between the microstrip lines and the TWP cable.

1.7 Contribution to Knowledge

I. The research presents an alternative test method for measuring the noise coupling performance of Ethernet cables in the mode-tuned reverberation chamber. This test method is suitable for both shielded and unshielded network cables, and the result can be extended to evaluate cable crosstalk and other noise parameters by cable professionals and installers.

II. Develop a test method that can help cable and system manufacturers assess the performance of their differential wares for EM emissions. The method which is for differential components and unshielded twisted pair cables can be extended to shielded cables, also.

III. Develop an approximate first step solution to predict the effect of twist nonuniformity due to manufacturing process based on the telegrapher's equation and modal decomposition.

1.8 Relating the Research Hypothesis to Cable Design

From the concept of mixed-mode analysis, it has been shown that if from the design stage cable wire pairs and differential transmission line components are made symmetrical (i.e. with equal dimensions), the chances are that such differential components and systems will not support DM-to-CM conversion and vice-versa. This will be demonstrated in the design and stimulation of balanced and unbalanced microstrip transmission lines (components) for cross-mode conversion using a 4-port VNA. The cross-mode conversion in the results will be related with that of a network cable for study.

1.9 Thesis organisation

The overall structure of the study takes the form of nine chapters including the literature review of previous research work and state of the art in chapter two. Chapter three is concerned with the methodology used for this study. The reverberation chamber test method is proposed as central in the test methods. This is emphasised in chapter three.

However, because of the need to include environmental noise in the tests, a balanced configuration of a 4-port VNA with a current probe was given consideration. The fourth chapter presents the measurement assessments for noise coupling to Ethernet cable. Chapters five and six deals with the measurement assessment on mixed-mode s-parameter on fabricated network components and cable. Chapter seven deals with measurements based on 1) coupling attenuation and 2) sensitivity of s-parameter matrix of Cat 6 UTP as test methods to establish the fact that the network cable can couple EMI to its environment and can be susceptible to external noise. The results and analysis of the research are presented in chapter eight. Chapter nine draws the conclusion and discusses future direction.

CHAPTER 2

LITERATURE REVIEW

This chapter provides some fundamental review of the concepts that shaped the research work. It also reviews current knowledge as well as theoretical and methodological contributions to the research topic. The subjects presented include a review of noise coupling to Ethernet cable, measurement techniques used, transient electromagnetic pulse emanation standard (TEMPEST), network cabling, intentional electromagnetic interference, IEMI, reverberation chamber and the mixed-mode s-parameter analysis.

2.1 Noise

Noise can be described as an unwanted signal which interferes with a desired signal. A noise signal can be transient or constant. Constant noise (e.g. electric/power line hum) can emanate from the predictable 50 Hz AC "hum" power line or from harmonic multiples of it and is capable of coupling to data communication cable when in close contact with it. Electrical noise coupling can take any of the following forms:

a) Galvanic

b) Electrostatic coupling

c) Electromagnetic induction

d) Radio Frequency Interference

Galvanic noise source can occur in data cabling when two signal channels in a signal data cable share the same reference conductor as common return path. In this way, the voltage drop across one channel appears as noise in the other channel and gives rise to interference. This form of noise coupling is often referred to as conductive common impedance coupling.

Electrostatic coupling occurs through various capacitances present in a network or circuit, between wires in a cable, between wires and ground, etc. The capacitances offer low impedance paths as noise voltages of high frequency are presented. This type is also referred to as capacitive coupling.

Electromagnetic induction expressed in terms of noise coupling is a course of action where a current carrying element located within a changing magnetic field creates a voltage across the current carrying conductor. As a result, this causes an induced current in the conductor.

Radio frequency interference, RFI, is the emission of RF energy from most electrical and electronic devices which can couple to adjacent circuits and are capable to impair or degrade the performance of such systems. The interfering signals can be emitted from devices such as switching power relays, personal computers, electronic printers, computing devices and laptops, etc.

Noise coupling to twisted pair cabling has been a growing concern to communication networks. This is so as communication speed continues to grow. It has been shown that to improve noise immunity and minimize radiation emission for UTP cabling is dependent on the type of balance of transmitted signal on the UTP. For a "perfectly balanced" UTP, (i.e. where wire-pairs are geometrically equal), induced voltages as a result of EMI are detected at the receiver and subtracted out. Consequently, the tendency of the UTP to act as an unintentional radiator is minimised by proper wire-pair balancing.

Hence, a perfectly balanced UTP will present absolute immunity and zero emission to noise.

2.2 Noise Coupling to Ethernet cable

Cables and wires have been known to be the most vulnerable parts of electrical and electronic equipment, hence this study is a contribution to numerous research works focusing on field-to-wire coupling in an electromagnetic (EM) field environment. In this chapter, experiments were conducted with two different network cables to determine the various levels of noise (EMI) coupling with respect to the frequency of interest. The tests were performed in a mode-stirred reverberation chamber, and the results were referenced to a standard receive antenna. The network cables selected for this test are Cat 5e UTP and Cat 6 UTP.

Category 5e UTP cabling is entirely backwards compatible and can be used in any application where a Category 5 cable would typically be used. However, apart from supporting the needs of Gigabit Ethernet, Category 5e UTP has enhanced channel performance. This improved cable performance quality was tested against Cat 6 UTP (for noise coupling) which can be used up to 250 MHz, and the results were compared.

Network cables are generally regarded as balanced transmission lines with a characteristic impedance of 100 Ω, and it used to be general practice to connect near ends of devices under test (i.e. the end connected to a 50 Ω coaxial connection cable) through a balun/balunless network for impedance balancing. A balun operates in the same way as a transformer and is normal because of unbalanced current (common mode current) induced on the exterior of the coaxial cable. However, conventional baluns with 1 MHz lower frequency tend to be limited to frequencies just a little above 1 GHz. Besides, a balun has restricted bandwidth, and this also affects the frequency characteristic of its use.

In this experiment, the test frequency in the reverberation chamber was chosen between 200 MHz - 6 GHz. This was to enable the chamber to have a high modal density and create a statistical uniform electromagnetic environment when stirred by the motorised stirrer. It is also to be noted that the DMU reverberation chamber has a lower functional frequency of approximately 200 MHz.

2.3 Measurement Techniques

This section reviews some widely used measurement techniques that are related to differential circuits. They are divided into analog techniques, RF/Microwave techniques, power measurement technique with baluns and scattering parameter measurement technique. Although the treatment of these techniques is not intended to be all-inclusive, it is presented to show the common types of measurement techniques typically used for differential circuits.

1. Analog Differential Measurement Technique

Conventionally, analog measurements of differential circuits involve direct measurement of voltages and currents which are restrained within audio range of frequencies [11]. This limiting factor is caused by the nature of distribution of circuits as frequency tends towards RF which affects the transmission line. The effects result in the voltage and current on the transmission which is dependent on the position on the line. Moreover, at RF frequency the parasitic inductances and capacitances become more meaningful and influence the performance of the device being measured. Accordingly, it is problematic to make apparent measurements of current and voltage at higher frequencies.

Typically, differential analog measurements use baluns (balanced – unbalanced transformer used as differential converters) to make an analysis of the DUT in differential mode. Nevertheless, these baluns (balance-to-unbalance) converters are not perfect, and they influence the correctness of the measurement which is difficult to remove [11] [12] [16]. One primary instrument used for analog measurement is the oscilloscope with input signals provided by a signal generator. Typically, the oscilloscope has high input impedance (usually 1MΩ), and this is ordinarily used for measuring voltages because the high impedance does not generally load the circuit. Figure 2.1 shows a schematic for an analog differential circuit measurement.

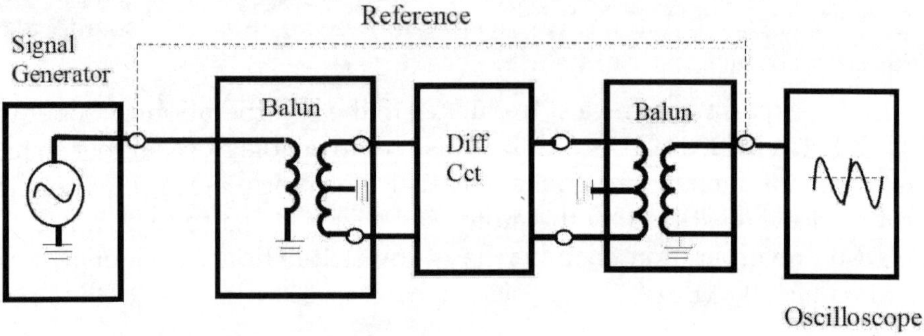

Figure 2.1 Analog Differential Measurement Technology

2. RF/Microwave Measurement Technique

With the RF/Microwave measurement technique, currents and voltages in differential circuits become unrealistic. In their place, proper measurements are made with the transmission of power waves [13].

However, the underlying problem with RF/Microwave measurement much like the analog measurement technique is the creation and reception of differential signals. Again RF/Microwave measurement technique requires baluns. Nonetheless, the significant difference with the baluns used for analog measurement is that the RF/Microwave baluns have greater non-ideal performance [14]. RF measurements can be made in differential-mode with the 180-degree phase shift RF power components like splitters and couplers.

These RF/Microwave measurements adopt single-ended inputs and outputs and are regarded as single-ended measurements [15].

3. Power Measurement Technique with Baluns

This is a broadly used type of RF measurement of differential circuits, and it can be used to determine the magnitude of the power. It can be implemented with a constant magnitude input applied across the frequencies of interest and gives rise to a gain against frequency characteristic. The diagram in Figure 2.2 shows a power measurement technique using a signal generator and a spectrum analyser.

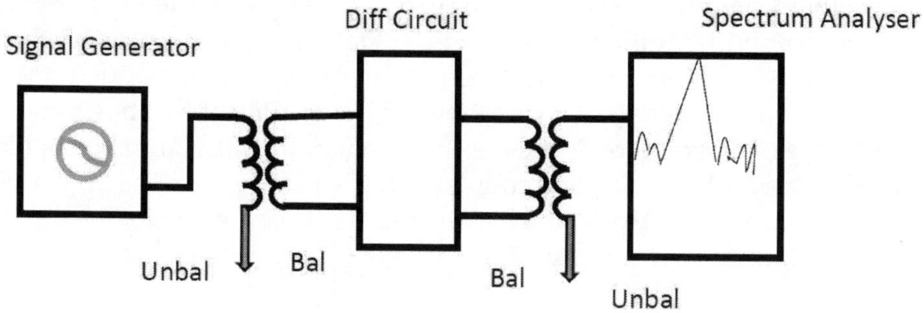

Figure 2.2 Power measurement technique using balun

The signal generator represents the RF source which passes through a balun and the differential circuit on to the measuring instrument, which is described here as a spectrum analyser. However, the use of the balun in this measurement technique introduces the balun effect earlier discussed in the analog method. This non-ideal balun effect which is specified in terms of loss, phase and magnitude imbalance are more challenging to remove than in the analog approach [16].

The RF balun in Figure 2.2 has an unbalance and a balanced side. At the balanced side, the single-ended input ideally is split into two equal amplitude with a 180-degree phase difference. With this equal amplitude split, a differential mode signal can be built.

Nevertheless, with the phase and magnitude imbalance, it means that the phase difference is not 180-degree and the magnitude of the split signal is not accurately equal. This also means that a clear difference signal will not be created with the power split.

At the spectrum analyser end, the phase and magnitude imbalance also affects the combination of the split signals in the spectrum analyser. This imbalance results in a false response to a common mode signal input into the spectrum analyser. However, the spectrum analyser cannot distinguish both the desired differential and the undesired common mode responses, and hence the overall performance accuracy is compromised.

For the spectrum analyser to be suitable for any application, its upper-frequency limit will have to be viewed. This is to ensure that the harmonics and the fundamental products of the measured quantity is displayed. To achieve this, the frequency range of the spectrum analyser must be extended beyond the fundamental frequency of the signal being measured. In most practical applications the figure used is about ten times the fundamental frequency.

4. Scattering Parameter Measurement Technique without Balums

Another common power measurement technique is the s-parameter measurement without the use of baluns [17] [18]. In this measurement approach, the s-parameter of a circuit is measured using single-ended input signals and output signals of a single-ended mode. One of the most typical applications of this method is the measurement of the differential response of a 180-degree 3dB branch line coupler using s-parameters. The approach uses a standard 2-port VNA which measures the s-parameters of the differential circuit as shown in Figure 2.3.

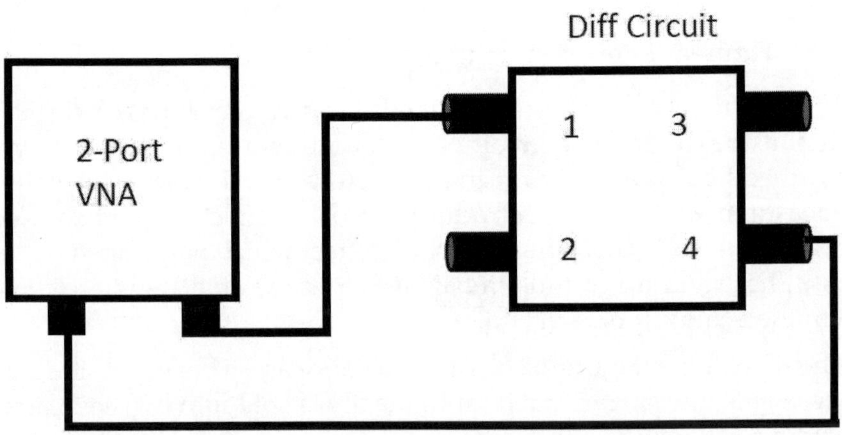

Figure 2.3 S-Parameter Measurement of a Differential Circuit without Balum

This measurement approach does not suffer from the effects of the use of a balun like the previous methods. Each arm of the transmission line is a quarter wavelength. The first port of the differential device is the input port; the second port and the third ports can as well be referred to as the isolated port and the direct ports, respectively. Apparently, due to symmetry, any of these ports can be used as the input port, but the output ports and the isolation port must be alternated accordingly. The magnitudes of *S31* and *S41* are typically equal, and their phase relationship is always 180 degree. The s-parameters are vector quantities and therefore represent both phase and magnitude measurements. However, one major limitation of this measurement technique is its inability to create a common and differential mode s-parameter response [19].

2.4 Transient Electromagnetic Pulse Emanation Standard

In this review, it is considered appropriate to discuss transient electromagnetic pulse emanation standard, TEMPEST, [20] because it borders on EMI emission and other compromise activities that could affect Ethernet and hard-wired IoT devices.

Wired devices and systems and their channels emit electromagnetic energy which can couple to adjacent networks and devices thereby causing EMC and TEMPEST issue.

EMC is defined as the ability of a device or system to function satisfactorily in its environment without affecting adjacent systems and devices or being affected by the environment.

TEMPEST which is a code name used by the USA National Security Agency (NSA) is a natural consequence of electromagnetic interference. TEMPEST is also being associated with monitoring of devices that diffuse electromagnetic radiation, EMR, theoretically that can be intercepted and reconstructed into understandable data. The analysis of apparent side-effects in the physical behaviour of a system which could lead to the failure of the system has been referred to as side-channel attack [21]. Regarding TEMPEST, detectable emissions in the form of electromagnetic signals from devices and the cache access pattern on a shared system could be reverse engineered to reproduce details of what is being emitted as electromagnetic emission. However, in the modern digital world, cryptographic algorithms have helped to secure information, but its efficiency on side channel attack is dependent on the capacity of an attacker monitoring the behaviour of a secured system.

The term TEMPEST originated in late 1960 with a code word used by the United States government. However, it later became an acronym for Telecommunication Electronic Material Protection from Emanation Spurious Transmission [22]. Today, the description of the concept has been replaced by (Emission Security), but the term TEMPEST remains popular. The National Communication Security Committee Direction 4 of the USA sets typically the TEMPEST standards, NACSIM 5100A.

One of the TEMPEST standards SDIP-29 [23] defines RED to mean electrical/electronic equipment, cables, systems and areas which process, transmit or store unencrypted or classified information. The standard also uses BLACK to indicate electrical/electronic equipment, cables, systems and areas that process or store encrypted or unclassified information. The standard also stipulates that a minimum of 10 cm separation distance should be maintained between RED and BLACK cable lines to avoid noise coupling. The relevance of separation could be explained due to the fact that increasing cable separation in an installation means a practical solution for decreasing cable crosstalk below the resonant frequency [24].

2.4.1 Practical TEMPSET Activities

In the proposed IoT, there are two significant ways to interconnect devices and systems to the internet. These are by wireless or hardwired (Ethernet). In either case, two things happen. One, electromagnetic noise is coupled through the medium into the communication channel. Two, inevitable electromagnetic radiation of waves in the form of conduction or radiation of electromagnetic radiated wave is often possible. This may result in information disclosure. Related research has shown that with appropriate equipment and technology, these "compromise emanations" from devices can be picked up and then reconstructed to reveal some confidential information on the original data being transmitted. Relevant research [25] [26] also show that IEMI receiver equipment located in about 1000-meter distance from the emanating radiation can pick up the emanation.

Computers and other forms of electronic devices are made of all kinds of transmission lines, signal processing circuits, clock circuits, displays, printed circuit boards, switch circuit, etc., which can be regarded as comparable antennas. In addition, computers contain power cords, telephone wires, ground wires, etc., which can also be a source of the leak of electromagnetic energy. Comparable antennas can propagate radiation of electromagnetic waves which can be regarded as a part of the communication system. In all these cases, the free space for transmission can be considered as a channel and the radiated emission as the compromise emanation. Compromise emission has been defined as an unintentional intelligence-carrying signal, which if intercepted and evaluated, can reveal the confidential information which is being transmitted [20]. Hence, to protect emanations from intelligible data from being intercepted and reconstructed, computers, laptops, cellular phones and most other portable devices need to be adequately shielded. It was in the light of the above that the work on shielding effectiveness of protective and pouch bags, though not covered in this documentation, was carried out.

In summary, TEMPEST represents a methodology to investigate, measure and analyse compromising emissions and the way to prevent processed information recovery.

2.5 Network Cabling

Network cables are typically used in local area networks LAN and are generally divided into two main groups – fibre and copper. Copper based cables are further divided into unshielded twisted pair (UTP), shielded twisted pair (STP) and coaxial cables. For decades, copper-based cable has been used for communication links, but more recently fibre optics communication has come into use because of its increased bandwidth and higher immunity to EMI. Fibre also offers a better resolution to connections above the most upper range of copper cabling.

Twisted pair cable contains eight copper wires that has each two-wires twisted together. Current flowing through each wire of the twists generates magnetic fields around the wire. When the wires are near and are each carrying current in different directions, the magnetic fields thus formed are the exact opposite of each other. The fields, therefore, cancel out. The field cancellation is enhanced by the cable twist. Among other measures introduced by cable designers and manufacturers to improve cable shield against EMI and crosstalk, twisting is fundamental to external noise cancellation. The Table 2.1 below gives a comparison among network cable types.

Table 2.1 Classification of Network cable

Type	Worth	Installation	Capacity	Range	Sensitivity to EMI
Co-axial (e.g. RG -11)	Below fibre & more than STP	Easy	Typically, 10Mbps	500 meters	Less than UTP
STP	Below Co-axial & greater than UTP	Fairly Easy	Typically, between 16 Mbps to 500Mbps	100 meters	Less than UTP
UTP	Comparatively cheaper than all types	Less expensive	Typically, 10 Mbps-10Gbps	100 meters	Most sensitive
Fibre	Topmost	Difficult & expensive	100 Mbps – 20,000 Mbps and more	10s of Kilometres	Very insensitive

The history of UTP cabling dates to 1881 when Alexander Graham Bell first used it in his telephone system. In EIA/TIA – 568 for Commercial Building Telecommunications Wiring Standards [27], the acronym "UTP" is specified as "Unshielded Twisted Pair" cable. The standard specifies among other things that the electrical properties such as attenuation and crosstalk of the UTP as well as other physical properties like cable diameter and colour coding. The standard is continually being revised to add new definitions to cable categories.

Each twisted pair of a UTP represents the "go" and "return" paths of a complete circuit. They may consist of stranded copper each covered with plastic coded colour insulation. In some applications, the two twisted wires are referred to as the tip and the ring wire.

2.7 Recent Standards development affecting Cat 5e and Cat 6

Most frequently, the UTP cable is referred to as Ethernet cable because it is the most common type of cable used in network connections. The name Ethernet is given to a set of standards for interacting related physical elements of a wired network [28] [29] [30] and how they handle data. The UTP has a characteristic impedance of 100 Ω, and the gauge of the copper conductors are 24 with a diameter of about 0.5106 mm. The transmission performance of the UTP is guaranteed up to 100 meters between devices. However, technically the distance restraint is 90 meters for structured cabling and a total of 10 meters for patched cord on either side [31]. However, for experimental purposes, a representative/typical 10-meter length has been used in most of the experiments reported in this work. This length of cable is considered long enough to highlight all the characteristics of the cable when tested.

2.6 Most Popularly Used UTP cables

Till date, Category 5e and 6 UTP remain the most popularly used UTP cable. Cat 5e (which represents the enhanced version of Cat 5) supports gigabit Ethernet (up to 1000 Mbps speed) over a short distance and is backwards compatible with structured Cat 5 [27] [32]. Cat 5e is specified for a bandwidth of 100 MHz. The Gigabit Ethernet Standards defines that Cat 6 cable has protocols that make it compatible with Cat 5e. Cat 6 is specified for performance up to 250 MHz. Accordingly, Cat 6 is a superior choice for 100Base-Tx (fast Ethernet), 1000Base-T/1000Base-Tx (Gigabit Ethernet) and 10GBase-T (10Gigabit Ethernet) [33]. The experiments in this work have also reported on the superior performance of Cat 6 over Cat 5e cable.

Cabling

Formally known as IEEE 802.3bz – 2016, 2.5G/5GBASE-T [34], the standard allows a signal speed fit for 2.5Gbps [34] to be transmitted across standard Cat 5e structured cabling. The standard also allows a 5Gbps speed of signal transfer in normal Cat 6 twisted pair. This creates an intermediate speed between the existing 1Gigabit and 10Gigabit Ethernet which cannot run on Cat 6 but requires specialised Cat 6a or Cat 7 cabling.

A clear majority of institutions, offices and homes are wired with category 6 and category 5e cabling for their network connection. It will, therefore, be costly to upgrade the speed of transmission of such structured cabling in other to avoid slowing down the rate of data transfer. The new intermediate 2.5G/5GBASE-T standard allows end users to transmit 2.5 gigabit of information per second (2.5Gbps) over the stipulated 100 meters using Cat 5e and 5 gigabits of data per second (5Gbps) over 100 meters for Cat 6. This higher speed means that all the 4-pairs will be used to transmit and receive data simultaneously. This is different from the 10BASE-T, and the 100BASE-TX where one twisted pair of the cable is used for transmission and another pair is used for reception, thus leaving the other two pairs as unused. Other moving stipulations of the new standard include the rolling out of Power over Ethernet standards PoE, (PoE+ and UPoE) [35] from Wi-Fi access points. The Table 2.2 below shows the stipulations of the new standards for Cat 5e and Cat 6 UTP.

Table 2.2 Compares Cat 5e and Cat 6 UTP Ethernet-based technologies

IEEE Std. 802.3bz	Cable type	Speed	No. of cable pairs	Bandwidth	Std Cable length	Cable Spec. (100m.)
2.5GBASE-T	Cat 5e	2500Mbps	4	100MHz	100 meters	100MHz
5GBASE-T	Cat 6	5000Mbps	4	200MHz	100 meters	250MHz
10GBASE-T	Cat 6A	10,000Mbps	4	400MHz	100 meters	500MHz

2.8 Intentional Electromagnetic Interference

Intentional EMI has been described as a malicious propagation of electromagnetic wave energy which can introduce noise into electrical and electronic systems, hence disturbing, complicating or damaging the systems either for illegitimate or extremist purposes [36] [37].

In [38] (IEMI) is identified by field strength (radiated) or voltage and current amplitude (conducted) with consideration to the distance between the source and its victim, only. The threat posed by IEMI is increasingly becoming a source of concern with electronics controlling many aspects of modern life from driverless cars to smart devices. Electronic components such as microprocessors, are functioning with progressively higher frequencies and lower voltages and have become more and more vulnerable to intentional EMI. Intentional EMI is conceivably striking since it can be embarked on clandestinely at some remote area from physical obstruction, such as walls and fences.

IEMI radiations may come in two forms. They may be in the form of high-power microwave (HPM), creating narrowband high-frequency energy, which can cause a 'front door' damage (e.g. in low noise amplifiers), or ultra-wide-band (UWB), high time-domain pulse energy, which can cause "back door" disruption (e.g. in control rooms), etc. [39].

High powered IEMI could cause disruption and damage when targeted to Financial Systems, Power Networks, Industrial Plants, Telecom Systems, Computer Networks, Traffic Control Systems, Medical Care, Radio/Television Networks, [40] etc.

In this study, EMI (noise), was generated and limited to the reverberation test chamber. The generated IEMI noise generated was confined in a test environment, and by mechanical stirring, a statistically uniform electromagnetic field thus created, provided the enabling test environment that replicated the DUT's working environment. The extreme noisy condition offered in the reverberation chamber provides a "worst case" environment akin to the operating environment of any device under test.

Options as per the standards [41] [42] such as the use of cable shields/fibre optic cables, ferrites, adding filters and surge arresters at connections to cables are suggested to mitigate IEMI. Nevertheless, the most economical approach is typical to employ electromagnetic shielding, which is suitable at frequencies above 1MHz.

In [43], a low-inductive 360°-feedthrough element was used to increase the shielding effectiveness of a screen room effectively as shown in Figure 2.4.

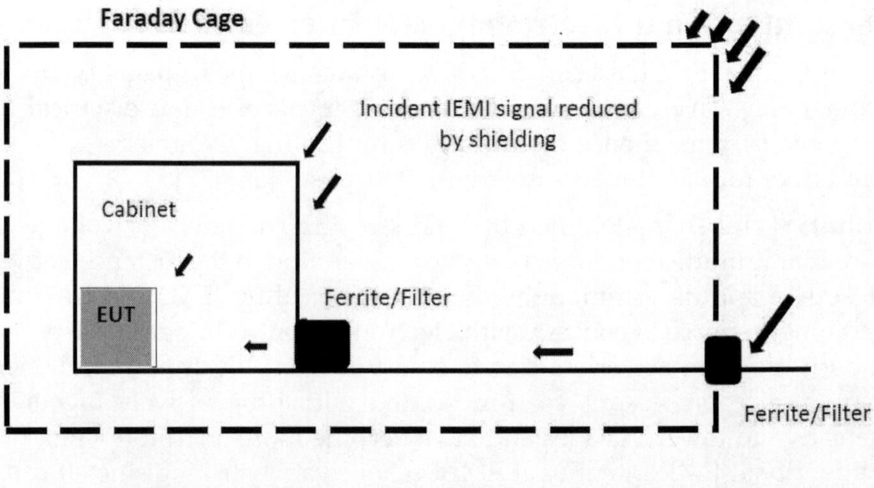

Figure 2.4 showing the concept of Faraday cage

However, no clear explanation was given on how the length of the cable inside the screen room would affect the SE. [44], suggested the use of pulse suppression devices as a possible defence against IEMI on network cables. However, the experimental results showed a lack of clarity on why speedy turn-on times were typically more extensive which may make the devices not suitable for very high frequencies.

2.9 The Reverberation Chamber Test Facility and Review of Literature on Noise Coupling and Cable Radiation Conducted in the Reverberation Chamber

This section of the literature review is dedicated to the reverberation chamber because it is intended to be central to the measurements made in this study. A good understanding of the theory of the reverberation chamber, the operation of the test environment and all the test instruments associated with it is vital to the accuracy of any test performed in the chamber. The section discusses the reverberation chamber facility in the Centre for Electronic and Communications Engineering of De Montfort University, Leicester, UK. Additionally, the segment also reviews measurements on EM noise coupling and Radiated Immunity tests which are all tied to the research topic.

2.10 Definition

The reverberation chamber has been defined as an electrically large, highly conductive resonant enclosure whose minimum dimension is significant relative to the wavelength at the lowest usable frequency and is used to perform EMC tests [45].

Primarily, it consists of a rectangular cavity with one or more metal mode stirrer having dimensions being substantial fractions of the dimension of the chamber [46]. When the chamber is stimulated with RF energy, the stirrer stirs the multi-mode EM environment to create the necessary field environment which is statistically uniform and statistically isotropic [47] [48].

2.11 Theory of the Reverberation Chamber

Over the past decades, most EMC tests have been carried out with the use of the reverberation chamber. Being a metallic enclosure, the reverberation chamber has a method of exciting modal structure changes within the enclosure with the use of stirrer. Its test environment represents a superposition of plane waves with random phase, which is continually being reflected by the metallic surfaces. Again, because of the actions of the stirrer, a statistical, isotropic and uniform electromagnetic environment is created inside the chamber which enables a robust, all aspect angle test, thereby eliminating the need for rotation or translation of the equipment under test. The test environment thus created emulates the real-world working environment of the equipment being tested.

EMC tests can be divided into four wide-ranging groupings: conducted immunity/susceptibility (CI), radiated immunity/susceptibility (RI), radiated emission (RE) and conducted emission (CE). This can be shown in Figure 2.5 below:

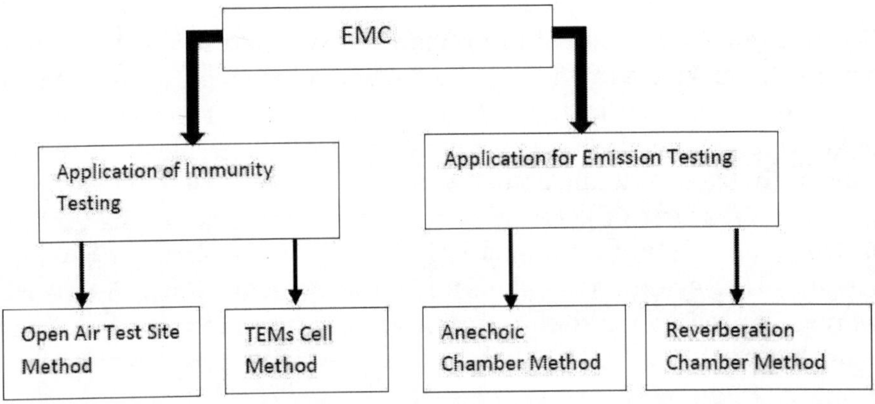

Figure 2.5 Two applications and four methods of EMC testing

Modes

The chamber functions like a multimode resonator whose modal resonant frequency is given by:

$$f_{m,n,p} = \frac{c_o}{2}\sqrt{\left(\frac{m}{l}\right)^2 + \left(\frac{n}{w}\right)^2 + \left(\frac{p}{h}\right)^2} \quad (2.1)$$

where c_o = speed of light

m, n, p = integers representing the number of half modes in a given direction.

l, w, h represents the length *(l)*, width *(w)* and height *(h)*, respectively (only one of which may be zero).

Additionally, the stirred EM environment alters the 'boundary conditions' within the chamber to cause a lot of changes in the standing wave pattern. These standing waves combine to create the modes (or maximums) and subtract to form the nulls [49]. These modes and nulls produce a field within the working volume that when averaged over one complete revolution, provide a statistically homogeneous and isotropic field that completely baths any object under test.

2.12 Operation

The standard (EN BS 61000-4-21) [46] recommends two methods of operation for the reverberation chamber.

Mode Tuned Operation

In this setup, the field energy is determined at several distinct individual frequencies for separate positions of the stirrer. Next, the stirrer is then relocated to another location, and the test is done again. The resulting set of measured data is then averaged over all stirrer positions with respect to the frequency of interest.

Mode Stirred Operation

This setup requires that the stirrer turns around at a continuous speed and a group of test measurements are made and averaged at each frequency before changing over to another frequency.

2.13 The Chamber Dimension and Operating Frequency

The lowest usable frequency of a chamber is a factor that determines how efficient a reverberation chamber will perform. [50] Stipulates that one of the methods used to determine the lowest usable frequency of a reverberant room is three times its fundamental frequency.

Theoretically and according to a generally accepted rule of thumb [51], the lowest operating frequency for the chamber to be used must support 60 modes. Since the DMU reverberation chamber has the dimensions of 5.00m x 2.95m x 2.36m, its lowest resonant frequency is approximately 174 MHz, although 200 MHz has always been adopted [52]. A further explanation regarding the chamber minimal mode density is that it shows how many modes a chamber needs to have for proper operation [53] and this can be determined by:

$$N_{s(f)} = \frac{8.\pi}{3} l * w * h \left(\frac{f}{c} \right)^3 - (l + w + h) * \frac{f}{c} + \frac{1}{2} \qquad (2.2)$$

where N_s = number of modes, f = frequency of propagation, l, w, h [53] are the dimensions of the chamber.

At a frequency of 1 GHz, therefore, the DMU reverberation chamber has a minimum mode density of approximately 10800.86, which is significantly higher than 60. This shows that the room has sufficient modes to support field uniformity beyond 200MHz frequency. Yet another critical parameter specified by the standard is the working volume.

2.14 The Chamber Working Volume

Often referred as the "uncluttered volume", this is defined as having $^{\lambda}/_{4}$ distance from the chamber walls, the transmit and receive antennas and the stirrer assembly. Since the DMU chamber has the lowest usable frequency of approximately 200 MHz, the chamber volume can be taken to represent the volume occupied by a distance of 1.5 meters from the chamber walls. For accurate measurements in the chamber, it is desired that devices under test be placed on non-conducting frameworks within the working volume.

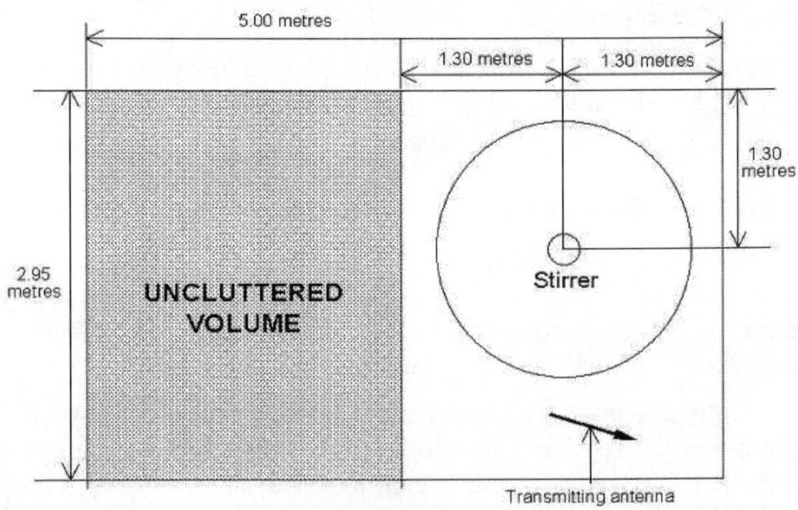

Figure 2.6 showing the test volume of the DMU reverberation chamber [52]

2.15 Stirring and Field Uniformity

The reverberation chamber can be fitted with one or more rotating reflective stirrers which rotates to alter the "boundary condition" within the chamber. The reverberation chamber test method has been known to show a reasonable level of comparable accuracy over a broad range of frequency because of its tolerance to minor changes. For instance, the results of susceptibility tests conducted using two similar, but different size reverberation chambers at NIST (National Institute of Standards and Technology) revealed that the results were comparable even when the input power requirements were different [54].

Hence, the statistical uniformity of the electromagnetic environment can be controlled by the stirring action of the motorised stirrer. The amplitude, phase, and polarisation at any position in the reverberation chamber is affected randomly by some steady statistical distribution principle [55]. Thus, tests conducted in the reverberation chamber can be regarded as a kind of random course, much as the reverberation chamber can provide the following:

a) Spatial uniformity: where the density of the energy in the chamber space is uniform in all directions.

b) Directional uniformity: where the energy flow in any direction is uniform

c) Random polarisation: where the phase angle of the electromagnetic waves and their polarisation are arbitrary.

The DMU reverberation chamber has a transmit and a receive antenna of the Bi-log type. The receive antenna is typically connected to a designated port 2 of a measuring instrument. Usually, the transmit antenna is stimulated by the RF signal from port 1 of the VNA. The chamber has an installed 2-Port VNA. At a designated RF power, the transmitter antenna directs RF wave energy into the room, and this electromagnetic energy is reflected by the walls of the room and the stirrer assembly. Since the reflected energy is limitedly absorbed, high intensity of electric field strength above 200 V/m can easily be generated by relatively less power input [55].

2.16 Comparing Reverberation Chamber Technique with Other Test Methods

Compared with the Open Area Site test (OAT) and the Anechoic Chamber (AC), the reverberation chamber test method is more sensitive to emission tests. The reverberation chamber is also capable of generating high field strength in immunity tests with modest amplifier power where power amplification is needed. Moreover, the cost per square meter of the reverberation chamber is cheaper than an anechoic chamber. This is because the reverberation chamber has no absorber materials on its walls. In emission testing, the reverberation chamber test method is the one technique that has the capacity to measure incidental path loss by regulating the reflected signals [56]. However, in the OAT and AC, the incidental path loss is controlled by the test environment [57]. This can be illustrated in Figure 2.7 (a) & (b) shown below.

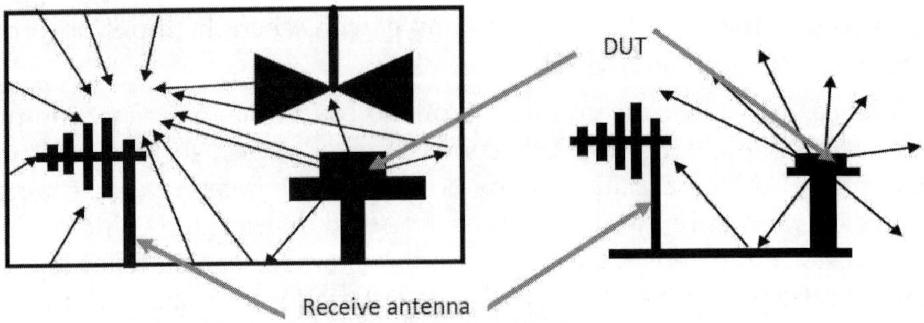

Figure 2.7 (a) showing RC Emission testing & (b) Open Area Testing

Figure 2.7 (a) illustrates emission testing conducted in a screened RC environment with the walls of the chamber and the stirrer assembly reflecting (regulating) the emitted signal from a DUT toward a receive antenna. Fig 2.7 (b) shows that much of the emitted signals from the DUT is lost to the environment except those from ground bounce and those incident on the receive antenna through line-of-sight. This is also the case in the AC where the emitted signals are absorbed by the absorber material the line the walls.

2.17 Reverberation Chamber & Review of Electromagnetic Noise Coupling

Twisted pair cabling is extensively used in network communication, signalling and computer technology, because they provide slight resistance to electromagnetic and alternating magnetic fields due to the proximity of the pair in the cable and the twist regime. The unshielded category of cables is the most widely used because they are cheap and not difficult to install; although some of the older legacy category cables have been superseded.

Legacy category cables [58] can be described as old communication cables that may still be in operation. From the introduction of low-speed analog Cat 1 which was used for transmission of voice and data at 100 KHz to Cat 3 cable, the speed of transmission of legacy category cable have been improved to about 16 MHz which was the frequency typically used for applications such as integrated service digital network, digital subscriber lines, LAN, and analog voice transmission. However, these legacy cables together with Cat 4 were replaced by Cat 5 which is specified for application requiring bandwidth up to 100MHz. Moreover, the Cat 5 (which is unrecognized by the standard TIA/EIA) may be unsuitable for 1000BASE-T gigabit ethernet and has itself been replaced by an enhanced Cat 5e version.

Following increased industrialisation, the demand for the use of Ethernet for automation and industrial systems control grew substantially. This enabled the use of Ethernet cable in industries for gathering real-time information on production and streamlining operations. Today Ethernet cables are found in other harsh environments like the medical environment where humidity, chemicals or other EMI are prevalent.

Cat 5e, which is an enhanced version of Cat 5 is still being used by installers for new installations. It has added qualities that support bi-directional communication and is compatible with Cat 6. It is also specified for 100 MHz. Backward compatibility makes it possible to use equipment without the need for new features.

In [59] the field-to-wire coupling of noisy electromagnetic fields that are statistical in nature was coupled to an unshielded twisted pair of wires and analysed. [60] Replicated the setup in an over-moded mode-stirred reverberation chamber and tested for the susceptibility of the twisted pair cable placed within the test volume of the chamber, at about one-quarter of a wavelength from the chamber antennas, the stirrer assembly and the chamber walls. The result showed that stronger twisted lines had more coupling occur at lower frequencies. However, this result did contain potential measurement error, though the author did highlight that without adequate explanation. In [61], the theory of transmission-line (TL) was used to model an electrically large cavity, and the problems of field-to-wire coupling were examined, and a semi-analytical solution was presented. Among the finding is that coupling of noise is dependent on the height above the ground and the matching at the load terminal. The paper revealed that if the load at one end is smaller than the characteristic impedance (load mismatch), that end can be regarded as short, or open if the load is higher than the characteristic impedance. But if one end is matched to the impedance of the line, then the coupling is most robust at that end when the other end is not matched (reflected wave energy because of mismatch). However, the paper did not provide information on the critical length at which this would occur since he used a model approach. [62] performed the same measurement test in a GTEM cell and concluded that a substantial spread of results could be predicted that strongly depends on the geometry of the wire and the direction of excitation. Comparing a system of two cavities [63], decided that the electric field energy distributed in a reverberation chamber cavity which follows a Rayleigh distribution, can couple to a small cavity through an aperture. It has been demonstrated

[64] that two apertures could be used to connect the two chambers and the result showed no excellent agreement with the expected double Rayleigh distribution. The study did not offer an adequate explanation for that result. Therefore, using nested reverberation chambers to determine the field coupling through multiple apertures should be treated with caution, as the coupled energy could emanate from other sources in the operational environment.

2.18 Reverberation Chamber and Review of Electromagnetic Radiation Tests

Electromagnetic radiation from cables and systems is believed to be mainly from unintentional common-mode signals distributing on lines bearing differential signals. Noise radiated from these sources would result in electromagnetic interference that can affect other electronic devices and systems in the adjacent environment. Such radiated noise can also be the source of radio-frequency interference that deteriorates the operation of digital radio systems including Wi-Fi and Bluetooth.

[65] experimented with how electromagnetic interference radiating from a cellular phone is coupled to medical devices and in aeroplane systems. Radiated immunity tests with (mobile telephone) GSM-modulated signals on equipment is always performed per IEC 61000-4-3. However, the choice of first investigating the radiation pattern of three different cellular telephones mounted on a turnable structure with both elevation and azimuth angles was explored in [64]. Perhaps the most severe disadvantage of this method is the choice of different makes of GSM phone for this test. It has been known that different types of GSM phones produce different radiation patterns. Hence, there will be inconsistencies in the generated radiation patterns. The 3D radiation patterns of the cellular telephones revealed this and the 2D cross-section does not seem to provide enough information on the radiation patterns.

In [66] the radiation pattern from different lengths PCB trace running on broadband harmonic frequency signals was investigated. Digital devices radiate a rich harmonic frequency component field which is responsible for the radiated emissions. Part of this radiated emission coupled to the PCB traces thereby making the PCB traces to begin to behave as unintentional radiators. From the results, the radiation intensities increased as the length of the PCB traces [65]. However, the exact formula to interpret these phenomena were not provided.

In [67], details of CISPR and IEC standards on different methods to determine the radiated interference on electronic equipment were explained to the extent that radiation tests conducted in a reverberation chamber should have the height of the receiving antenna to vary between 1 meter to 4 meters. The receive antenna should also be mounted on a turntable. This is to enable the receive antenna pick up both the "line-of-sight" signal from the EUT and the bounce off from the ground. A specified number of sampling points are recommended by these standards for determining the maximum radiated fields. This implies that for frequencies above 1 GHz, various sampling methods could be used to predict the highest radiated electric field. From the result, the highest radiated E-field strength showed good agreement when compared with the simulated effect. However, not much information is made available to the reduced number of sampling that was used in the experiment.

The use of a high-powered microwave (HPM) radiation to cause permanent damage to electronic equipment. The methodology used consists of the smallest power density needed to damage an object within a frequency range, by means of a reverberation chamber (RC). A modest battery-powered electronic circuit was generally tested in this experiment. The EM power density needed to cause permanent damage to the performance of the circuit was determined with respect to the pulse length. Although the author got some impressive results below the pulse width of 3 μs, at the frequency of about 2 GHz, the results show that with the pulse length of about 3 μs, the experiment could not achieve adequately high field strength to destroy all circuits. One of the limitations of this account is that it does not explain why sufficient destructive EM energy could not be generated in the RC.

Since full analysis of noise coupling is likely to rely on the mixed-mode s-parameter analysis in order to determine the common and the differential noise coupling modes (CM & DM), the next phase of the work is devoted to reviewing the literature of s-parameter mixed mode analysis, with emphasis on cross conversion mode.

In the radiation experiments explained in chapter 7, a 4-port VNA configured in 1-balanced and 1-single was used with a current probe to investigate the electromagnetic radiation from Cat 6 UTP cable. The same mixed-mode s-parameter approach was used to examine the susceptibility of the same cable to external interference. More like the reverberation chamber test method, the balanced VNA with the current probe approach also took into account the environmental noise factor.

2.19 Mixed-mode S-Parameter Analysis Reviewed

The history of mixed-mode s-parameter analysis began in 1995 with Bockelman and Eisenstadt who pioneered the method to interpret differential-mode DM, common-mode CM and differential-to-common mixed-mode DM-CM conversion for a case with no coupling [69]. The duo later in 1997 presented a method of converting from the traditional single-ended to mixed-mode s-parameter. [70] later simplified the theory of [69] so that mixed-mode s-parameter can be functional not only to differential circuits with differential ports but likewise to other networks with single-ended ports as well. This conversion method has been extensively used ever since in many publications [71] [72 [73]. [74] noted that a network transmission line should be designed to have noise coupling between the pairs such that outside noises are coupled in common mode. Nevertheless, in strongly coupled differential networks, neither the common nor differential mode impedances are equal to the characteristic impedance [75] of the network line. Thus, the commonly used conversion method causes inaccuracy when used for networks with differential signalling [76].

The scattering parameters (s-parameters) are used to represent the dispersal or uneven distribution of a signal by a DUT. The dispersed signals are the transmitted and reflected electromagnetic signal waves that are generated when the DUT is excited by an incident wave. Mixed-mode s-parameter analysis provides an understanding of the contributions of the differential and the common mode circuit characterization of a DUT at each stage in terms of attenuation/insertion loss, return loss, and cross conversion, etc., as though the device is functioning in its intended environment.

In this study, the DUT includes fabricated differential transmission lines in symmetrical and asymmetric configurations and a network cable structure. The aim is to investigate the cross-mode conversion in the structures and to identify the property(s) of the structures that is responsible for mode conversion.

The mixed mode scattering parameter analysis provides a transformation matrix that takes care of the odd (differential) and the even (common) mode impedances and hence averts mismatch and distortion in the balanced network. However, if the edge-to-edge spacing of the conducting paths of the fabricated structures and the signal pattern being transmitted through the differential lines (in this case, the out-of-phase differential and the in-phase common mode signals from the VNA) are to vary, the characteristic impedance of the line would change. This would make the line become a coupled transmission line.

In general, to determine mode conversion in differential structures, two methods are used: i) modal impedance matrix method, and ii) s-parameters (mixed-mode) method. In this study, the mixed-mode s-parameter method is used because of ease.

2.20 UTP Cable Twist Nonuniformity

Several authorities have investigated the effects of external electromagnetic field coupling to twisted pairs of wires where the frequency-domain response of the CUT was illuminated by a plane wave electromagnetic field was derived in closed form. [77] generalised the concept for arbitrary incident and polarised angle and [78] proposed a worst-case model to address the field-to-wire coupling problem while [79] restated the TL model by solving the Taylor inhomogeneous TL equation in closed form for a single TWP in free space. One criticism with the afor-mention contributions is the assumption of the TWPs running in free space which does not seem to agree with real practical application where TWPs are installed in close proximity to planer metallic "ground" structures, e.g. onboard spacecraft, thus enabling the coexistence of DM and CM voltages and currents.

[80] formulated an analytical solution for radiated electromagnetic field from coupled traces based on mode decomposition technique and far-field Green's function. This solution was used to predict the EMI from different differential microstrip pairs with time domain input signals having different slew rate and varied amount of skew. [81] proposed a circuit presentation of mode conversion by introducing the concept of weak imbalance using the microstrip line as the wiring structure.

In both [80] and [81], microstrip lines were used as the wiring structure with geometric imbalances resulting from different skew or asymmetry on the line length. In this work, it has been assumed (and rightly too) that real-world TWPs present a certain amount of nonuniformity, i.e. asymmetry in the line length. Moreover, in recent times, new generation of cables have been introduced with TWPs intentionally manufactured with random twist nonuniformity to optimise cable crosstalk performance [82] [83] [84].

The question then arises if attempting to optimise cable crosstalk performance by introducing twist nonuniformity may not lead to compromising the immunity of the TWP cable.

Chapter Summary

In this chapter, different analog and RF/Microwave measurement techniques have been reviewed bringing out the non-ideal balun effect which is specified in terms of loss, phase and magnitude imbalance.

Also, conventional network cabling has been studied particularly the widespread use of Cat 5e and Cat 6 UTP even in recent times. The study has also dealt with the contemporary standards development affecting Cat5e and Cat 6 cabling in terms of Gigabit Ethernet.

The study has also attempted to summarise the perception of transient electromagnetic pulse emanation standards (TEMPEST) as it ties up with the research topic. It has been shown that the concept which originated as a code word represents a methodology to investigate, measure and analyse compromising emanations and the way to avert processing information recovery. Compromise emanations (radiations) are elements of unwanted noise signal which, though may contain some intelligence, can couple to the adjacent circuitry; hence investigating its cause in terms of mode conversion is central to this research work.

The DMU reverberation chamber is used to create the IEMI research environment where DUTs are tested as though in their intended operational environment. Therefore, understanding the principles of operation of the chamber is paramount in this research.

Mixed-mode s-parameter analysis offers an arrangement to investigate the parameters of a DUT. Depending on the configuration of a 4-port vector network analyser, it can be used to make various cable parameter measurements. As part of the analyses performed in this study, it was used in conjunction with a current probe to determine the emissions from both Cat5e and Cat 6 UTP cables in 3-port configuration.

Also, the sensitivity of the mixed-mode s-parameter matrix of Cat 6 UTP was tested in 4-port configuration to ascertain how susceptible the cable is to external noise.

Finally, the question of twist nonuniformity in TWP cabling was considered. Since real-world TWPs present certain apparent degree of non-uniformity in twisting, the question of its role in the compromise of the TWP immunity was then introduced. This will be thoroughly discussed in chapter seven.

CHAPTER 3
METHODOLOGY

This chapter presents the different approaches used in the experiments conducted in this research and articulates the reasons for choosing a particular test procedure. It also explains how data was acquired and interpreted for each method.

Basically, three significant experiments were documented to justify the research topic. They include 1) Tests on noise coupling to Ethernet cables at higher frequencies. For this study, the decision on the test method was made following feedback from the industry who showed interest to investigate the performance of Cat 5e and Cat 6 network cables in harsh environment as networks expand. It was considered that the best simple approach to adapt for this investigation was the potential divider method with specified impedances to connect the CUT through 50 Ω SMA-to-BNC connectors to a 2-port VNA which served as the test instrument. The whole setup was to be mounted in a mode-stirred reverberation chamber. 2) Mixed-mode s-parameter noise analysis of network cable with a four-port vector network analyser. The mixed-mode s-parameter method is one of the more practical ways of investigating signal mode conversion. Using the test method on the experiment of noise coupling to Ethernet cable, the result agreed with the fundamental concept that noise can couple to any transmission line. As a result, it was further decided that the best method to investigate whether the coupled noise can make the transmission line act like an unintentional radiator, capable of radiating interferences, was by using the mixed-mode s-parameter analysis. One advantage of the method was that it gave a measure, in dB, of what differential signal (desired signal) could convert to common mode signal (noise) and vice versa. The configuration used in the experiments enabled the sixteen element mixed-mode performance characteristics of the cable which was used in the analysis. 3) The use of the current probe method to investigate the TWP cable emission and susceptibility. Following through from 2), the current probe method was used to characterise the emission of EMI in both Cat 5e and Cat 6 network cable using the s-parameters. The configuration used in the test setup was a one balanced, and one unbalanced three-port configuration with the fourth port of the test instrument terminated in 50 Ω impedance. One consideration for setting up the 3-port test instrument in a test bench instead of conducting the experiment in a reverberation chamber was that the DMU reverberation chamber test facility has an installed 2-port VNA. Moreover, it was easier to include the instrument noise floor in the measurement when the setup was configured outside the chamber. Overall, the methodology used which also consists of the test setups in each experiment can well divide into three:

- The reverberation chamber test method with a 2-port VNA
- The 4-port mixed-mode s-parameter test method
- The current probe test method using a 3-port configured VNA

However, before the use of any of these test methodologies, the measuring instrument was first calibrated for impedance anomalies, and the test instrument was set to a reasonable low noise floor.

3.1 Instrument Calibration

Test instruments are usually calibrated for accurate measurement. To calibrate an instrument, a standard that has got a considerable level of accuracy of the DUT is required. Over time, test instruments are knocked "out of calibration" when the significant parameters of the test (e.g., reference voltage, current, etc.,) radically shift or fluctuate. This shift could be typically negligible and frequently harmless when instruments are well calibrated on schedule. Mostly, the process of calibration is to detect and apply impedance corrections.

3.2 Calibration Procedure for 2-Port and 4-Port VNAs

Calibrating an instrument against known impedance standards helps to reduce the error terms of the test instrument to a negligible value. A full 2-port calibration of the 2-port VNA test instrument was done manually with a calibration kit using the SOLT (short, open, load, thru) standards of 50 Ω characteristic impedance. With the SOLT calibration standard, the forward and converse transmission and reflection quantities of the measuring instrument was calibrated. To do this, the ZV Z19 Series of the test ports RF coaxial cable and the standard calibration kits were used. One after the other, each standard was connected to the reference plane. After that, the two orientation planes were connected as one to make a through (thru) final measurement. The SOLT calibration has the advantage of addressing each of the sources of error across a broad band of frequencies. Figure 3.1(a) show the calibration of a 2-port VNA being calibrated for use.

For the 4-port configuration used in this study, an auto calibration was applied. After connecting the analyser to the calibration unit and initializing, all the ports were then connected to the calibration unit using the RF connectors. The ports were then selected and by means of the calibration wizard, the calibration was performed. The RF test cables were then removed from the unit and replaced by the DUT and calibration was performed. Figure 3.1 (b) shows the 4-port VNA being calibrated. Internally, the analyser compares measurement data of the standards (standard cal) against their ideal performance when a DUT was connected. The difference was used to generate system errors and to obtain a set of system error rectification data. The generated error information was then used to fix the measurement results of the DUT. Figure 3.1 shows (a) Calibrated 2-port and (b) 4-port VNA.

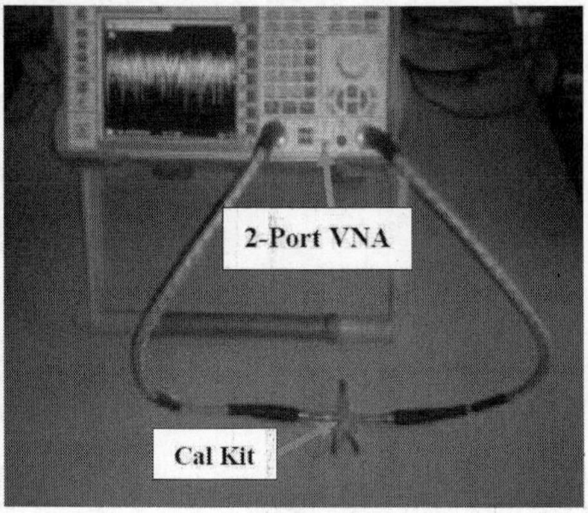

(a)

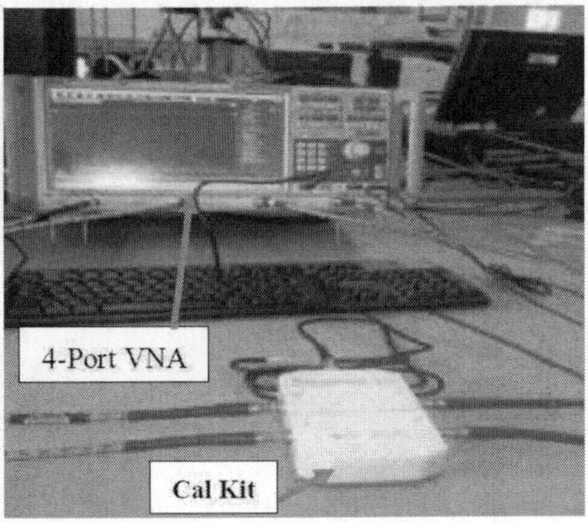

(b)

Figure 3.1 Showing (a) a 2-port and (b) a 4-Port VNA being calibrated

3.3 Instrument Noise Floor setting

The noise floor can be described as the lowest level at which signals can no longer be discerned. It is basically the inherent noise contribution of the instrument in any measurement. Although the 2-port and 4-port VNA were used in the test methods, the technique of setting the instrument noise floor also applied to the use of the Agilent CAS N1996A Spectrum Analyser in the work on the SE for protective bags (not documented in this research). For a general noise floor setting of the test instruments, the following steps were employed:

- Adjust the resolution bandwidth of the test instrument to show how significant a signal can be displayed in the manifestation of the instrument internal noise level.

- Apply averaging on the displayed noise signal. Noise and measurement errors could be random and systematic in nature. By averaging, the values of the uncertainties in the instrument true reading of the noise floor measurement is made smaller.
- Continue to reduce the resolution bandwidth so that the integrated bandwidth will continue to diminish and hence, the integrated power is also reduced
- Reduce the instrument power reference level to 10dB by reducing the attenuation of the instrument
- Finally, the optional internal preamplifier of the instrument may be engaged to raise the input signal above the instrument noise, thereby making it easy to view low signal amplitudes.
- The reduced noise floor can then be viewed by turning on the power spectrum density to appropriately adjust the y-axis to display power level in dBm/Hz.

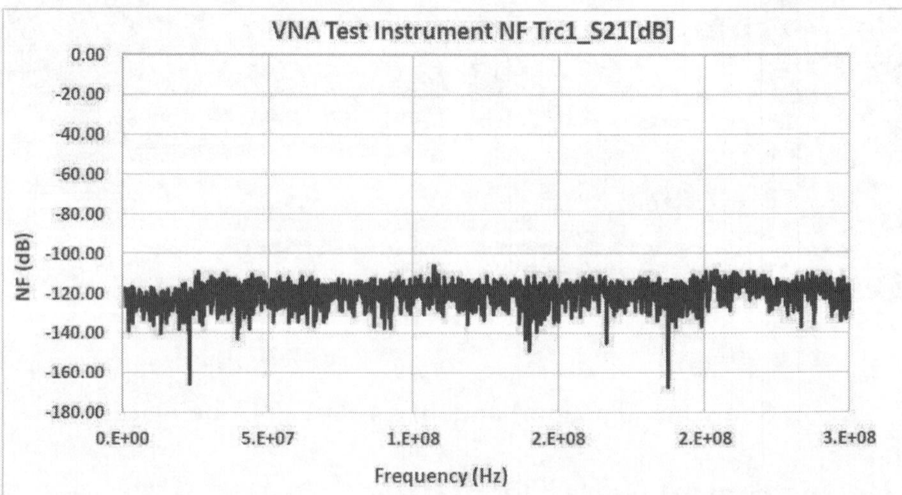

Figure 3.2 Showing typical noise floor measurement

Fig 3.2 shows the instrument noise floor for the Rohde & Schwarz ZNB 8 VNA between 200 MHz - 250 MHz set to between (-110.5 dB and -120 dB).

3.4 The Reverberation Test Method with 2-Port VNA

EN 61000-4-21 standards [46] endorses that for EMC tests performed in a mode-stirred reverberation chamber, stepped stirrer movement be used because of the dwell time requirement of the equipment under test. In this test, the mode-stirred method (2.3) was used, and the stirrer was positioned at a specific angle of rotation while measurements are taken. This method ensures continuous rotation of the stirrer and provides that the equipment under test remains uniformly exposed to the chamber electric field strength for the duration of the test. Nevertheless, manually staying the stirrer at each test just to record results and start all over again require a longer time. Because of the enormous amount of time involved in this stepping movement, the standards recommend that at least 12 exclusive stirrer positions be used.

A different approach to stepping the stirrer is to operate the stirrer in a continuous mode. In it, the stirrer is continuously rotated while the test is on. This can significantly curtail the test time and, eliminates any mechanical crackling effect associated with the start-stop operation in the stepped movement [85]. However, the tradeoff in both stirring methods is that the mode-tuned operation is generally better for application within 0.2 GHz to 2 GHz frequency where the density of modes in the chamber is not as high, while the mode-stirred approach is more superior for some application above 2 GHz frequency [86].

3.5 Measurement Setup

Figure 3.3 shows a typical experimental setup for the reverberation test method. It consists of a mode-stirred reverberation chamber of dimension 5 m x 2.95 m x 2.36 m. The setup also had a 2-port Rohde & Schwarz ZVL Vector Network Analyser (VNA), a Bi-Log transmitter antenna, UTP cable under test, a test bench and a function generator which generated the pulses that triggered the stirrer motor. An N-type to BNC connector was used to connect the VNA using a 50 Ω RF coaxial cable through the chamber bulkhead. The transmit antenna was positioned at one of the edges of the chamber working volume and was excited by the RF signal generated from the output port of the chamber VNA.

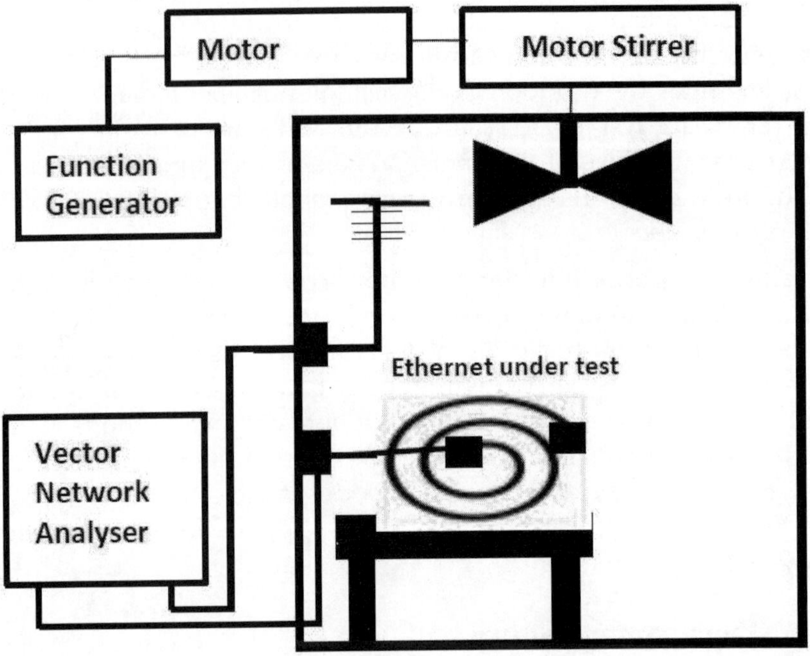

Figure 3.3 Typical experimental setup for the RC test method

Figure 3.4 Showing cable under test in the reverberation chamber

The chamber walls and other support devices inside the chamber reflected the exciting fields and created a multipath environment (wireless environment) throughout the chamber volume. The transmit antenna was located to point away from the cable under test to prevent direct coupling (Gaussian coupling) [87]. The cable under test was situated in the working volume (the valid test volume of the chamber) where it experienced in full, the Raleigh channel (reflections from the channel walls) [88]. However, after one complete revolution of the stirrer, the average received power can be described as constant (isotropic), irrespective of the transmit antenna location and orientation. This meant that the device under test received an equal amount of field energy from all directions of the incident wave in a rich isotropic reference environment. The benefit of using the reverberation chamber in this experiment was that it had the ability to create statistically uniform and statistically isotropic test environment.

3.6 Measurement Specification

The measuring instrument was specified as hereunder:

Instrument specification	
Start Frequency	200 MHz
Stop Frequency	6 GHz
Power Input (dB)	-10 dBm
Instrument reference level	0 dB Meas.
BW	10 KHz
Instru. Noise floor	-110.5 dB
No of Meas. Points	401

In making this specification, the nature of the CUT, the type of the test undertaking (in this case environmental noise coupling at high frequencies) and the test instrument limits to obtaining an accurate measurement were considered.

3.7 The 4-Port S-Parameter Test Method

The test method for a four-port s-parameter specifies the mixed-mode s-parameter test method. It was preferred for its ease of interpretation, completeness and accuracy to characterise a device under test. In mixed-mode measurement, only 2 ports are involved. Each of these ports was aggregated as balanced ports (theoretically carrying both common mode and differential mode signals). The measurement approach helped to characterise the behaviour of the device under test.

The study of the four-port s-parameter measurement of the microstrip lines was used to gain insight into the transmission behaviour of balanced and unbalanced lines. Since the Cat6 UTP is generally regarded as balanced line, the result of the s-parameter measurement of the microstrip was considered helpful in understanding the transmission behaviour of the cable. Nevertheless, both the cable and the microstrip lines were not tested at the same frequency because the Cat6 UTP is specified at different frequency, but the s-parameter results showed good ground to gain knowledge of the behaviour of the Cat6 UTP cable, especially in the cross conversion mode. As a result, the mixed-mode s-parameter performance results of the test fixtures were related to the cable and the results were used to approximately interpret the cable behaviour.

First, a balanced (symmetric) and unbalanced (asymmetric) microstrip lines were fabricated as shown in Figure 3.5 with 4-ports and characterised using the 4-port VNA. Both were configured as balanced lines and their behaviour as transmission lines were investigated. The purpose of the experiment was to examine mode conversion in both the balanced and the unbalanced lines.

Second, a representative 10 meter Cat 6 UTP cable was characterised using a test head designed using CST MWS suite and fabricated by the author at the PCB Router facility of De Montfort University Interfacing Laboratory. The behaviour of the cable was also investigated. Additional tests were also carried out to investigate the sensitivity of the cable s-parameter to external noise. Details of the test head fabrication are discussed in chapter 7.

For the 4-port VNA test method, a differential mode impedance of 100 Ω and a common mode impedance of 25 Ω were used. However, the reference impedance of the measuring ports is 50 Ω. These were selected as the default impedance values from test instrument measurement menu. The implication of this selection is that the phase difference of the forward DM and DM-to-CM s-parameters (S_{dd21} and S_{cd21}) has automatically been set to 1800. Likewise, the phase difference for the CM and the CM-to-DM forward s-parameters (S_{cc21} and S_{dc21}) have equally been set automatically to 0° by the measuring instrument. All the measurements were made in a single sweep across frequency resulting in a magnitude (dB gain/loss) versus frequency characteristics. Details of the test specifications are shown below, and the results are discussed in chapter seven.

Figure 3.6 shows a differential microstrip line under test. Figure 3.7 shows the Cat 6 UTP being tested.

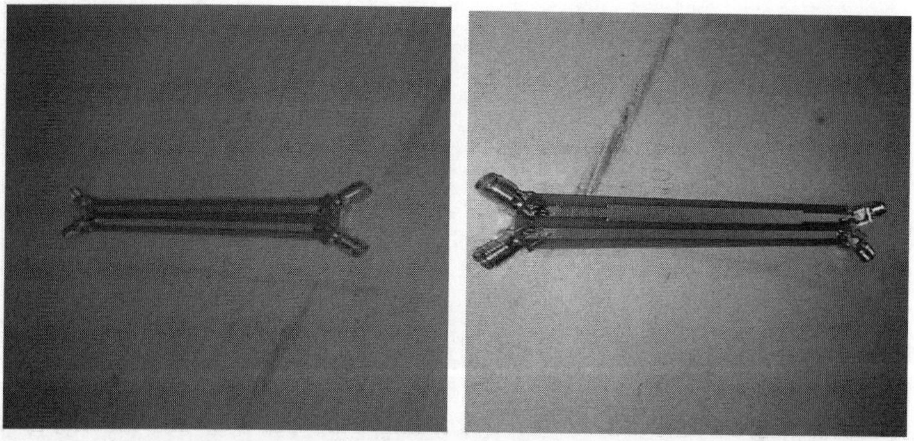

Figure 3.5 (a) Symmetric (balanced) & (b) Asymmetric (unbalanced) structures

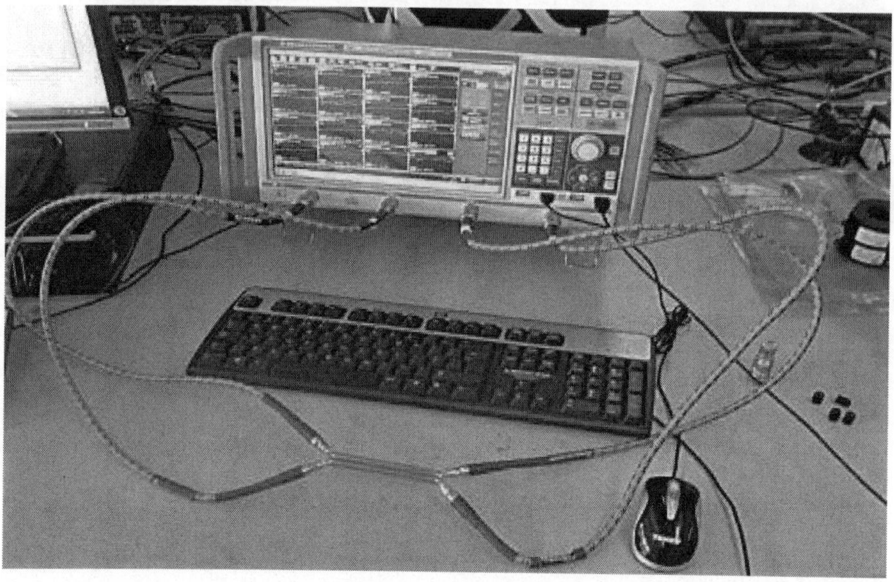

Figure 3.6 Showing the symmetric & the asymmetric structures as DUT

By connecting the microstrip lines in balanced configuration to the measuring instrument, all the 4x4 mixed-mode s-parameter matrix of the test fixture was measured by the VNA. Each of these 16 s-parameters matrices reveals separate characteristic behaviour of the same test fixture which can be very useful especially to the design and installation personnel. However, care must be taken in ensuring good symmetry and geometry of the test fixture for a better performance.

Figure 3.7 Mixed-mode s-parameter measurement of Cat 6 UTP

The instrument specifications listed below were based on the specification for the Cat 6 UTP cable under test and the configurations for a balanced mixed-mode measurement. A differential signal power of 10 dBm was carefully chosen as the input signal power into the cable to display appreciable mixed-mode signal amplitudes. Both CM and DM impedances were selected as default impedance settings of the test instrument. A high data point was chosen so that the relationship between those data points would be high.

Instrument Specification	
Start frequency	1 MHz
Stop frequency	250 MHz
Number of Meas.points	1601
Port Configuration	2 x Balanced
Instru. Ref. Impedance	50 Ω
CM Impedance	25 Ω
DM Impedance	100 Ω
Input Power	10 dBm
Meas. BW	100 KHz

3.11 The Current Probe Test Method Using a 3-Port Configured VNA

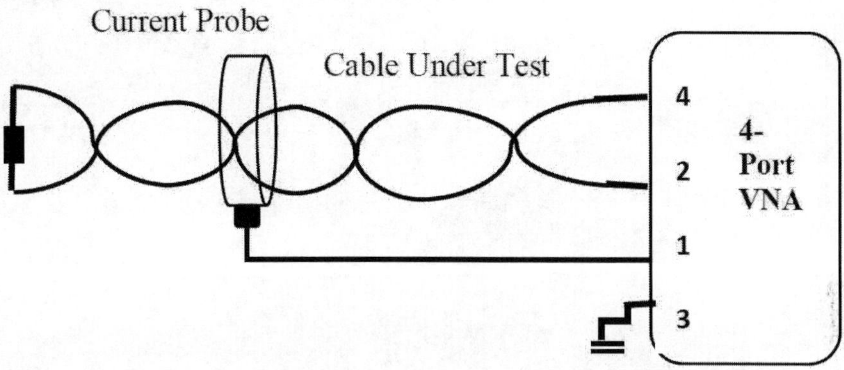

Figure 3.8 Showing sketch of the experiment 3-port VNA setup

Figure 3.8 (which test setup is pictured in Figure 3.9) was based on a 3-port configuration and used to measure the coupling attenuation of the CUT. The current probe was connected to port 1 of the VNA to measure the emitted noise from the cable which may have been occasioned by the cable imbalance. The instrument specification was almost the same with that explained in 3.10, except for the instrument configuration. A stepped frequency was selected in preference to continuously sweep frequency so as to measure all in-band signal frequencies including the fundamental of the noise and the harmonics.

Instrument Specification	
Start frequency	1 MHz
Stop frequency	250 MHz
Number of Meas. Points	1601
Port Configuration	1 unbalanced port (1) and one bal. (ports 2 & 4)
Ref Impedance	50Ω
	CM 25 Ω
	DM 100 Ω
Input Power	10dBm
Freq Sweep Mode	Stepped
Meas. Bandwidth	(fast sweep 100 KHz)

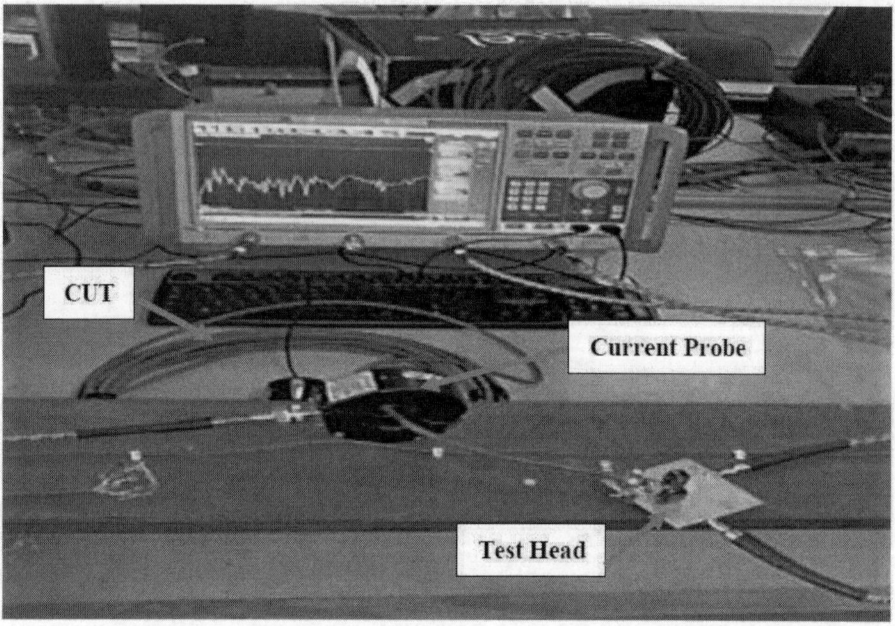

Figure 3.9 Showing the current probe test method

Figure 3.9 shows the experimental setup for the current probe injection method.

In this test method, mixed-mode analysis was used to investigate noise coupling in both differential mode, and common mode for cables exposed to external signals injected using a current probe to represent localised noise. The test method described a test configuration that uses a current probe to inject mock external EM noise to wire harnesses. The noise injector port P1 and the wire harness terminal ports P2 and P4 were the ports for an N-port circuit which made it relatively easier to obtain the N-port s-parameter of the network.

A 10 m long network cable under test which was kept stretched and straight and was clamped with the current probe at selected positions. The representative 10 m length of the CUT was chosen because it was long enough to characterise the behaviour of the cable under laboratory setting. All the unused 3-pairs were terminated in a network of 50 Ω and 25 Ω resistive loads as shown in Figure 3.10 at both ends in such a way that each pair was referenced to the other.

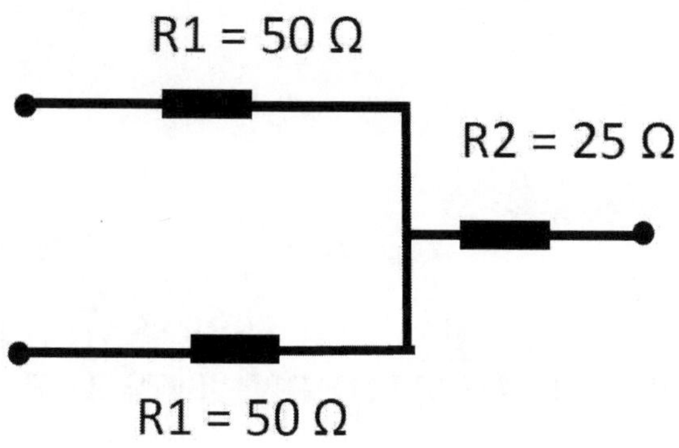

Figure 3.10 Network Termination

Referring to Figure 3.10, the total resistance of the series resistors R1 (50 Ω +50 Ω) =100 Ω represent the differential mode characteristic impedance which is equal to the impedance of the network cable under test.

Its common mode counterpart is 50 Ω in parallel with 50 Ω plus 25 Ω (R2) in series. It is noteworthy, however, that the common mode characteristic impedance is not specified by the standards, but typically varies between 25 Ω and 75 Ω [89]. Typically, a middle common mode reference value of 50 Ω is always used.

Chapter Summary

Chapter three has described the specific procedures or methods used to identify noise coupling and analyse noise conversion using mixed-mode s-parameters. It has also explained how data used in the analysis were generated or collected.

In experiment one, the potential divider test method was used with a differential impedance termination for impedance matching. Data was acquired using the *.2sp data file* of the 2-port VNA and represented graphically for the analysis.

In experiment two, the current probe test method was used with the VNA configured in 3-port for data acquisition.

In experiment three, the same current probe test method was used but with the VNA configured in a balanced 4-port. Data was acquired through the *.4sp data file* of the test instrument for both experiments two and three plotted in graphs for the analysis.

All the data points in experiments two and three were swept in both forward and reverse directions for each sweep points, e.g. (S_{dc12} and Sdc_{21}).

CHAPTER 4

THE TEST PROCEDURE AND ASSESSMENT FOR NOISE COUPLING TO ETHERNET CABLE

In this chapter, the coupling performance of two Ethernet cables, Cat 5e and Cat 6 UTP were investigated. The two network cables were chosen for test because both represent the most popular network cables in use. Besides, industry had increasing interest in the coupling performance of both popular cables due to growing usage and is keen on simple test methods.

It is generally known that Cat 6 UTP performs better in terms of noise coupling than Cat 5e. The main point about this experiment is on the test method used.

The design of the test method is based on a simple voltage divider principle as shown in Figure 4.1. However, it is worth noting that only a single pair was testing (the Blue Pair) and the result was used to assess the performance of the cable over a range of 200 MHz to 6 GHz frequency.

First, the 2-port vector network analyser was calibrated to obtain a very low noise floor measurement. Discussion on how to achieve a very low noise floor in a measuring instrument has been made in chapter 3, section 3. This was done without any source connected to the instrument. Since the noise floor represents the level of background noise introduced by the instrument below which no meaningful measurement can be obtained, it was most reasonable to reduce the noise floor level to the lowest minimum.

As in [90] [91], the twisted cable under test was prepared as shown in Figure 4.1.

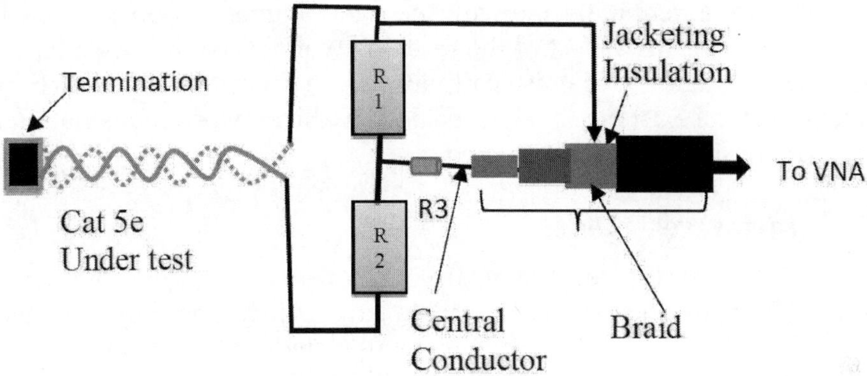

Figure 4.1 Cable under test prepared for testing in the RC

Like in [92], all the unused pairs at the far ends of the cables were terminated in 100 Ω pure resistive loads representing the cable nominal characteristic impedance. R1 and R2 are 50 Ω each, and their series connection, which is 100Ω, matched the differential termination to the pair under test. Their parallel connection, which is 25 Ω, plus (R3) 25 Ω, also matches the 50 Ω impedance of the RG 213 coaxial cable that links the VNA. It even presents a terminal impedance of 50 Ω which is equal to the input impedance of the measuring instrument. Hence, the presence of impedance discontinuities or mismatches and signal reflections are avoided. By this connection, any impinging external noise on the cable under test can be measured by the measuring device as common mode (unwanted) noise.

Suitable N type-to-BNC connectors were used to connect the VNA with the pair under test through the chamber bulkhead.

Since a representative 10 m length is long enough to characterise the behaviour of the CUT, it was considered informative understanding the character of the cable below that length.

Therefore, the tests were conducted using 2.5 meters, 5.0 meters and 10 meters lengths of each cable type with the following aims:

1. To investigate if noise coupling to network cables is length dependent
2. To investigate if noise coupling to network cables is predisposed to the cable lay pattern
3. To investigate if exposing the cable ends and terminations (not screened) to direct illumination of noise in the reverberation chamber could dominate the noise coupling

4. To compare noise coupling in both cable types with a standard reference antenna. In line with the overall aims and objective of this research, this aspect of the research work serves to give a baseline understanding of noise coupling to the Ethernet cable which indicates the existence of an unbalance in the network cable that makes it possible for the cable to couple noise.

4.2 Test Assessment

In this test assessment, the coupling performance of various lengths Cat 6 UTP were investigated. The cable lengths included 2 m, 5 m and 10 m lengths of Cat 6 UTP and they were all tested with ends and terminations screened from direct illumination of the generated noise signal in the reverberation chamber. The cable lengths were also experimented with the cables laid in zigzag pattern. From the results, different lengths of the CUT couple differently. The results also showed that the shorter lengths of the CUT coupled less noise than the longer lengths when tested in a mode-stirred reverberation chamber. Figures 4.3 and 4.4 also revealed that the electromagnetic noise coupled to the ethernet cables was length dependent. In common sense term, the longer the cable, the more noise energy it couples. This tended to suggest that the noise coupling performance of the CUT was an inherent property of the cable rather than because of the test methodology. However, the development of the simple test method that confirmed this result remains the focus.

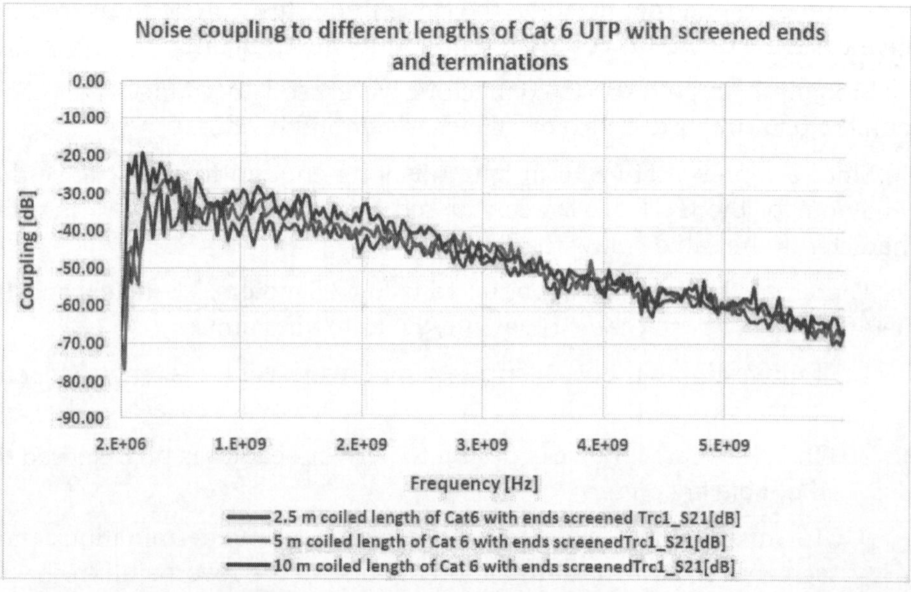

Figure 4.2 Showing noise coupling to different lengths of Cat 6 UTP.

Figure 4.3 also shows that network cables with unscreened ends and terminations are capable of increased noise coupling.

In the next experiment, the effects of screened ends and terminations against direct illumination of noise was investigated. To this end, all the exposed cable ends and terminations were insulated with paper tapes and insulating/metallic foil materials from direct noise coupling. This was to avoid direct coupled noise through those sections from influencing the measurements. The results are as shown in Figure 4.4.

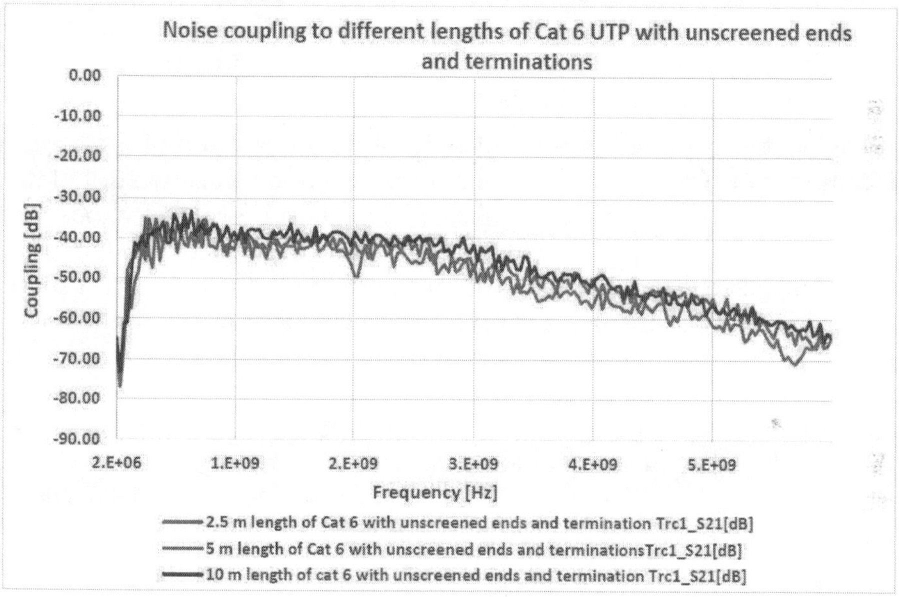

Figure 4.3 Showing noise coupling to unscreened ends and terminations

From the results of Figure 4.3 and Figure 4.4, the mean coupling performance of the different lengths of the CUT screened and unscreened at 6 MHz can be shown in Table 4.1 below.

Table 4.1 Comparing noise coupling in both screened and unscreened ends and terminations of CUT at 6 MHz.

Maximum Frequency over range	Cable type	Cable lengths	Unscreened cable ends and terminations	Screened cable ends and terminations
200MHz – to-6GHz	Cat 6 UTP	2.5m	-66.2dB	-69.9dB

200MHz-to-6GHz	Cat 6 UTP	5.0m	-66.5dB	-68.3dB
200MHz-to 6GHz	Cat 6 UTP	10.0m	-64.4dB	-67 dB

The results showed that screening exposed ends and terminations with insulating materials/metal foils is capable of screening off the communication cable from direct noise coupling which might degrades its performance. This would probably result in less interference/corruption to the desired signal content borne by the cable. Hence, it is generally a good practice to screen exposed cable ends and terminations from EM noise mainly when the cable is signal bearing.

The next experiment was to investigate the orientation of the cable in the chamber during testing for noise coupling. To do this, two orientation patterns were selected, viz laying the cable in zigzag form and choosing to coil the CUT. The Cat 6 UTP was singled out for test, and the 10 m length of it was selected. The CUT was laid out in the pattern chosen and placed in the working volume of the reverberation chamber. From the results in Figure 4.5, it can be seen that there was no significant difference in coupling in the two different cable orientations, especially at higher frequencies. Hence, it was concluded that noise coupling to network cables was unaffected by the cable orientation.

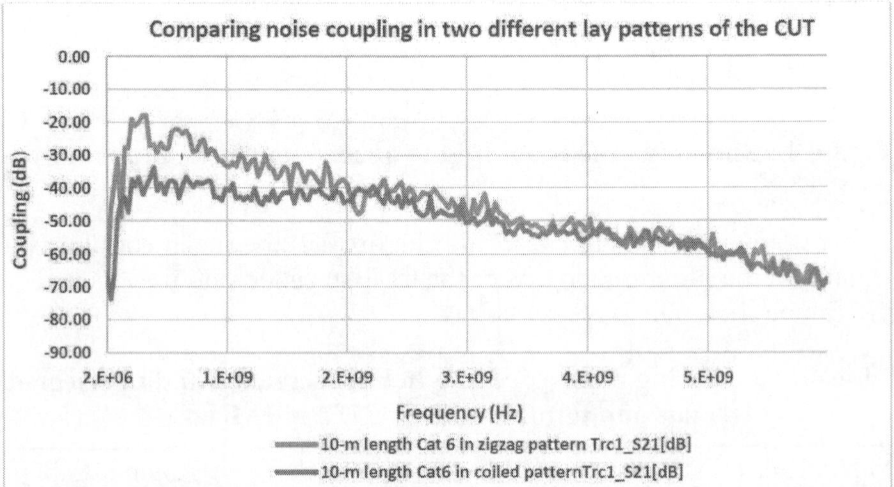

Figure 4.4 Showing noise coupling in two cable orientations of Cat 6 UTP

In the next experiment, noise coupling into Cat 6 and Cat 5e UTP was compared with the standard reverberation chamber reference antenna.

The aim of the study was to investigate the noise coupling performance of both cable category types. A representative 10 m each of both cables were used and terminated as described in section 4.1 and the process of screen was illustrated as shown in Figure 4.5.

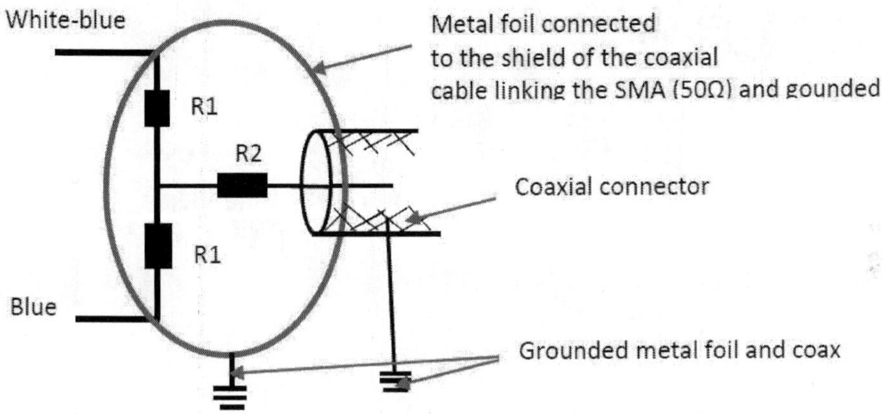

Figure 4.5 Illustration of the screening of the exposed cable ends and terminals

Figure 4.5 illustrates how the exposed ends and terminations of a pair of the UTP cable were screened. First, the terminated ends were covered with insulation tape and paper before being wrapped up with metal foil. The foil was then connected to the braids of the coaxial cable that combined with the SMA-to-N-type connector. The N-type connector was used to connect to the bulkhead of the chamber at the other end. Above all, care was taken to ensure that the gap between the braid connection and the metal foil was minimal to avoid unnecessary loops.

Again, with all the ends and terminations screened from direct EMI illumination, the experimental setup was made in the reverberation chamber working volume. The result of the test comparing the coupling performance of both types of cable with a standard reference antenna is shown in Figure 4.6. As can be seen, Cat 5e couples more noise than Cat 6 UTP. Also, as the frequency increased the coupling also increased. However, towards 200 MHz (the chamber LUF), the differences in coupling was less distinguishable. Table 4.2 also reveals the coupling data when compared with the standard chamber reference receive antenna.

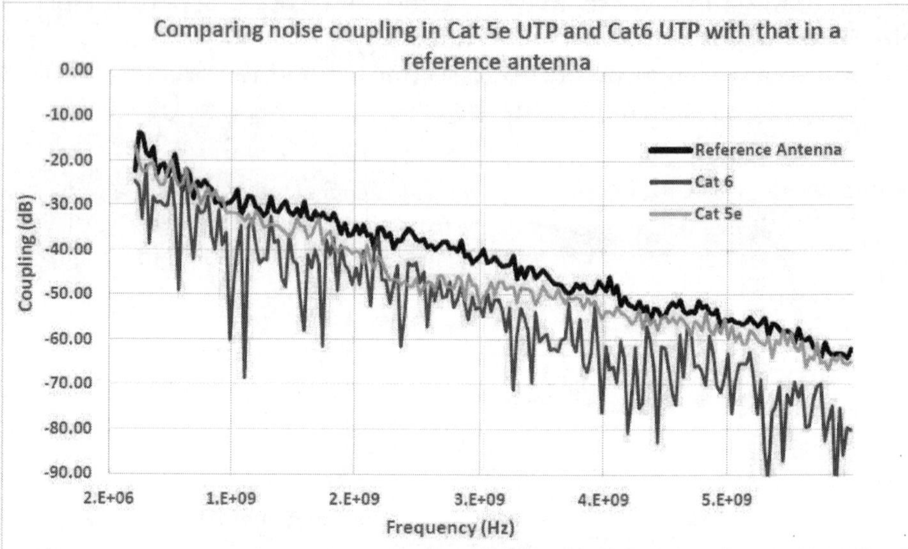

Figure 4.6 Showing noise coupling in both Cat 5e and Cat 6 UTP cabling compared with that of a reference antenna

Table 4.2 Comparing Noise Coupling between Cat 6, Cat 5e UTP with a Standard Reverberation Chamber Reference Antenna

Frequency (Hz)	Reference Antenna Measurement (dB)	Cat 6 UTP Measurement (dB)	Cat 5e UTP Measurement (dB)	Coupling in Cat 6 (with ref to Ref Antenna)	Coupling in Cat 5e (with ref to Ref Antenna)
210 MHz	2.24	2.47	1.68	-0.23	0.56
300MHz	1.84	2.11	2.25	-0.27	-0.41
420MHz	2.12	2.93	2.56	-0.81	-0.44
510MHz	2.13	2.72	2.40	-0.59	-0.27
630MHz	2.20	2.46	2.21	-0.26	-0.01
720MHz	2.47	3.03	2.69	-0.83	-0.42
810MHz	2.57	2.81	2.63	-0.24	-0.06
960MHz	2.97	3.62	3.18	-0.65	-0.21
1.02GHz	2.86	4.77	3.18	-1.91	-0.32
2.01GHz	3.44	4.11	4.02	-0.67	-0.58
2.40GHz	3.63	5.41	4.70	-1.78	-1.07

3.00GHz	4.13	5.27	5.23	-1.14	-1.10
4.02GHz	4.91	6.14	5.36	-1.23	-0.45
5.10GHz	5.62	6.83	5.87	-1.21	-0.25
6.00GHz	6.22	8.02	6.50	-1.80	-0.28

From the experiments described above, the following deductions could be made.

EM noise can always couple to network cables irrespective of their lengths and orientations. Moreover, the longer the cable, the more noise was coupled to it. However, noise coupling is not directly proportional to the length of cable because increasing the cable length increases the attenuation and other constructive and destructive interference issues. This was also true irrespective of the cable orientation pattern.

The results also showed that it is good practice to always terminate and screen terminations against direct noise coupling. This will screen off exposure terminations from dominating the coupling.

Comparing power ratios of the coupled signals from Table 2, it can generally be deduced that Cat 6 UTP cabling coupled less EM noise when compared with Cat 5e UTP. Overall, less than 3dB of more noise was coupled by Cat 5e than Cat 6 UTP between 210 MHz to 6 GHz.

$$\frac{\sum_{(from 210MHz)}^{(to 6GHz)} (Coupling in Cat6(w.r.t\ \mathrm{Re}-Antenna))}{\sum_{(from 210MHz)}^{(to 6GHz)} (Coupling in Cat5e(w.r.t\ \mathrm{Re}-Antenna))} = 2.36dB$$

This figure was more influenced at higher frequencies since noise coupling at low frequencies was comparably low. A possible explanation for this might be that Cat 6 has a better twist regime than Cat 5e. However, this figure could be lower because of the considerable nulls in the plot for Cat 6 UTP which was not immediately clear.

It can also be adduced that the higher the performance category, the better the cable. Hence, Cat 6 UTP performs better in terms of noise immunity than Cat 5e.

Chapter Summary

In this chapter, an investigation into the phenomenon of noise coupling to Ethernet cable using the mode-stirred reverberation chamber has been studied. It has been shown that within the operating frequencies of the mode-stirred reverberation chamber, noise coupling to Ethernet cabling is length dependent. This can be related to the working environment where the cable is subjected to ambient noise.

It has equally been shown that a marginal difference in coupling existed between Cat 5e and Cat 6 UTP due to the orientation of the category cables when tested in the reverberation chamber.

Also, screening the cable ends and terminations gave a better coupling performance and prevented direct coupling of noise from dominating the result.

Finally, compared to a standard reference antenna, Cat 6 UTP yielded a better coupling performance than Cat 5e UTP over 200 MHz to 6 GHz. This was attributed to some design features (inclusion of pair separator) and better twist regime in Cat 6 which aid to minimise pair crosstalk. Moreover, the coupling performance became better as the frequency increased.

CHAPTER 5

MIXED MODE SCATTERING PARAMETER MEASUREMENT

This chapter introduces other performance parameters used to evaluate passive networks and their components in the frequency domain using a vector network analyser (VNA). The mixed-mode s-parameter analysis is required especially in differential systems to provide comprehensive information on system performance. The scattered information which includes the reflected and transmitted electromagnetic signals are created when a device is excited with an incident signal. Practical knowledge of the application s-parameter will be demonstrated in this chapter by the fabrication and measurement of the s-parameters of balanced and unbalanced microstrip transmission lines. It is hoped that this will provide insight into the propagation behaviour of network cables (UTP cabling), often regarded as balanced transmission lines.

Although s-parameters have been used to analyse and characterise differential circuits, this work attempts to relate this knowledge to mode-specific representation with respect to the natural mode of operation of network cables. The whole idea is to investigate if any intra-pair skew (i.e., any difference in the dimension of a given pair resulting from pair twisting), will give rise to signal mode conversion that may lead to EMC (radiation) and Signal Integrity (susceptibility) issues.

The scope of measurement will be limited to balanced differential circuits. This will include symmetric and asymmetric differential line structures as well as Cat 6 UTP cable often regarded as a differential balanced line.

5.1. Single-ended and Differential Measurements

Single-ended circuits are known to be referenced to a common ground and therefore prone to distortion and noise at high frequencies. On the other hand, balanced networks which normally has a pair of symmetrical transmission lines are referenced to each other and in this way, capable of attenuating common mode noise at its output end as much as possible.

For example, $(V^+ + noise) - (V^- + noise) = (V^+ - V^-)$. This represents the two swings of a differential signal with added noise. When the upper swing with added noise is subtracted from the lower, the result is the desired differential signal with an increased dynamic range. This is contrary to a single-ended implementation where the maximum voltage swing is less than the supply voltage. The benefit of this is that when systems are implemented in differential circuits, the available voltage/signal swing, and indeed the dynamic range, are increased.

5.2 Single-ended Measurement with Baluns-the Analog Method

In the recent past, the two-port VNA has been used to make measurements on balanced networks by connecting each port of the analyser to the ports of the DUT via a balun as shown in Figure 5.1. In this connection, the balun transfers the single-ended stimulus to balanced stimulus and vice versa. One major weakness of this connection is that only the differential-to-differential parameters are measured. Other parameters such as the common mode-to-common mode, common mode-to-differential and differential mode-to-common mode do not account. Also, the use of baluns has not been ideal as their effects are included in the measurement results. These non-ideal performance effects are typically specified as losses and may consist of phase and magnitude imbalance which are hard to eradicate. Also, in the past traditional RF and Microwave methods have been used to restrain the existence of numerous modes in a circuit. This gave rise to non-consistencies in measurements, designs and analysis of differential microwave and RF circuits.

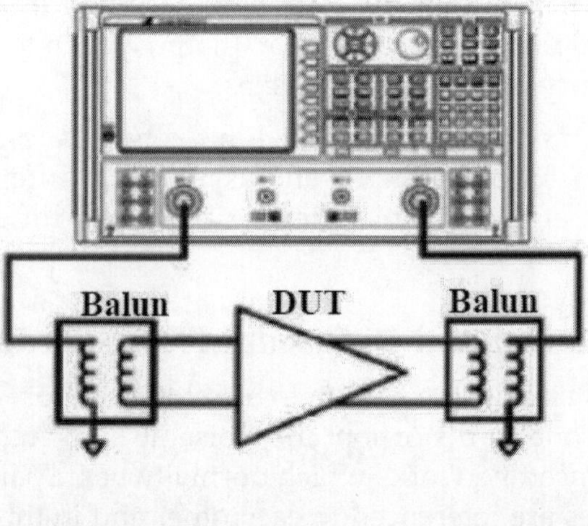

Figure 5.1 DUT Measurement Using Balun [93]

5.3 Coupling and Mode Conversion

In single-ended lines, noise coupling is associated to mutual inductance (L_m) and capacitance (C_m) that exist connecting the lines.

Inductive Coupling

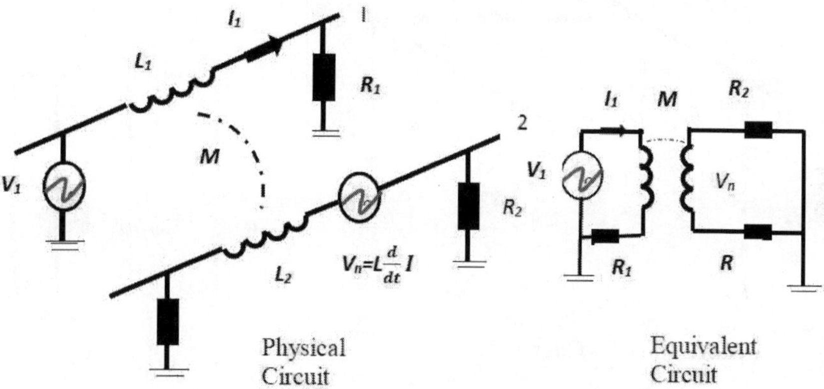

Figure 5.2 Inductive Coupling between two transmission lines

Figure 5.2 represents inductive coupling between two conductors 1 and 2. R_1 and R_2 represents the circuits connected to the lines and are not stray components, while R is the impedance of line 2. V_1 represents the source of interference. M is the mutual inductance between lines 1 and 2. With approximations [94], V_{noise} is the induced noise resulting from the magnetic field of flux density (derived from Faraday's Law) and is given by

$$V_{noise} = L_m \frac{d}{dt} I,$$

where V_{noise} is the noise voltage, and I is the operational line current.

Capacitive Coupling

Similarly, Figure 5.3 represents capacitive coupling between two conductors. C_{12} is the stray capacitance between conductors 1 and 2. C_{G1} and C_{G2} are the capacitances between conductors 1 and 2 and ground, respectively. R which is not a stray component results from the circuitry connected to conductor 2. V_1 represents the source of interference affecting the receptor circuit line 2. It is to be noted that the effect of C_{G1} connected directly across the source can be neglected as it has no influence on the noise coupling. Hence, with approximation, the noise voltage V_n produced between conductor 2 and ground can be expressed as

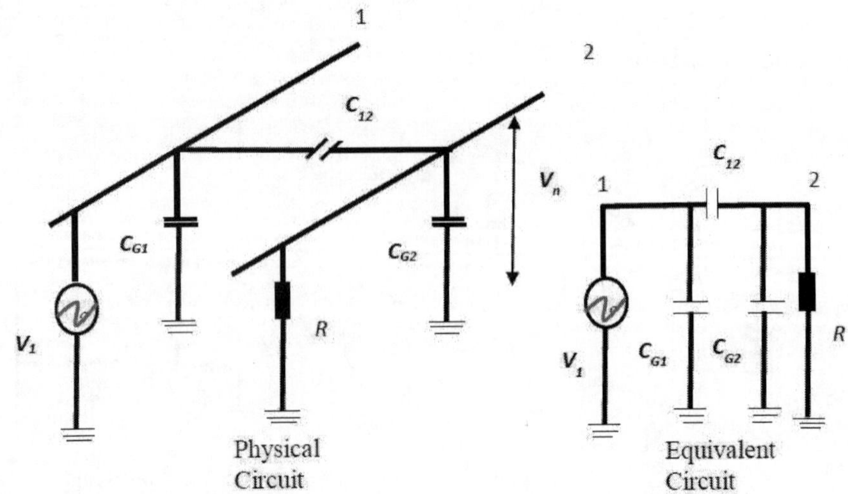

Figure 5.3 Capacitive coupling between two transmission lines

$$I_{noise} = C_m \frac{d}{dt} V$$

where I_{noise} is the noise current on the adjacent line, V represent the operational line voltage.

Noise coupling depends on the amount of layout of the lines and the form of the signal on the line, hence the odd and the even modes. Odd-mode can be described as the signal between two adjoining lines with the same amplitude but with 180 degrees phase difference, while even-mode is the driving signal lines with the same amplitude and phase. These are often referred to as differential and common mode noise signal respectively.

For the two neighbouring lines, the coupling noise voltage can be approximated as

$$V_1 = L_o \frac{d}{dt} I_1 + L_m \frac{d}{dt} I_2$$

$$V_2 = L_o \frac{d}{dt} I_2 + L_m \frac{d}{dt} I_1$$

Where L_o = lumped-self inductor and L_m = mutual inductor due to coupling

In the odd mode, propagation of signal is in opposite direction, i.e. $I_1 = -I_2$. Hence,

$$V_1 = (L_o - L_m)\frac{d}{dt}I_1$$

$$V_2 = (L_o - L_m)\frac{d}{dt}I_2$$

This shows that with signal coupling, the total inductance reduces with mutual inductance [94].

In similar manner, the noise current can be estimated. For the two neighbouring lines

$$I_1 = C_o\frac{d}{dt}V_1 + C_m\frac{d}{dt}(V_1 - V_2)$$

$$I_2 = C_o\frac{d}{dt}V_2 + C_m\frac{d}{dt}(V_2 - V_1)$$

where C_o = lumped element capacitance

C_m = mutual capacitance joining the lines

Since propagation in odd-mode is in opposite direction, i.e. $V_1 = -V_2$

$$I_1 = (C_o + 2C_m)\frac{d}{dt}V_1$$

$$I_2 = (C_o + 2C_m)\frac{d}{dt}V_2$$

This also shows that the overall capacitance grows with mutual capacitance [94]. The same analysis applies in the even-mode where signal propagates with equal magnitude and phase $V_1 = V_2$ and $I_1 = I_2$ with the following

$$V_1 = (L_o + L_m)\frac{d}{dt}I_1$$

$$V_2 = (L_o + L_m)\frac{d}{dt}I_2$$

And for the currents in the line

$$I_1 = C_o \frac{d}{dt} V_1$$

$$I_2 = C_o \frac{d}{dt} V_2$$

Mode conversion is possible where a stimulus of a pure mode generates a response of more than one mode [95]. For instance, when a pure differential stimulus drives a DUT and both differential and common-mode responses are created, at that point mode conversion has taken place.

The s-parameter has been described as a mathematical representation of how RF energy is propagated in a multiport network [96]. It symbolises an arrangement to store information, the quality of which depends on the instrument of measurement, its calibration, test fixtures, input information and other geometry information. It also defines the relationship of two normalised power waves, namely the response and the stimulus.

5.4 Other Network Parameters and the S-parameter naming convention

The Z (impedance) parameters are members of other comparable parameters used in electrical/electronic and communication systems to describe the electrical behaviour of network systems. Others include the "Y" (admittance), "ABCD" and the "h" (hybrid) [97].

Mixed-mode s-parameters are a broadening of regular s-parameters mode for balanced measurements. The vector network analyser is often used to determine the mixed-mode parameters once a balanced circuit configuration is nominated.

Mixed-mode s-parameters are used to differentiate the following three port modes [98]: s: single-ended (for unbalanced ports), d: differential mode (with balanced ports) represented, c: common mode (for balanced ports) [98].

A typical mixed-mode s-parameter representation can take the following order: $S_{<m\text{-}out><m\text{-}in><out><in>}$, where $_{<m\text{-}out>}$ and $_{<m\text{-}in>}$ mean the output and input port modes, $_{<out>}$ and $_{<in>}$ signify the output and input port numbers [99]. The naming convention of the mixed-mode s-matrix can be shown as in Figure 5.4 where S_{dd11}, for example, means a differential response, at port 1 because of a differential stimulus at port 1.

	Differential mode stimulus		Common mode stimulus	
	Port 1	Port 2	Port 1	Port 2
Diff mode Port 1	S_{DD11}	S_{DD12}	S_{DC11}	S_{DC12}
Response Port 2	S_{DD21}	S_{DD22}	S_{DC21}	S_{DC22}
Common mode Port 1	S_{CD11}	S_{CD12}	S_{CC11}	S_{CC12}
Response Port	S_{CD21}	S_{CD22}	S_{CC21}	S_{CC22}

Figure 5.4 Mixed-mode naming convention

Describing networks with their scattering waves is important, especially under increased frequency of operation, so those circuit elements are made a significant fraction of a wavelength (i.e. one-tenth of a wavelength). S-parameters are easy to measure with network ports terminated in its characteristic impedance. The practical implications of this are immense since open and short-circuited circuits are challenging to accomplish at microwave and RF frequencies owing to the effects of distributed elements.

5.5 Need to Use Mixed-mode Analysis

Characteristically, differential circuits had been intended and evaluated in the past with old-fashioned analogue techniques, which involve lumped element assumptions. Also, the traditional means of testing differential circuits required the application and measurement of voltages and currents, which is problematic [100] at RF and microwave frequencies [100] for determining impedance.

At RF and microwave frequencies, it is suitable to explain a given network in terms of the ratio of incident and outgoing waves rather than voltages or currents. This is defined in equation (5.16).

$$S_{ij} = \left. \frac{b_i}{a_j} \right|_{a_k = 0 \text{ for } k \neq j} \qquad (5.1)$$

From (5.1) it is, therefore, necessary that port *j* must be energised in other to measure the response at port *i*. However, for differential circuits (e.g., balanced microstrip lines, power splitters and combiners, couplers, etc.), that use differential modes like differential and common mode, a straightforward application of standard s-parameters does not readily yield comprehensible definitions of a general differential network. It is, therefore, necessary to evaluate these differential circuits to guarantee best circuit and system operation. Combining the DM and the CM (mixed-mode s-parameters) is known to be a most accurate method to characterise linear circuits at RF frequencies. Hence, the mixed-mode method is preferred for symmetrical differential circuits instead of the standard s-parameter due to its simplicity.

Another characteristic of the mixed-mode s-parameter is that it not only defines how a device under test modifies a stimulus or its response in either forward or reverse direction but also stipulates the resolution of the common and the differential mode signals, which represent the sum (common mode) and differences (differential mode) of the two signals.

5.6 Modal/Single-ended s-parameter representation of a two-port differential line

Consider a single link shown in Figure 5.5. The sketch is used here to represent a twisted pair with one line running between input-end **X** and output end **V**. The second runs between Y and U. These two lines are capable of coupling. Incident and reflected power waves are specified by the conventional representation of **a** and **b** individually. The regular single-ended s-parameter for line **X-V** as shown in Figure 5.5 can be written as S_{xx}, S_{xv}, S_{vx}, S_{vv}. Additionally, the **Y-U** can be expressed as S_{yy}, S_{yu}, S_{uy}, S_{uu}. Given that the two lines are capable of coupling, the relationship between the incident and reflected waves of ports that are not coupled through the lines can be defined using the scattering parameters. As a result, in every incident port x,y,u,v two new relations of the s-parameters are possible. Hence, there are eight additional s-parameter terms to be merged with the conversant eight transmission line s-parameter terms to create a comprehensive single ended 4 x 4 scattering matrix as shown in equation (5.2).

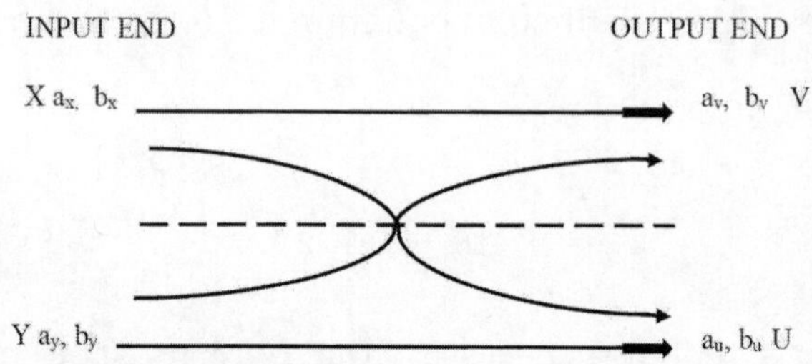

Figure 5.5 Physically coupled lines

From the representation in Figure 5.4 [101], it is possible to originate all the sixteen single-ended s-parameters and their notations [101].

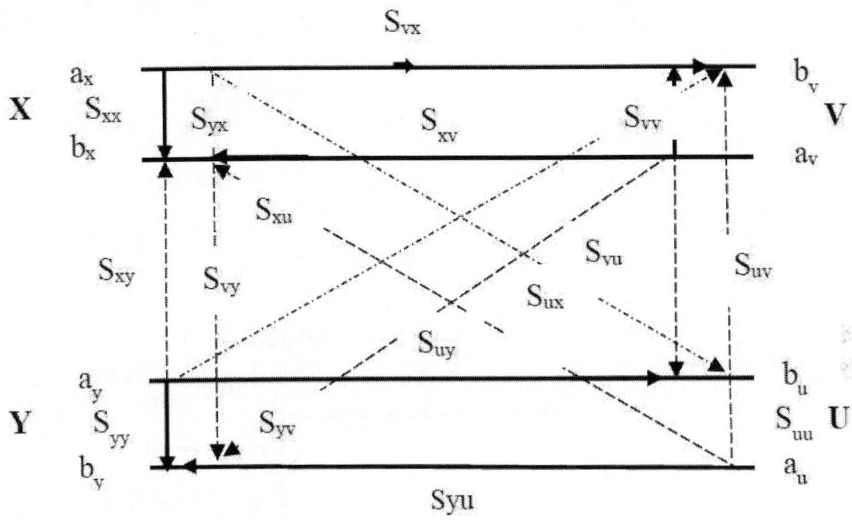

Figure 5.6 Calibrating Single-ended s-parameter notation for a coupled pair [102] *(Web sourced)*

5.7 Generalised Single-ended and Mixed Mode S-Parameter Notation

Standard two-port VNA can be employed to make measurements of mixed-mode s-parameter. This may involve making measurements of the DUT to measure 4-port single-ended s-parameter and perform a conversion. The conversion will then generate results as though the ports were driven in pairs. However, a mixed-mode measurement using a 4-port VNA that is configured in the balanced mode for balanced networks is required to correctly determine the mixed-mode transition in a physical differential test structure.

For a 4-port single-ended DUT shown in Figure 5.7, it is possible to arrange its ports as a differential two port DUT shown in Figure 5.8, where ports 1 and 3 and ports 2 and 4 (of the single-ended DUT) are configured as balanced ports 1 and 2, respectively. A complete s-parameters matrix for Fig 5.6 can be written as in (5.2) to describe all potential combinations of responses divided by the stimuli. The single-ended s-parameter matrix is given in (5.2).

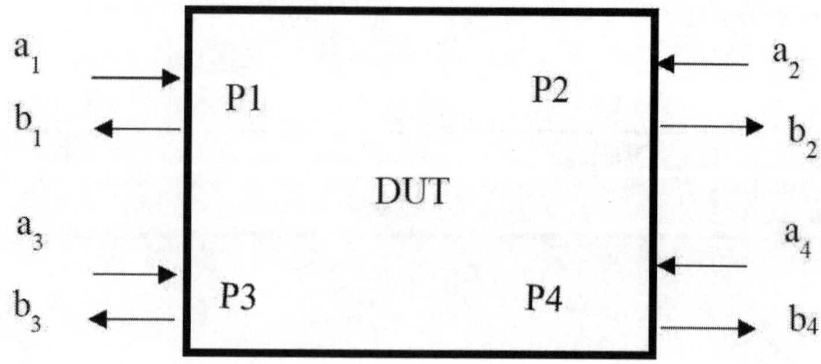

Figure 5.7 A 4-Port Single-ended DUT

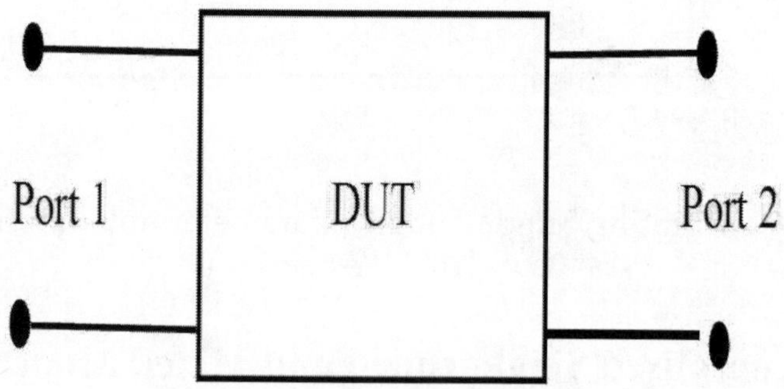

Figure 5.8 Differential 2-port DUT

$$\begin{bmatrix} b1 \\ b2 \\ b3 \\ b4 \end{bmatrix} = \begin{bmatrix} S_{11} & S_{12} & S_{13} & S_{14} \\ S_{21} & S_{22} & S_{23} & S_{24} \\ S_{31} & S_{32} & S_{33} & S_{34} \\ S_{41} & S_{42} & S_{43} & S_{44} \end{bmatrix} \cdot \begin{bmatrix} a_1 \\ a_2 \\ a_3 \\ a_4 \end{bmatrix} \qquad (5.2)$$

The expression in (5.2) can also be represented as $B_{std} = S_{std} .A_{std}$.

In this wise, A_{std} and B_{std} stand for the stimulus and response wave matrix, respectively. S_{std} represents the single-ended four-port s-parameters solution. These are shown individually in (5.3).

$$B_{std} = \begin{bmatrix} b1 \\ b2 \\ b3 \\ b4 \end{bmatrix}, \; A_{std} = \begin{bmatrix} a_1 \\ a_2 \\ a_3 \\ a_4 \end{bmatrix} \text{ and } S_{std} = \begin{bmatrix} S_{11} & S_{12} & S_{13} & S_{14} \\ S_{21} & S_{22} & S_{23} & S_{24} \\ S_{31} & S_{32} & S_{33} & S_{34} \\ S_{41} & S_{42} & S_{43} & S_{44} \end{bmatrix} \quad (5.3)$$

As shown in Figure 5.6, it is possible to give a description of the common and differential mode voltages and currents (i.e. the power waves–stimulus and response). Hence, following the manner of (5.3), a mixed-mode s-parameters can also be constructed where each row will represent the response, and each column will describe the stimulus condition. This can be given in (5.4) as a generalised mixed-mode s-parameter and is written as

$$\begin{aligned} b_{d1} &= S_{11}a_{d1} + S_{12}a_{d2} + S_{13}ac_1 + S_{14}ac_2 \\ b_{d2} &= S_{21}a_{d1} + S_{22}a_{d2} + S_{23}ac_1 + S_{24}ac_2 \\ b_{c1} &= S_{31}a_{d1} + S_{32}a_{d2} + S_{33}ac_1 + S_{43}ac_2 \\ b_{c2} &= S_{41}a_{d1} + S_{42}a_{d2} + S_{43}ac_1 + S_{44}ac_2 \end{aligned} \quad (5.4)$$

where subscripts $_1$ and $_2$ are for ports 1 and 2, correspondingly. From (5.4), the mixed-mode s-parameter format can also be constructed as

$$\begin{bmatrix} bd1 \\ bd2 \\ bc1 \\ bc2 \end{bmatrix} = \left[\begin{array}{cc|cc} Sdd_{11} & Sdd_{12} & Sdc_{11} & Sdc_{12} \\ Sdd_{21} & Sdd_{22} & Sdc_{21} & Sdc_{22} \\ \hline Scd_{11} & Scd_{12} & Scc_{11} & Scc_{12} \\ Scd_{21} & Scd_{22} & Scc_{21} & Scc_{22} \end{array}\right] = \begin{bmatrix} ad_1 \\ ad_2 \\ ac_1 \\ ac_2 \end{bmatrix} \quad (5.5)$$

where S_{ccij} and S_{ddij} $(i, j = 1,2)$ are the pure common-mode and pure differential s-parameters, correspondingly. S_{cdij} and S_{dcij} for $(i, j = 1,2)$ are the cross-mode s-parameters. In (5.5) with S_{ddij} $(i, j = 1,2)$, all the elements of the quadrant characterise the performance of the differential stimulus and response. All the elements of the S_{ccij} $(i, j = 1,2)$ quadrant also describe the performance of the common mode stimulus and response. The elements of the S_{cdij} $(i, j = 1,2)$ and S_{dcij} $(i, j = 1,2)$ also describe the mode conversion performances of the stimuli and responses, separately.

Again, as in the manner of the single-ended mode, equation (5.5) can also be expressed as $B_{mm} = S_{mm}A_{mm}$ (5.6), where B_{mm} is the mixed mode response wave, S_{mm} is the mixed-mode s-parameter, and A_{mm} is the mixed mode stimulus. The single-ended s-parameters of (5.2) can also be related to the mixed-mode equation of (5.5).

5.8 Transformation from the Single-ended mode to Mixed-mode S-parameters

Using the sketch of Figure 5.8 and considering the pairs of nodes 1 and 3 as combined differential port and nodes 2 and 4 combined as another differential port where a_i and b_i (i =1 to 4) represent the wave signals taken at ports 1 to 4. a_i (i = 1 to 4) describe the incident waves while b_i (i =1 to 4) describe the reflected waves.

The choice for the difference and the sum of the wave expressions in (5.7) for the differential and common mode waves are understandable (+ for common mode, - for differential mode). The inverse of root 2 in the equation (5.7) represents a normalization factor to keep power levels equivalent [103]. (a_{d1}) and (a_{c1}) describe the incident normalized power wave for the differential and common modes of the mixed mode port, while (b_{d1}) and (b_{c1}) describe the reflected normalized power wave for the differential and common mode of the mixed mode ports, respectively.

$$a_{d1} = \frac{1}{\sqrt{2}}(a_1 - a_3)$$

$$a_{c1} = \frac{1}{\sqrt{2}}(a_1 + a_3)$$

$$b_{d1} = \frac{1}{\sqrt{2}}(b_1 - b_3)$$

$$b_{c1} = \frac{1}{\sqrt{2}}(b_1 + b_3)$$

$$a_{d2} = \frac{1}{\sqrt{2}}(a_2 - a_4) \qquad (5.7)$$

$$a_{c2} = \frac{1}{\sqrt{2}}(a_2 + a_4)$$

$$b_{d2} = \frac{1}{\sqrt{2}}(b_2 - b_4)$$

$$b_{c2} = \frac{1}{\sqrt{2}}(b_2 + b_4)$$

From (5.3) the mixed-mode incident waves A_{mm} [103] and the mixed-mode response [103] waves B_{mm} can be used to develop the mixed-mode s-parameter matrix S_{mm} [103] if the conversion matrix M and the inverse conversion matrix, M^{-1} are considered. Matrices for the mixed-mode waves, the mixed-mode s-parameter matrix and the conversion as well as the transpose are expressed in equations (5.8 – 5.12).

$$B_{mm} = MB_{std} = \begin{bmatrix} b_{d1} \\ b_{d2} \\ b_{c1} \\ b_{c2} \end{bmatrix} = \frac{1}{\sqrt{2}} \begin{bmatrix} 1 & 0 & -1 & 0 \\ 0 & 1 & 0 & -1 \\ 1 & 0 & 1 & 0 \\ 0 & 1 & 0 & 1 \end{bmatrix} \cdot \begin{bmatrix} b_1 \\ b_2 \\ b_3 \\ b_4 \end{bmatrix} \quad (5.8)$$

$$A_{mm} = MA_{std} = \begin{bmatrix} a_{d1} \\ a_{d2} \\ a_{c1} \\ a_{c2} \end{bmatrix} = \frac{1}{\sqrt{2}} \begin{bmatrix} 1 & 0 & -1 & 0 \\ 0 & 1 & 0 & -1 \\ 1 & 0 & 1 & 0 \\ 0 & 1 & 0 & 1 \end{bmatrix} \cdot \begin{bmatrix} a_1 \\ a_2 \\ a_3 \\ a_4 \end{bmatrix} \quad (5.9)$$

$$M = \frac{1}{\sqrt{2}} \begin{bmatrix} 1 & 0 & -1 & 0 \\ 0 & 1 & 0 & -1 \\ 1 & 0 & 1 & 0 \\ 0 & 1 & 0 & 1 \end{bmatrix} \ \& \ M^{-1} = \frac{1}{\det M}[M] = \frac{1}{\sqrt{2}} \begin{bmatrix} 1 & 0 & 1 & 0 \\ 0 & 1 & 0 & 1 \\ -1 & 0 & 1 & 0 \\ 0 & -1 & 0 & 1 \end{bmatrix} \quad (5.10)$$

According to [103] [104], expressing the mixed-mode matrix in terms of the conversion matrix in the form of $S_{mm} = MS_{std}M_{-1}$ can be written as S_{mm} =

$$\text{From (5.6) } B_{mm} = S_{mm}A_{mm} = \begin{bmatrix} b_{d1} \\ b_{d2} \\ b_{c1} \\ b_{c2} \end{bmatrix} = \begin{bmatrix} Sdd_{11} & Sdd_{12} & Sdc_{11} & Sdc_{12} \\ Sdd_{21} & Sdd_{22} & Sdc_{21} & Sdc_{22} \\ Scd_{11} & Scd_{12} & Scc_{11} & Scc_{12} \\ Scd_{21} & Scc_{22} & Scc_{21} & Scc_{22} \end{bmatrix} \cdot \begin{bmatrix} ad_1 \\ ad_2 \\ ac_1 \\ ac_2 \end{bmatrix} \quad (5.11)$$

$$\begin{bmatrix} \frac{S_{11}-S_{12}-S_{21}+S_{22}}{2} & \frac{S_{11}+S_{12}-S_{21}-S_{22}}{2} & \frac{S_{13}-S_{14}-S_{23}+S_{24}}{2} & \frac{S_{13}+S_{14}-S_{23}-S_{24}}{2} \\ \frac{S_{11}-S_{12}+S_{21}-S_{22}}{2} & \frac{S_{11}+S_{12}+S_{21}+S_{22}}{2} & \frac{S_{13}-S_{14}+S_{23}-S_{24}}{2} & \frac{S_{13}+S_{14}+S_{23}+S_{24}}{2} \\ \frac{S_{31}-S_{32}-S_{41}+S_{42}}{2} & \frac{S_{31}+S_{32}-S_{41}-S_{42}}{2} & \frac{S_{33}-S_{34}-S_{43}+S_{44}}{2} & \frac{S_{33}+S_{34}-S_{43}-S_{44}}{2} \\ \frac{S_{31}-S_{32}+S_{41}-S_{42}}{2} & \frac{S_{31}+S_{32}+S_{41}+S_{42}}{2} & \frac{S_{33}-S_{34}+S_{43}-S_{44}}{2} & \frac{S_{33}-S_{34}+S_{43}+S_{44}}{2} \end{bmatrix}$$

(5.12) [103] [104]

This brings together the established relationship between normalised mixed-mode waves, i.e. (a_{d1}, b_{d1}, a_{c1}, d_{c1}) and the single-ended waves (a_1, b_1, a_2, b_2) whose mode-specific transformations are listed from (5.13) to (5.16). The conversion formula follows the linear transformation approach of [105].

1. Differential mode – to – Differential mode terms,

$$\begin{aligned} S_{dd11} &= \frac{1}{2}(S_{11}-S_{21}-S_{12}+S_{22}) \\ S_{dd12} &= \frac{1}{2}(S_{13}-S_{23}-S_{14}+S_{24}) \\ S_{dd21} &= \frac{1}{2}(S_{31}-S_{41}-S_{32}+S_{42}) \\ S_{dd22} &= \frac{1}{2}(S_{33}-S_{43}-S_{34}+S_{44}) \end{aligned} \quad (5.13)$$

2. Common mode - to- Common mode terms,

$$S_{cc11} = \frac{1}{2}(S_{11}+S_{21}+S_{12}+S_{22})$$
$$S_{cc12} = \frac{1}{2}(S_{13}+S_{23}+S_{14}+S_{24})$$

$$\begin{aligned} S_{cc21} &= \frac{1}{2}(S_{31}+S_{41}+S_{32}+S_{42}) \\ S_{cc22} &= \frac{1}{2}(S_{33}+S_{43}+S_{34}+S_{44}) \end{aligned} \quad (5.14)$$

3. Common mode - to- Differential mode terms,

$$S_{dc11} = \frac{1}{2}(S_{11} - S_{21} + S_{12} - S_{22})$$

$$S_{dc12} = \frac{1}{2}(S_{13} - S_{23} + S_{14} - S_{24})$$

$$S_{dc21} = \frac{1}{2}(S_{31} - S_{41} + S_{41} - S_{42})$$

$$S_{dc22} = \frac{1}{2}(S_{33} - S_{43} + S_{34} - S_{44}) \quad (5.15)$$

4. Differential mode – to - Common mode terms,

$$S_{cd11} = \frac{1}{2}(S_{11} + S_{21} - S_{12} - S_{22})$$

$$S_{cd12} = \frac{1}{2}(S_{13} + S_{23} - S_{14} - S_{24})$$

$$S_{cd21} = \frac{1}{2}(S_{31} + S_{41} - S_{32} - S_{42})$$

$$S_{cd22} = \frac{1}{2}(S_{33} + S_{43} - S_{34} - S_{44}) \quad (5.16)$$

5.9 Interpreting the Mixed-mode s-parameters as it relates the Single-ended Mode

An interpretation of (5.12) shows that mixed-mode s-parameters are related to regular four-port s-parameters by a linear similarity transform. This similarity transformation gives extra information about the character of the mixed-mode s-parameter. Again, it demonstrates that the operator *M* is a matrix transpose operator which indicates that the operator is unitary

$M\,(M^*)\,T = 1$ (5.17) (* is a complex conjugate).

In unitary transformation, one orthogonal base can be transformed into another. This apparently means that the two sets of orthogonal s-parameters are two different ways of representing the same information about the same device. This fact would be better appreciated as the touchstone s-parameter data files, and the plots of the parameters are examined.

Equation (5.12) also indicates that a single-ended four-port VNA (with each measurement port stimulated in turn) can be used to measure a differential network and the subsequent s-parameters transformed to mixed-mode for ease of analysis. For example, Figure 5.9 examines the plots of a differential stimulus at a differential port 1 and a differential response taken from a differential port 2 measured directly from a balanced 2-port VNA and its transformation from single-ended measurement as given below:

$$S_{dd21} = 0.5\,(S_{31} - S_{41} - S_{32} + S_{42})$$
$$= 0.5\,(\text{Trace 9} - \text{Trace13} - \text{Trace10} + \text{Trace14})$$
$$= (\text{Trace 17})$$

This transformation which is implemented by the *Trace Maths Function* of the R & S VNA is in line with equation 5.13.

However, it is noteworthy that the VNA does not deliver exact balanced measurement when both inputs of a differential device is stimulated. Instead, only single-ended balanced measurements are made, and outputs from a stimulated input are individually measured. Using the Maths formulas modelled in equations 5.13 – 5.16, the VNA calculates the differential and common mode inputs from a DUT in the frequency domain using complex phase and magnitude values.

As can be seen in Figure 5.9, the direct measurement method has a slight accuracy advantage over the transformation method, especially at lower frequencies.

This result is approximately consistent with the earlier studies in mode transformation which demonstrates that single-ended 4-port measurements can be done with a VNA and the result transformed to mixed-mode s-parameters for analysis. The result also shows that direct measurement of mixed-mode s-parameters has an advantage over the converted measurement for differential circuits. Because of this, direct measurements with the 4-port ZNB 8 VNA was the preferred option in all the mixed-mode s-parameter measurements in this study for more accurate characterization of the DUT.

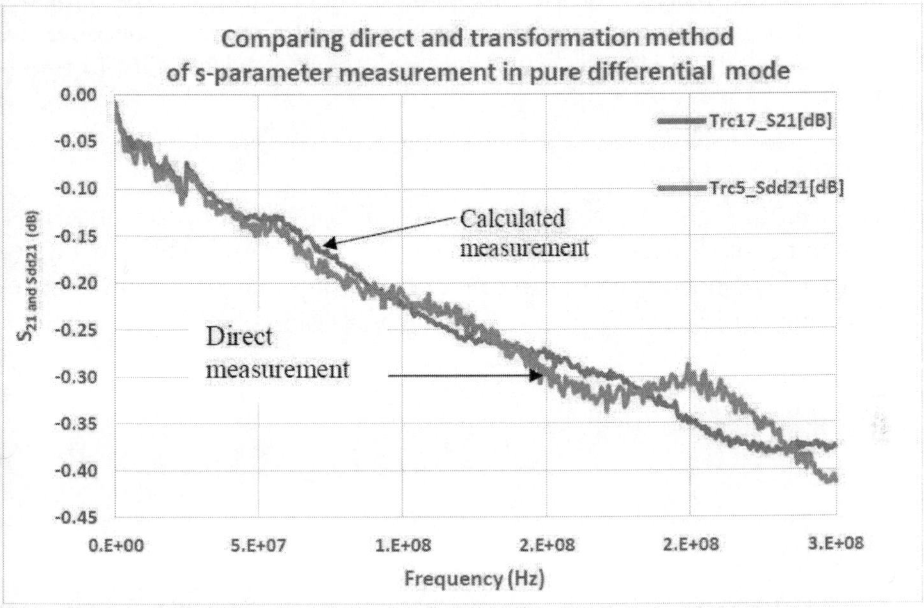

Figure 5.9 Comparing direct Mixed-mode s-parameter and Transformation method from single-ended measurement

However, the slight inconsistency in the plots especially at high frequency can be explained by the effect of the terminal resistors used to balance the impedance of the line. Precision type resistors with very low impedance tolerance could perform better.

5.10 Properties of a Network

1. Network Reciprocity

Any network that has got no active devices, no transistors, vacuum tubes (valves), tunnel diodes, etc. (i.e., entirely passive) is regarded as a reciprocal network [106].

For a reciprocal network

$[S] = [S]^T$, where T is the transpose.

This can be rewritten as

$$\begin{bmatrix} S_{11} & S_{12} \\ S_{21} & S_{22} \end{bmatrix}^T = \begin{bmatrix} S_{11} & S_{21} \\ S_{12} & S_{22} \end{bmatrix}$$

From the expression for the transpose of this matrix, the rows for the matrix has become the columns, and similarly, the columns become the rows. This matrix can apparently serve as a test for reciprocity in a network.

2. Return Loss

The loss of signal power via reflection as a result of impedance mismatch can be used to describe return loss, RL. With return loss, the higher the value of RL in dB specification the better [106]. Like, insertion loss, return loss is expressed in decibel (dB). The expression of RL is given below.

$$RL = -20\log\left|\frac{Vr}{Vi}\right|dB$$

$$= -20\log S_{11}\ dB$$

$$= -20\log \Gamma_1\ dB$$

Alternatively, RL can be expressed as the ratio of reflected power to incident power, i.e.,

$$RL = 10\ \log\frac{P\ reflected}{P\ incident}\ dB$$

Return loss can be affected by port terminations during measurements. All input and output ports need to be terminated in the characteristic impedance. Input and output ports not properly terminated will result in poor input RL and output RL, respectively.

For a perfectly matched system where the reflection coefficient is zero, the return loss is infinity [107].

If a port is completely mismatched, all the signals will have to be returned, and the RL will be zero dBm. This is further explained for the two cases below:

CASE 1	RL
Perfectly matched	$\infty(\Gamma_i = 0)$
CASE 2	
Mismatch	0dB $(\Gamma_i = 1)$

It is desirable for all designs to have high values of RL (i.e., - ∞dB), but this is extremely unachievable. In reality, it is difficult to have a perfectly matched network. So, as much as possible a high RL value is required across all frequencies.

3. Insertion loss

The loss of signal power (attenuation) due to the insertion of a device is known as insertion loss, IL. The expression can be written as follows

$$IL_{ij} = -20\log \frac{Vout}{Vin} \text{ dB}$$

$$IL_{21} = -20\log S_{21} \text{ dB}$$

Alternatively, it can be stated as the relation of the output power to the input power, i.e.

$$IL = 10 \log \frac{P \text{ output power}}{P \text{ input}} \text{ dB}$$

In order words, it is a measure of the decrease in signal strength that results from introducing a circuit into a network. IL through a passive device is ideally considered as a low loss, i.e., the magnitude of loss remains constant at all frequencies. However, in reality, this loss may vary several tenths of a dB across the frequency band of interest. With IL a small value is generally preferred. One characteristic of IL in a passive network is that it is the same if the signal is propagated from input to output or from output to the input port of the device being tested.

5.11 Unbalanced and Balanced Port Configuration

Single-ended ports are largely regarded as unbalanced ports. Unbalanced-to-balanced conversion is possible using transformers (baluns) which separate the input signal into differential and common mode equivalents. However, measuring instruments like the vector network analyser measures the unbalanced state and translates the results into mixed mode balanced parameters. In this work, no basic transformers were required. For balanced measurement, two network analyser ports were aggregated to form a logical port. The balanced port of the DUT was then connected to the configured balanced port of the network analyser. Moreover, any two arbitrary ports of the VNA can be chosen to form a balanced port with independence reference impedance values. A balanced port configuration can be defined as the combination of the pairs of any physical ports to form balanced ports with the two reference impedances defined as differential and common mode at each balanced port. Figure 5.10 shows the diagram for unbalanced (single-ended) ports and balanced port configuration.

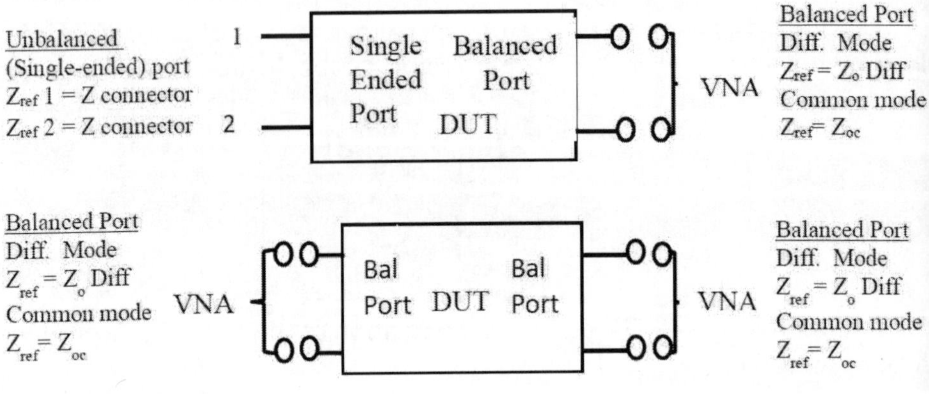

Figure 5.10 Unbalanced and Balanced port configurations

Chapter Summary

This chapter has discussed the merits of using the s-parameter over other parameter techniques in characterising differential networks. The chapter has presented the derivation of network parameters using a single-ended link and showed how the connection can be employed to originate all the sixteen single-ended s-parameters of a DUT. The standard conversion technique of a 4-port single-ended mode to the mixed-mode differential measurement using the idea of linear similarity transformation has also been discussed.

In the next chapter, attention will be devoted to the application of the concept to practical differential circuits. This leads to the design and fabrication of RF differential transmission lines (symmetric/balanced and asymmetric/unbalanced) and the measurement of the mixed-mode characteristics.

CHAPTER 6

THE FABRICATION AND TESTING OF DIFFERENTIAL STRUCTURES

From the knowledge of the fundamentals of balanced differential line propagation, this chapter deals with the fabrication of the RF differential structures (symmetrical and asymmetrical) for the purpose of relating the performance of the CUT to the performance of the test structures. In chapter 5, the concepts of mixed-mode s-parameter were established. In this chapter, these concepts and measurement systems will be applied to the analysis of some test structures and circuits. The chapter will focus on the s-parameter measurement and analysis of symmetric/balanced and asymmetric/unbalanced structures which will provide insight into the performance of unshielded twisted network cable. Although the twisted pair cables are generally regarded as balanced transmission lines, there is a possibility that the nonuniformity in the rate of cable twists could make the line unbalanced. It could be argued, however, that the unbalance in the twist rate is supposed to be taken care of by the test instrument calibration. Nevertheless, measuring instruments do have residual error even after calibration.

The test structures are constructed to give good examples of the practical usage of the mixed-mode s-parameter concept in measuring and analysing RF differential devices. Moreover, they can provide a reasonable degree of confidence in the accuracy of the measurement results. These test fixtures offer vital evidence about the implementation of practical differential structures and the results obtained will be used as a reference for testing and analysing the s-parameters of unshielded twisted pair cables.

In this study, the test fixtures (symmetrical and asymmetrical) were fabricated and experimented upon to investigate their performance in terms of mode-specific behaviours such as noise conversion and coupling. The structures were made with copper microstrip on FR4 substrate (relative permittivity, $\varepsilon_r = 4.3$, loss tangent = 0.025), and the microstrip widths were defined with a characteristic impedance of 50 Ω. The 50 Ω unique impedance of the transmission line was calculated using macros which is a numerical tool for computing impedances of transmission lines with respect to relative permittivity, absolute permittivity, frequency, trace thickness, etc. However, the width of the microstrip can be determined directly using the expression given below

$$w = \frac{7.48 * h}{e\left(z_o \frac{\sqrt{\varepsilon_r + 1.41}}{87}\right)} - 1.25 * t$$

where z_o = reference/single-ended impedance,

w = width of trace

t = trace thickness

h = dielectric thickness

ϵ_r = relative permittivity

Both fixtures were considered as weakly coupled transmission line because the thickness of the substrate was much smaller than the edge-to-edge spacing between the top copper lines [108]. Moreover, in fabricating these microstrip designs, each signal path was designed disregarding coupling between the two adjacent signal [109] paths. Hence, both the differential-mode and the common-mode characteristic impedances were assumed to be 50 Ω right from the design process, thus allowing consideration for weakly coupled transmission paths. Table 6.1 shows the related dimensions and materials of the test fixture parameters. The designs and fabrication of the transmission fixtures used in the experiments were done by the author. All the structures were fabricated using the PCB Router facility of De Montfort University Interfacing Laboratory.

The choice of using FR4 substrate type was influenced by availability and cost. However, Rogers substrate type would give a better performance considering the range of frequencies used in the experiment.

Table 6.1 Test Fixture Geometric Parameters

	Balanced line	**Unbalanced line**
Copper thickness	0.035mm	0.035mm
Copper width	3.137mm	Stepped 1.5mm; 5mm
Line impedance, Z_o	50Ω	50Ω
Spacing between track	3.137mm	3.340mm

Substrate thickness	1.6mm	1.6mm
Substrate type	FR4	FR4
Dielectric constant	4.3	4.3
Loss tangent	0.025	0.025
Metal conductivity	5.96e+007[s/m]	5.96e+007[s/m]

6.1 Fundamentals of Differential Circuit Propagation

For ease of understanding, Figure 6.1 shows the response of a *perfect* differential transmission line. It shows a simultaneous propagation of two signal modes – mixed mode - (notably common and differential modes) to a coupled transmission line. For most practical applications, differential circuits will include some form of reference conductor. This reference ground makes it easy for the common mode signal to be propagated. The capacity of differential circuit to propagate both differential and common mode signals makes it easy to characterise other modes transmitted at the same time.

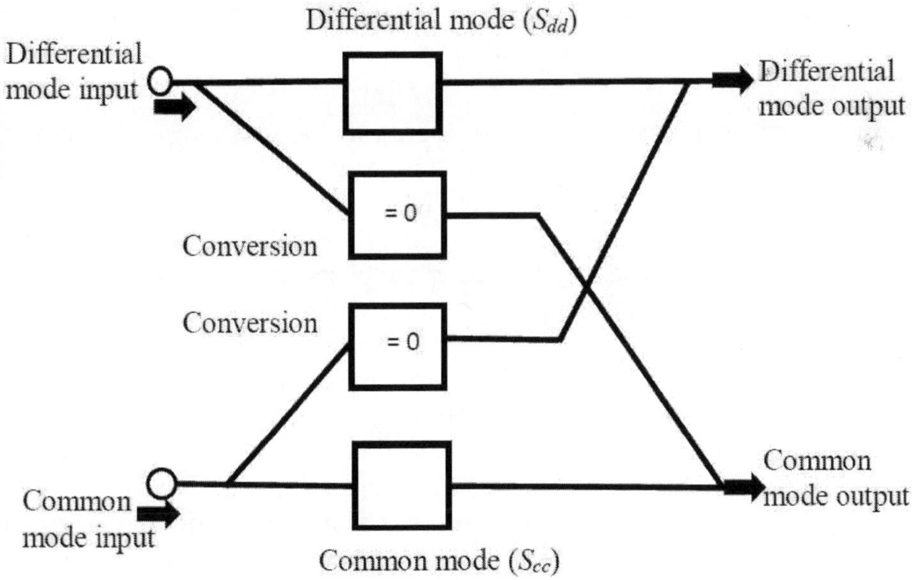

Figure 6.1 Description of the response of a *perfectly* balanced transmission line

It has been shown [110] [111] [112] that totally symmetric (or balanced) differential circuits show no mode conversion. If therefore the investigation is restricted to symmetric circuits alone, (i.e., by ignoring asymmetry), the occurrence of mode conversion can be entirely disregarded. Mode conversion happens when a stimulus of a pure mode produces a response with more than one mode. For instance, if a pure differential signal drives an active device, and both a differential-mode and common-mode response signals are produced, then some transformation from differential to common mode has taken place. Understanding mode conversion is an essential experience in RF systems, and it helps to predict the performance of differential circuits. As in the literature [113], mode conversion has been shown to affect the maximum attainable common-mode rejection ratio (CMRR). CMRR is a significant parameter of differential active devices which specifies the capacity of the active device to reinforce differential signals and discard common-mode signals.

6.2 Symmetric Differential Structure Test

It is worthy of note that the idea behind the test fixtures was to relate the performance of the cable to the performance of the structures since a balanced microstrip line, like a twisted pair cable, can both be regarded as balanced lines. It was also envisaged that the test results of the microstrip lines could be used to interpret the cable data. As well, the test fixtures can also be referred to as coupled structures because the microstrip transmission lines were lined so reasonably adjacent to each other [114].

In this manner, they can be considered as being a single differential transmission line. The lines can also be regarded as balanced because the pair had a constant cross-section over its length. Thus, the impedance of each transmission line was designed with a minimal characteristic impedance of 50 Ω to match the impedance of the ports of the measuring instrument. The width of each transmission path was 3.137 mm, and the edge-to-edge spacing between them was also 3.137 mm. The two signal paths can, therefore, be said to be symmetrical (within production tolerance) with the phase and magnitude balance between the two being 1800 (for differential stimulus). The gap, between the ends of the test structure and the edges of the conducting copper track, was also copper and 3.137 mm, and this has been added to reduce parasitic resonance at high frequency as much as possible. The bottom of the stripboard was metalised with pure copper to form the ground plane. Hence, both the differential and common mode waves can propagate on the differential line structure according to the relationship between the common mode current and voltage.

However, if the two paths were not symmetrical, remarkable levels of mode conversion could be expected. In that case, a source of differential mode voltage can produce a common mode current on the line which is capable of causing radiation from the differential line.

Figure 6.2 shows the fabricated test structure of the balanced differential transmission line.

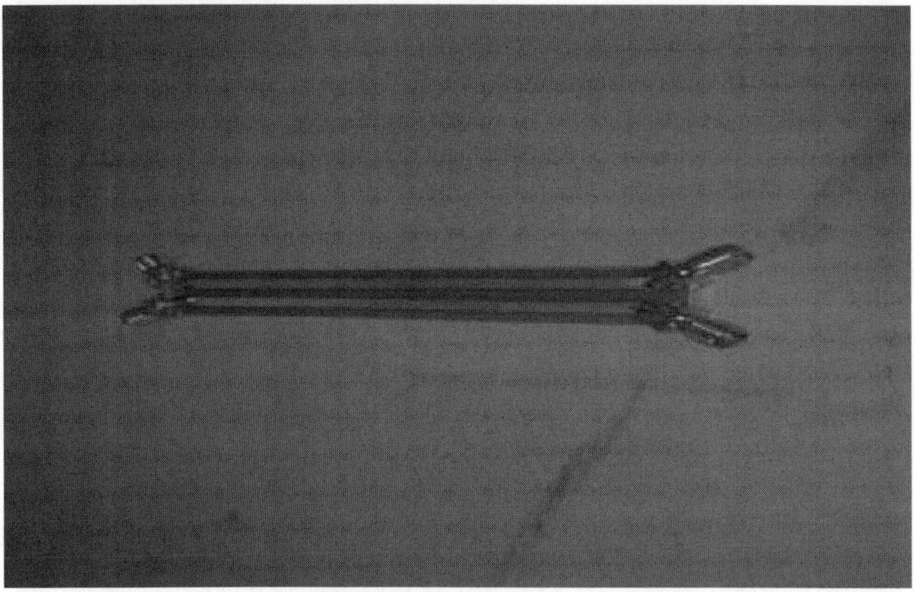

Figure 6.2 Showing the Microstrip Symmetric/balanced test structure

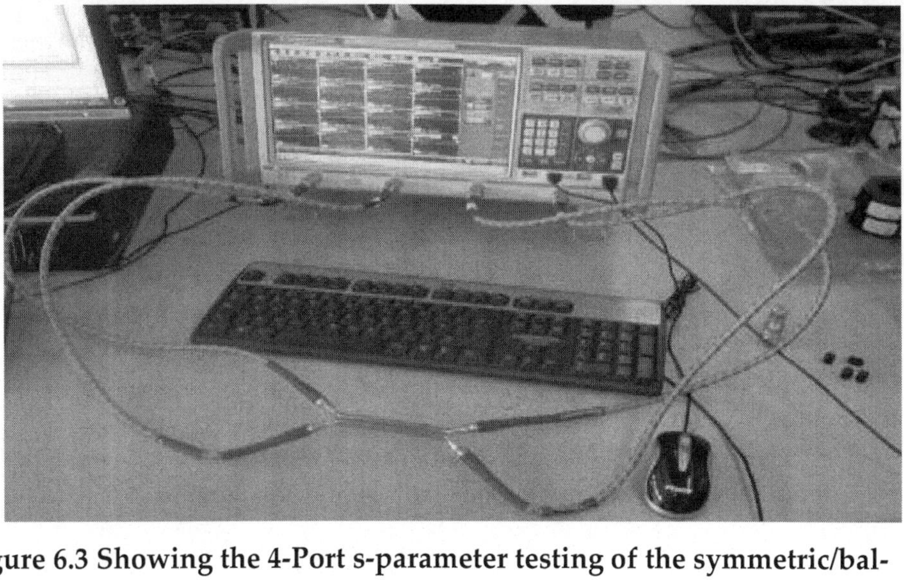

Figure 6.3 Showing the 4-Port s-parameter testing of the symmetric/balanced test structure

The instrument setting and test specification have already been discussed in 3.7. All the measurements were made in a single sweep across frequency resulting in a magnitude (dB gain/loss) versus frequency characteristics.

From the result matrix, the *dd* quadrant describes the basic functioning in the pure differential mode setup. The *cc* quadrant describes the fundamental performance in pure common mode operation. The *dc* describes common mode stimulus to differential response while the *cd* quadrant depicts the conversion of the differential to common mode. Both *dc* and *cd* quadrants represent the cross-conversion modes. The test was conducted between 250 MHz – 550 MHz frequency with differential input signal of 10 dB in ports 1 and 3, while the response was monitored in ports 2 and 4 of the VNA. This frequency range was chosen in line with the design calculation of the impedance of the microstrip line.

6.3 Mixed-Mode S-parameter Measurement for the Symmetric Microstrip Line

The microstrip conductor lines were designed to have a cross-section of 3.137 mm along the entire length of the structure with an edge-to-edge spacing of 3.137 mm and a total length of 100 mm (which makes the structure symmetric). From the default setting of the test instrument, a differential-mode impedance of 100 Ω and a common-mode impedance of 25 Ω were selected. Figure 6.4 shows the linear magnitude plots in dB for the pure differential-mode responses of the balanced structure against frequency.

6.4 Balance Microstrip Parameter Plot in dB Magnitude

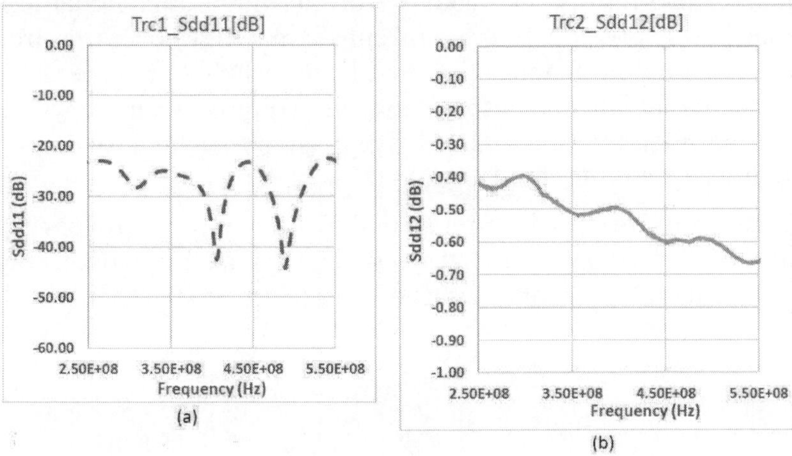

Differential Return loss = -23.3dB at 550 MHz

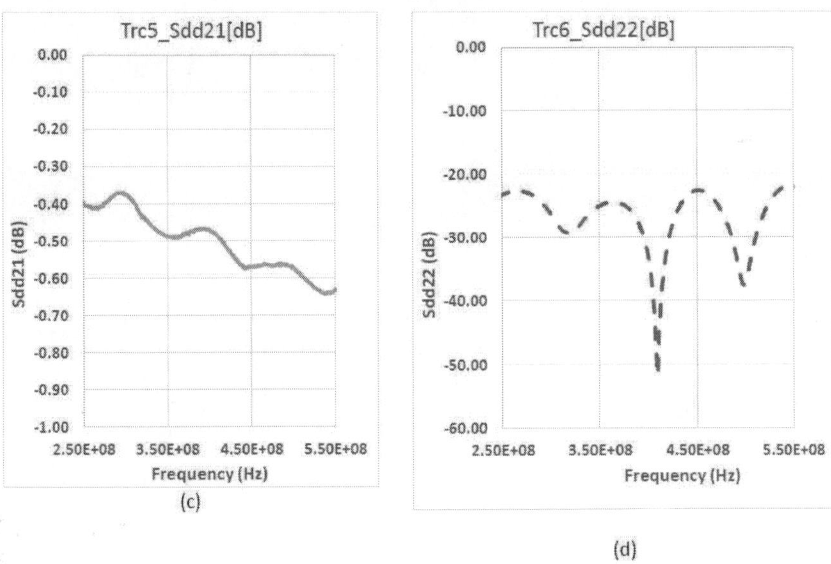

Differential Insertion loss = -0.63dB at 550

Figure 6.4 Measurement of symmetric mixed-mode s-parameter in pure differential (*dd*) mode

As anticipated, individual subdivision of the matrix (see also the touchstone data in section 6.4) exhibits the quality of a reciprocal and symmetric DUT. As can be seen from Figure 6.4 (a), the pure differential return loss is between -23 dB to -23.4 dB across the 250 MHz – 550 MHz frequency range.

This represents power loss through signal reflection due to impedance mismatch. It also represents about 7% of the differential signal loss due to mismatch. It is possible that the mismatch may have occurred from the default differential impedance (selected from the VNA) for the test which is 100 Ω, while the instrument reference impedance remains at 50 Ω. The structure can, therefore, be said to behave like a matched, low-loss transmission line to the differential signal.

The structure also has the minima in the differential return loss of -44dB at about 490 MHz. At 550 MHz (representing the max frequency), however, the structure has a differential insertion loss of about - 0.635dB.

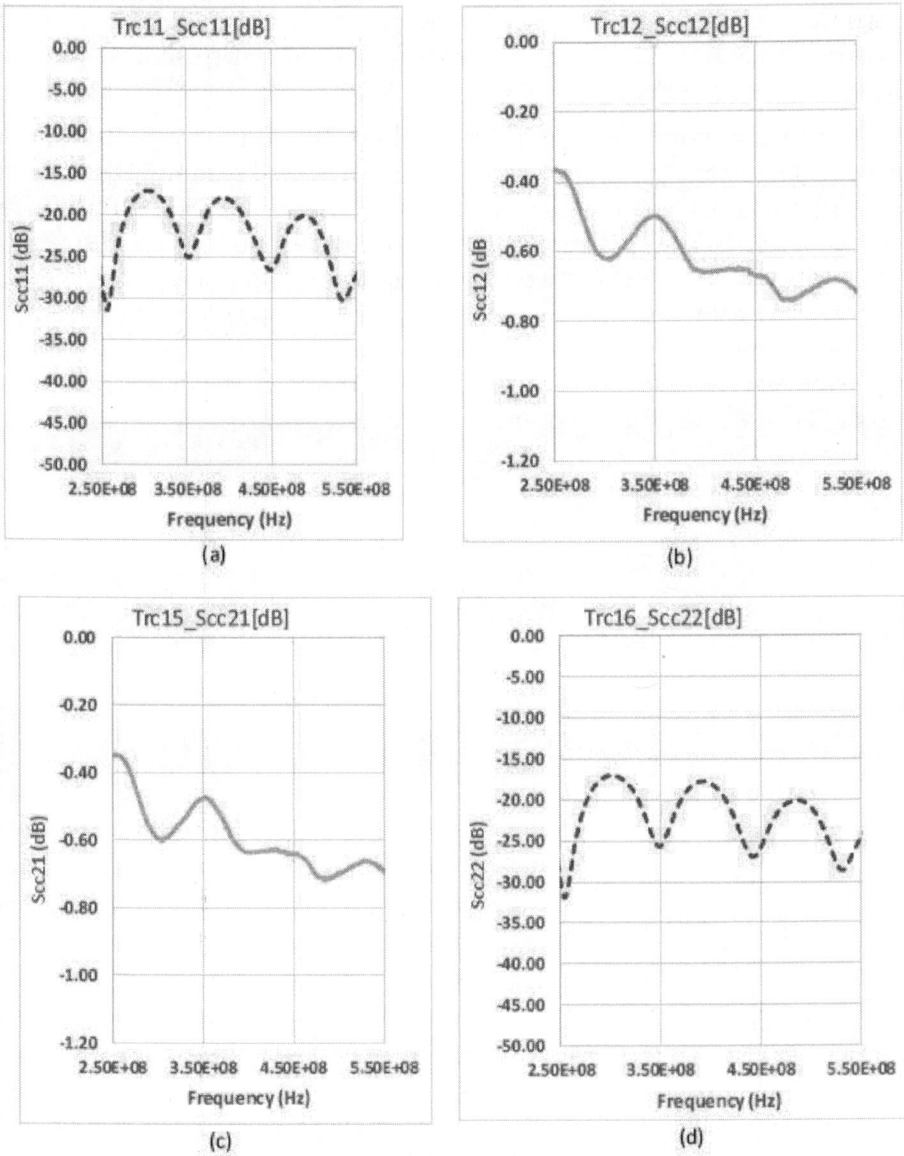

Figure 6.5 Measurement of symmetric mixed-mode s-parameters in pure common (*cc*) mode

In the common-mode s-parameters (Figure 6.5), the magnitudes in dB of the common mode responses are plotted against frequency. The differential test structure exhibits a mismatch in the common-mode characteristic impedance of 25 Ω as selected in the 4-port VNA. The plot of the return loss element in the first quadrant of the pure common mode shows some periodic variations which displays an indication of an impedance mismatch from what the set reference is. However, the two reflection parameters (forward and reverse) are very nearly the same which shows evidence of good port symmetry as expected.

In summary, both the pure differential-mode and pure common-mode insertion losses Sdd_{21} and Scc_{21} are approximately the same (-0.36 dB to -0.65 dB) and (-0.42 dB to -0.63 dB) within 250 MHz to 550 MHz test frequency range. This represents a measure of the decrease in signal strength that results when the microstrip structure is in use. In line with the generally accepted rule of thumb for insertion loss measurement, this value is bound to be mostly small.

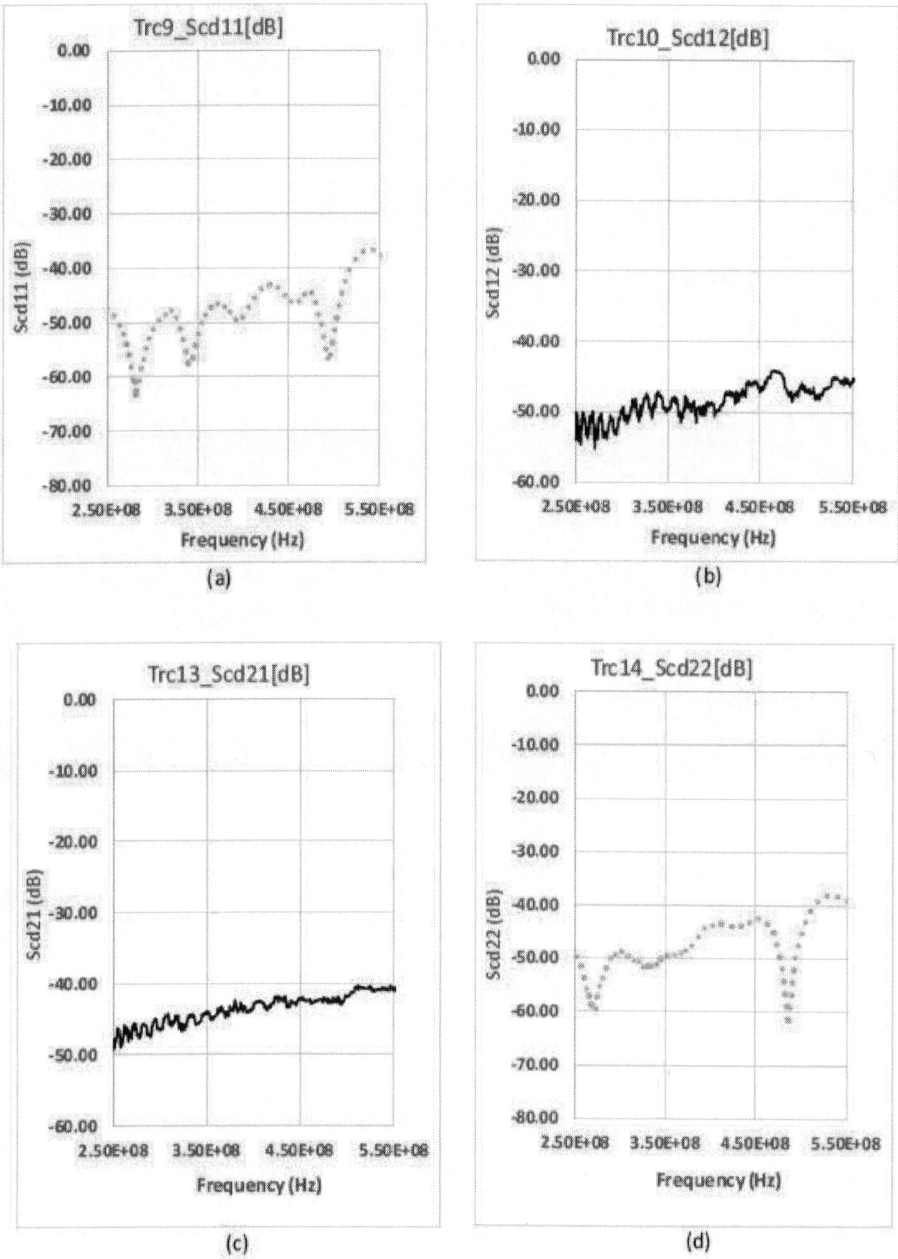

Figure 6.6 Measurement of symmetrical mixed-mode s-parameters in differential-to-common mode (c*d*) conversion.

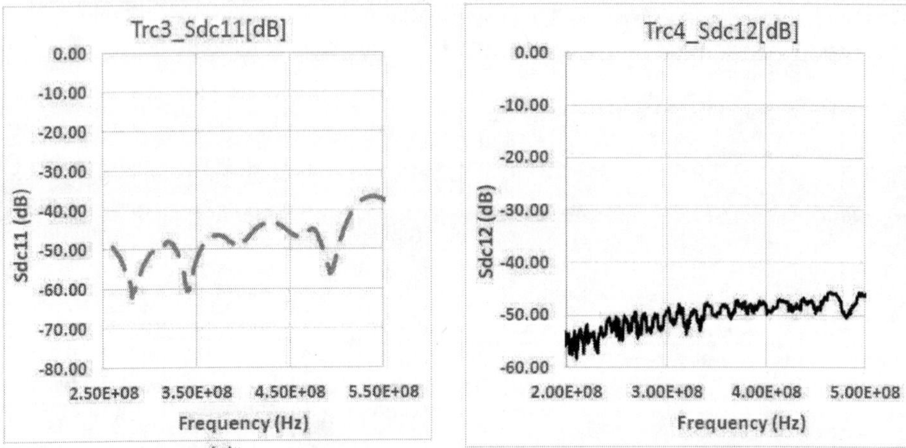

(a) (b)

N/B: The return loss in both conversion modes (DC and CD) are indistinguishable. They look very much the same. Both show the relatively low level of conversion in the reflection parameter (-37.1dB and -37.8dB at max freq).

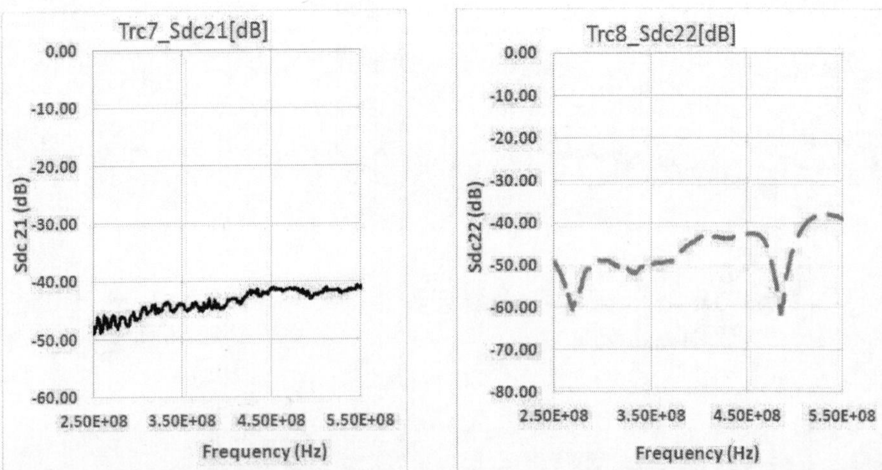

(c) (d)

Figure 6.7 Measurement of symmetric mixed-mode s-parameters in common-to-differential mode conversion (*dc*) mode.

In Figures 6.6 and 6.7, the cross-mode conversion response plots in dB magnitude are plotted against frequency. Unlike the pure differential and pure common-mode s-parameters (S_{dd} & S_{cc}) explained above, the results show very strong symmetry of the differential structure. The plots show a reasonably low level of mode conversion in the reflection parameters.

From section (6.1), *perfect* symmetric structures do not support mode conversion. However, very low level of transformation could be observed in the insertion loss plots of Figure 6.6 and 6.7 between 250 MHz to 550 MHz with the peak insertion loss occurring at 550 MHz. A possible explanation for this may be due to manufacturing issues in the microstrip lines. From the data in equation (6.1), it can be seen that the level of conversion between the propagation modes in the transmission parameters of S_{dc21} and S_{cd21} is very low at 550 MHz (about -40 dB). This represents 1% conversion loss of the differential signal to common mode signal and vice versa. Hence, the mode transition parameters (S_{dc21} and S_{cd21}) of the symmetric structure thus supports the fact that there is insignificant transform (mode-conversion) between the two modes.

Furthermore, since there is theoretically an insignificant mode conversion in symmetrical structures, differential and common-mode signals at the output port are practically the same as the input ports [114] [115].

6.4 (a) Touchstone File Data for the Symmetric Microstrip Line at 550 MHz

$$\begin{array}{c|c} S_{dd} & S_{dc} \\ \hline S_{cd} & S_{cc} \end{array} = \left[\begin{array}{cc|cc} -31.5\angle-178 & -0.14\angle160 & -38.5\angle69.5 & -43.3\angle-112 \\ -0.12\angle-161 & -31.1\angle-177 & -40.2\angle112 & -38.5\angle-69.5 \\ \hline -38.5\angle69.7 & -43.1\angle-113 & -31.2\angle-177 & -0.15\angle160 \\ -40.3\angle-112 & -38.5\angle69.4 & -0.13\angle-160 & -31.8\angle-179 \end{array}\right] \quad (6.1)$$

It is worthy to note that the 550 MHz frequency is not a unique reference frequency, but the upper test frequency used in this experiment. In other words, at frequencies outside 550 MHz, the results of the test would not be the same, i.e., the data file will read differently.

Equation 6.1 represents the *.s4p data file* for the s-parameter at 550 MHz. Each division of the submatrix shows the passive, reciprocal, port symmetry property of the DUT. S_{dd} shows the differential s-parameter of the symmetrical test fixture with 100 Ω differential impedance. S_{cc} shows the common mode s-parameter of the test fixture with 25Ω impedance. S_{cd} and

S_{dc} show the cross-conversion mode for the test fixture with low mode conversion between propagation modes.

6.5 Mixed-Mode S-parameter Measurement for the Asymmetric Microstrip Line

This asymmetrical structure is like the balanced test structure except that the midsection of one of the transmission lines is increased in width, while the other remains unchanged. Like the symmetric/balanced test structure, both ends are designed with a characteristic impedance of 50 Ω. However, the midsection of one of the transmission lines is 60 mm long while the lengths of the two ends are 40 mm. Although more would have been learnt by investigating an asymmetric structure with three different length sections, this was not considered since the later part of the research looked on imbalance due to length nonuniformity.

Hence, like in the case of the balanced structure, the total length of the test fixture is 100 mm. Since the midsection of one of the transmission lines is different in width with the other transmission line, the differential structure is considered as unbalanced/asymmetrical. Figure 6.8 shows the test structure of the unbalanced microstrip test structure with the stepped midsection cascaded in-between the narrower ends. However, the narrower ends have the same impedance as the reference 50 Ω impedance.

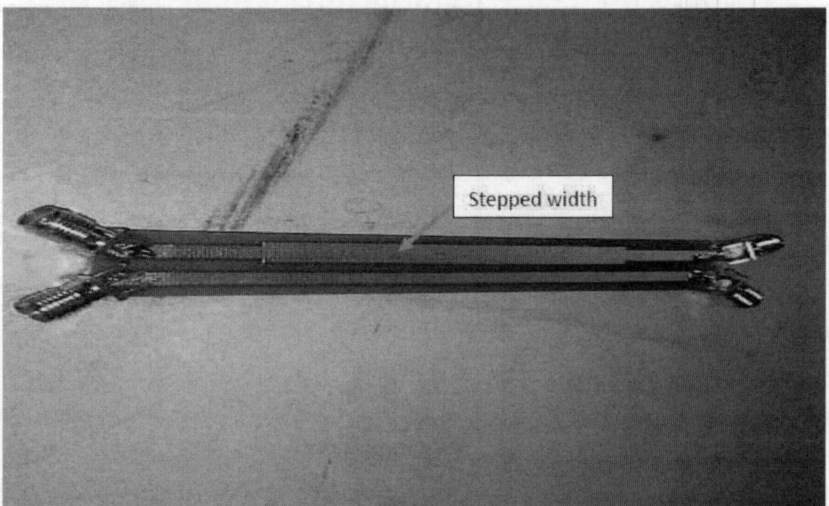

Figure 6.8 Test structure of an asymmetric microstrip test structure

Measurement results obtained from S_{dd}, S_{dc}, S_{cd} and S_{cc} are shown and analysed below.

6.6 Mixed-Mode S-Parameter Measurement of the Asymmetric Microstrip Line

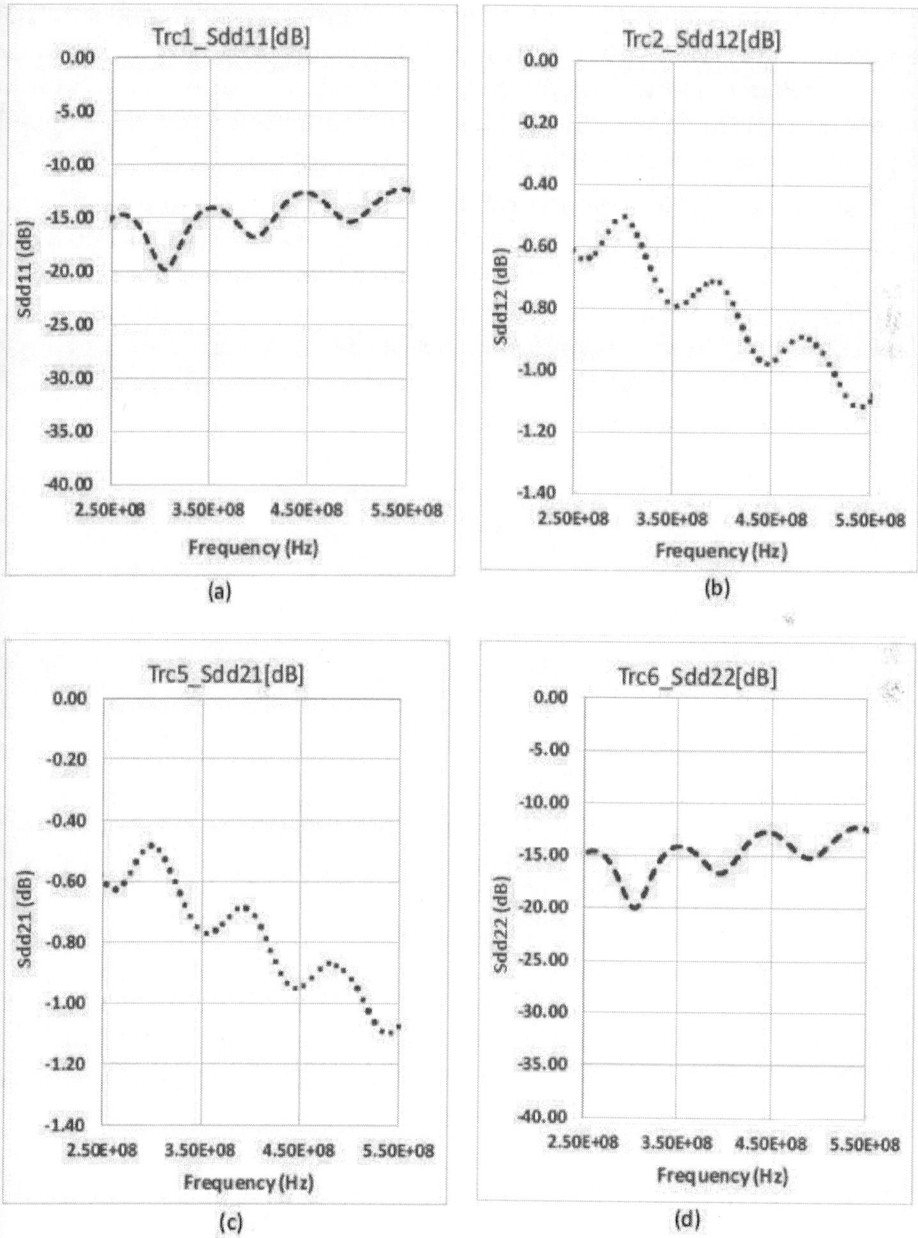

Figure 6.9 Measurement of asymmetric mixed-mode s-parameters in pure differential *(dd)* mode

Despite being an asymmetric structure, results of the measured pure differential-mode responses (*dd*) show that the structure is a good differential line. The differential return loss is between -15 dB to -12.3 dB within 250 MHz and 550 MHz and it tends to increase with frequency. This represents a 24% maximum return loss of transmitted signal at 550 MHz due to mismatch. However, unlike the symmetric structure, it shows more pronounced periodic variations. It can thus be suggested that the stepped impedance in one of transmission line is responsible for this.

A significant noticeable occurrence is that the minima in the differential return loss of this structure are at a slightly lower frequency (-20 dB at 308 MHz) when compared with that of the balanced structure (-43 dB at 490 MHz). This fundamental difference can also be explained in part by the stepped increase in the dimension of one of the microstrip lines.

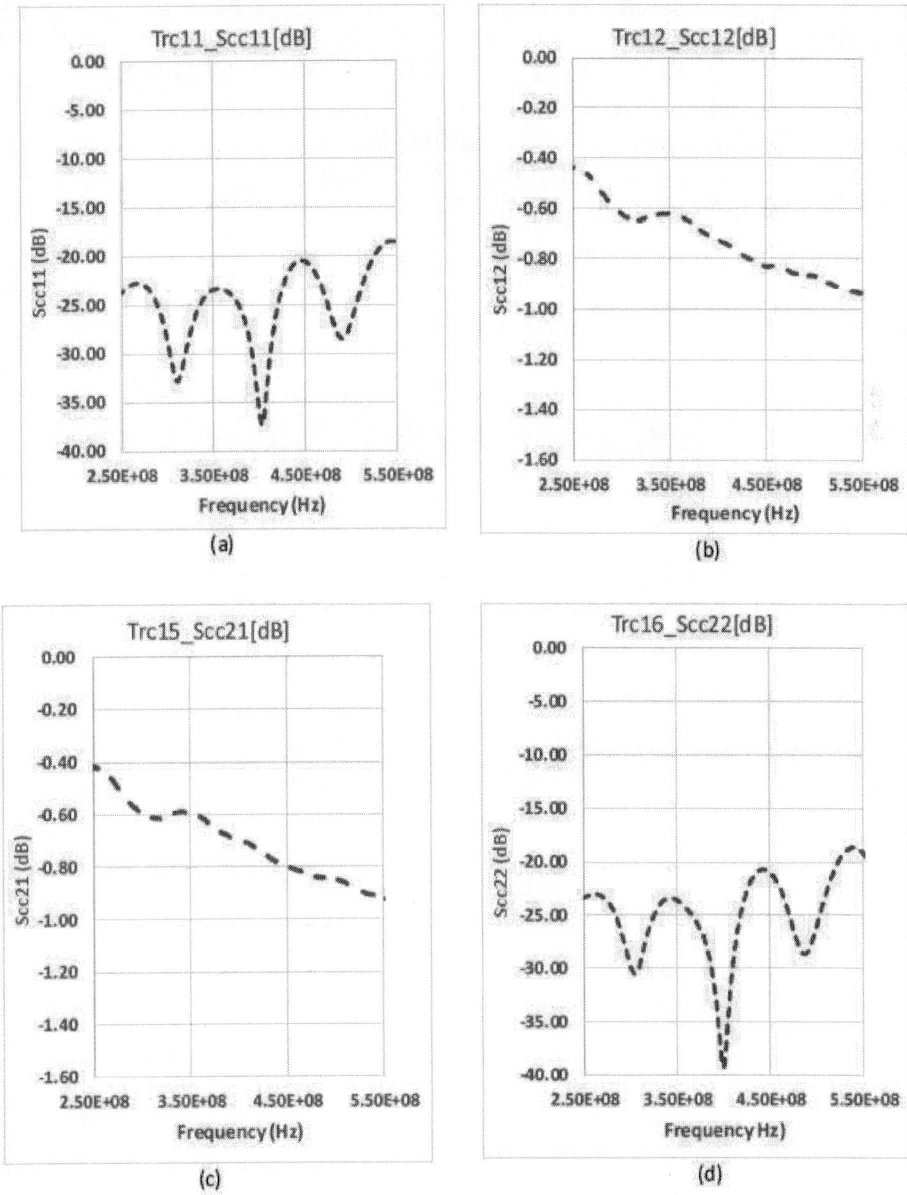

Figure 6.10 Measurements of asymmetrical mixed-mode s-parameters in pure common mode (*cc*).

Figure 6.10 shows the measured responses of the unbalanced (asymmetric) line in the common mode. The response is almost comparable to that of the balanced line. However, the major/significant difference is in the return loss parameters, especially at lower frequencies. While the minima of the return loss of the common mode occur at significantly higher frequencies (-37 dB at about 402 MHz), that of the symmetric structure occurs at a lower frequency (-31.6 dB at 256 MHz). These results are also likely to be related to the difference due to increased step impedance in one of the microstrip lines which results in the lack of field symmetry. Also, the differential-mode electrical length of the midsection of the asymmetrical fixture is less than its same physical length.

Generally, it can be seen from Figures 6.9 and 6.10 that both the pure differential and common mode transmission ratios, Sdd_{21} and Scc_{21}, decreased with frequency. This result may be related to attenuation effect due to structural asymmetry.

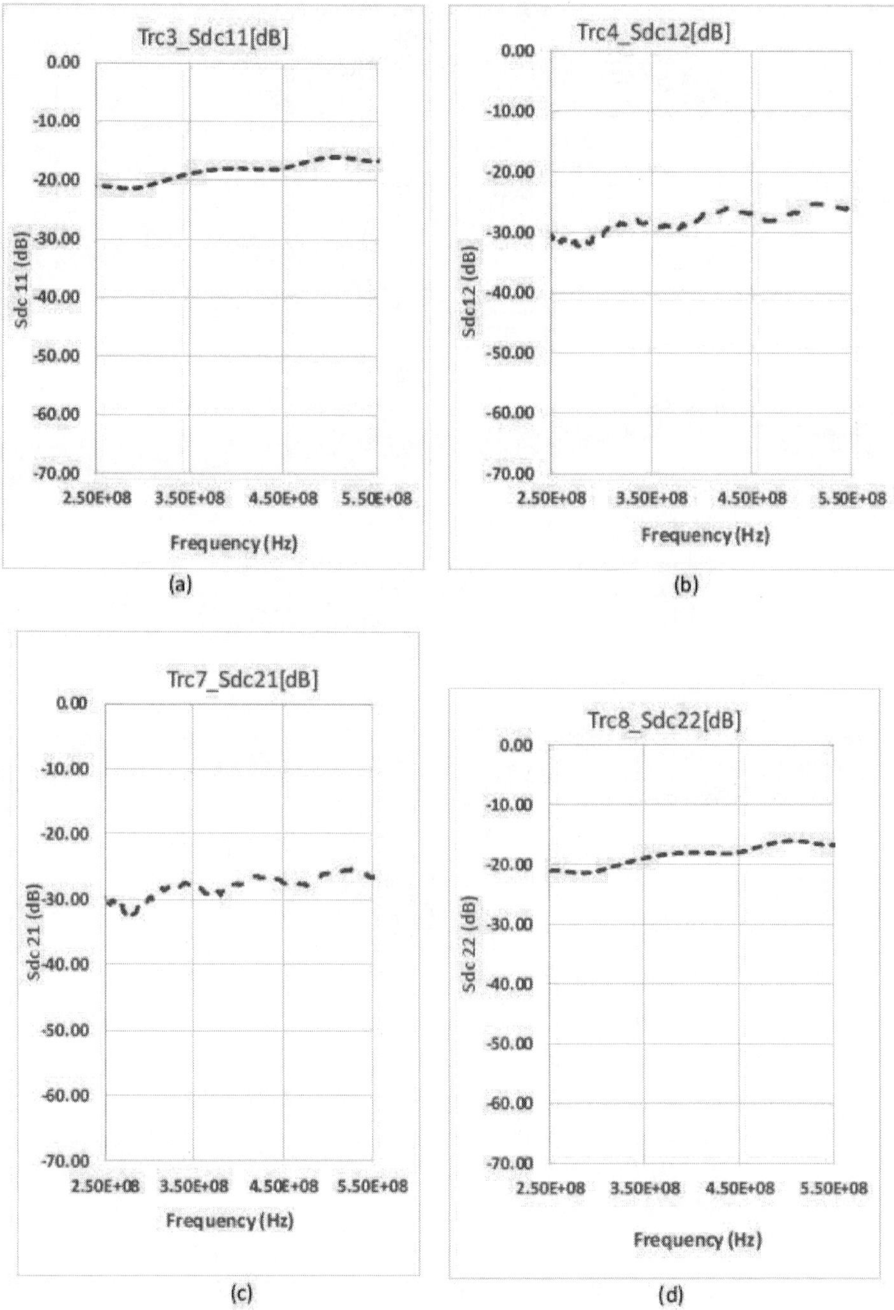

Figure 6.11 Measurement of asymmetric mixed-mode s-parameters in common-to-differential conversion mode (*dc*).

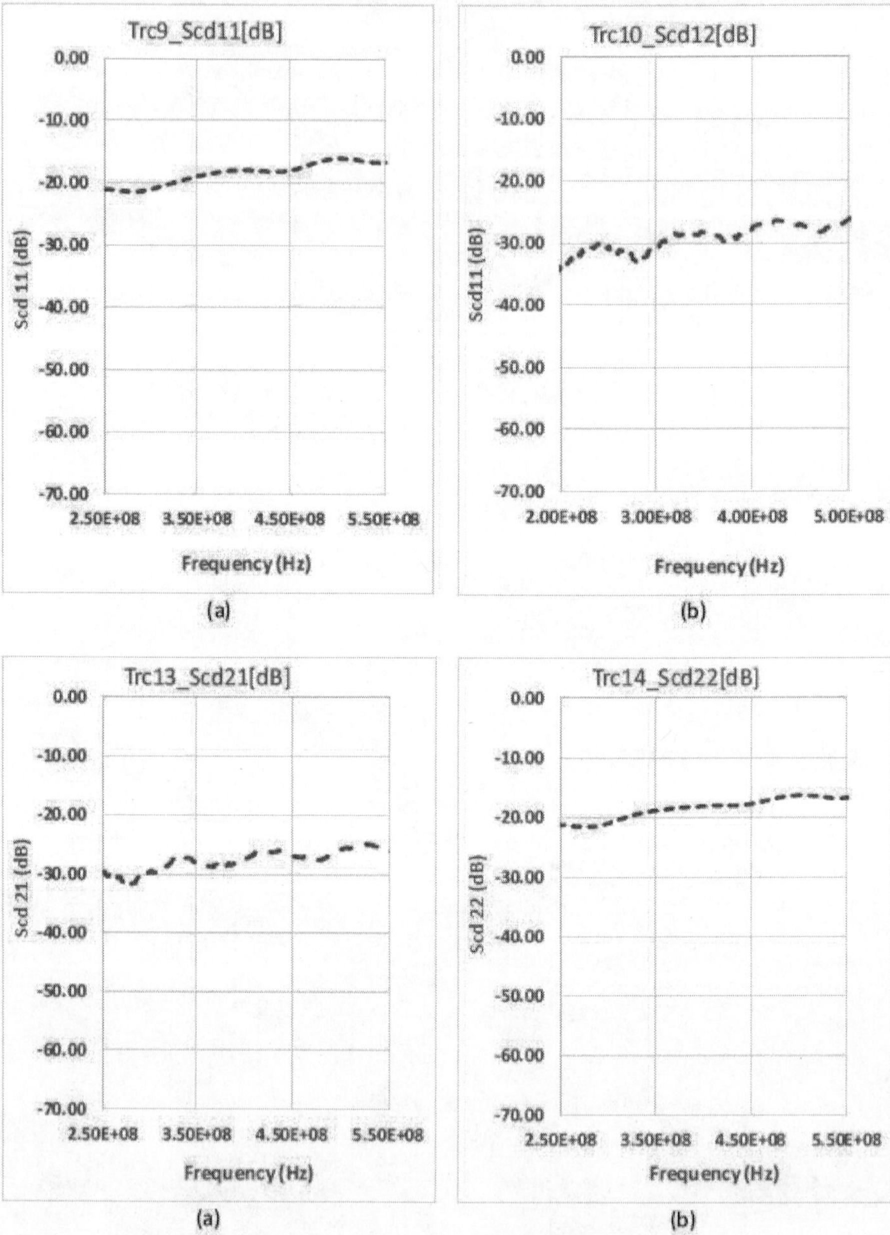

Figure 6.12 Measurement of asymmetrical mixed mode s-parameters in differential-to-common mode conversion (*cd*).

Figures 6.11 and 6.12 represent the mode conversion parameters (*dc* and *cd*) of the asymmetric transmission line test structure. The results of the cross-mode conversion of the asymmetric structure indicate an increase in the conversion level across the test frequency. Compared with the symmetric structure, the conversion level is very high especially in the return loss or the reflection parameters (about -16.7 dB) as against about – 37.5 dB at the highest frequency, respectively. This indicates an appreciable mode conversion for the asymmetric structure when compared with that of its symmetric counterpart.

Moreover, in the insertion loss parameters of Figures 6.11 and 6.12 (i.e. Sdc21 and Scd21), the symmetric structure measured -40 dB (about 1%) and the asymmetric structure measured -26 dB (about 5%) at the highest (550 MHz) frequency. This shows that about 5% more of signal cross conversion takes place in the asymmetric structure compared with that of the symmetric structure at the maximum frequency.

Compared with the mixed-mode s-parameter measurement for the symmetric (balanced) line, the stepped width of the asymmetric structure substantially affected the mode conversion responses. However, the pure differential mode (S_{dd}) and the pure common mode (S_{cc}) responses were less affected. Nevertheless, slightly higher level of signal strength was attenuated in the pure differential parameter of the asymmetric structure (S_{dd21} = 1.09 dB) than in the symmetric structure (S_{dd21} = 0.635 dB). It can thus be suggested that the imbalance in the step impedance was responsible for the s-parameter mode conversion responses in the asymmetric test structure.

The results also show some increased amplitude variations in the insertion loss of the cross-conversion mode. It may well be the case therefore that these variations may as well have been caused by the imbalance in one of the differential lines.

One significant outcome of this result is that the magnitude of S_{dc21} and S_{cd21} tend to increase (deteriorate) with frequency. One possible explanation for the case of S_{cd21} is that a differential stimulus at port 1 has increasingly been converted to common mode response at port 2 with rising frequency. This is supported by a corresponding increase in all the common mode values as evidenced in Figure 6.12. Although, at port 2 both the common mode and the differential mode signals happen, some portion of the energy in the differential mode has been transformed to common mode. This could result in a significant amount of common mode noise which may interfere with adjacent systems causing signal integrity issues as well.

6.7 Data file for the Asymmetric Microstrip Line

The data in equation 6.2 describes the behaviour of the asymmetric structure at the maximum frequency of about f = 550MHz. The data file with subscript "$_{mm}$" shows the parameters are in mixed mode format; the vertical bars specify the values of the magnitude terms, and ∠, the angle sign, represents the phase of the parameter. Equation 6.2 also shows evidence of good reciprocity in the parameter terms and port symmetry.

$$S_{mm} = \begin{array}{c|c} S_{dd} & S_{dc} \\ \hline S_{cd} & S_{cc} \end{array} = \begin{array}{cc|cc} -12.3\angle -109 & -1.09\angle -131 & -16.3\angle -141 & -26.3\angle 96.8 \\ -1.07\angle -131 & -12.5\angle -107 & -26.5\angle -97.6 & -16.6\angle -142 \\ \hline -16.5\angle -141 & -26.1\angle -96.1 & -18.9\angle -19.7 & -0.94\angle -128 \\ -26.1\angle -97.6 & -16.7\angle -142 & -0.91\angle -128 & -19.3\angle -13.3 \end{array} \tag{6.2}$$

As can be seen, the results show there is significant cross mode conversion between the propagation modes of S_{dc} and S_{cd} when compared with that of the symmetric structure. The data also shows that all the terms in the two conversion sub-matrices are very nearly equal, demonstrating equal mode conversion from differential to common and from common to differential modes.

The table below gives a summary of the consequence of cross-mode conversion on the return loss and the insertion loss for both differential lines.

Table 6.2 Effect of Cross-mode conversion on Differential Return and Insertion looses

Cross mode Return loss	Maximum test frequency	Symmetric line	Asymmetric line
S_{dc11} S_{cd11}	550 MHz 550 MHz	-38.65 dB -38.65 dB	-16.7 dB -16.7 dB
Cross conversion Insertion loss			
S_{dc21} S_{cd21}	550 MHz 550 MHz	-40.2 dB -40.3 dB	-26.5 dB -26.1 dB

Return loss has been define as the ratio of the power received to the power transmitted and as usual, should be as small as possible. Expressed in dB, however, the return loss should be as significant a negative number as possible. Hence, from Table 6.2, the cross conversion return loss attests to the robustness of the test method. Also, the insertion loss which is a measure of attenuation in the transmission line is lower in the symmetric structure than in the asymmetric structure. This is also in line with the known principle and shows how good the test method is. It also has led to a further understanding of the effects of mode conversion on both return loss and insertion loss parameters.

From this result, it can be deduced that asymmetric structures are capable of signal mode conversion which could result in both EMC and Signal Integrity issues. In this test, the cause of imbalance had been linked to the asymmetric nature of the transmission line where the midsection of the transmission line had a different character with the rest of the line.

From here onwards the cause and effect of imbalance in differential structures is extended to unshielded twisted pair cabling. The aim is to investigate if imbalance resulting from unequal pair twisting can as well give rise to EMC and Signal Integrity issues as noticed in differential structures.

6.8 Fundamentals of Differential and Common-Mode Signals in Unshielded Twisted Pair Cables and Electromagnetic Compatibility Issues

Twisted pair cables are generally regarded as balanced lines and have wire pairs wound around each other in a helical structure as shown in Figure 6.13. In Figure 6.13, the first diagram shows the flow of the differential mode current which flows into the terminal load and back by the return path. This is denoted by $I_{\textit{differential current}}$. The second diagram represents the combinational flow of current from the first and second loops, I_{c}, and a ground return. This is designated as $I_{\textit{common mode}}$ and is often completed by parasitic capacitance (the gap between each twist wire and a reference return path).

Unshielded twisted pairs are found mostly in telephone and Ethernet networks and have copper wires covered with some jacketing material. In this section, the mixed-mode s-parameters of a Cat 6 UTP is tested and used to provide an example of signal mode conversion in network cables.

It is known that when a pair of the twisted cable is stimulated with pure differential mode stimulus, the currents in each wire will travel in opposite direction [115] and generate equal and opposite magnetic fields around the pairs. In an ideal case, however, if the pair has a uniform twist, the generated magnetic fields will cancel out. In that case, each twist reverses the direction of the induced magnetic field. Nonetheless; if there is no uniformity in the induced field, the generated magnetic fields will not precisely cancel out.

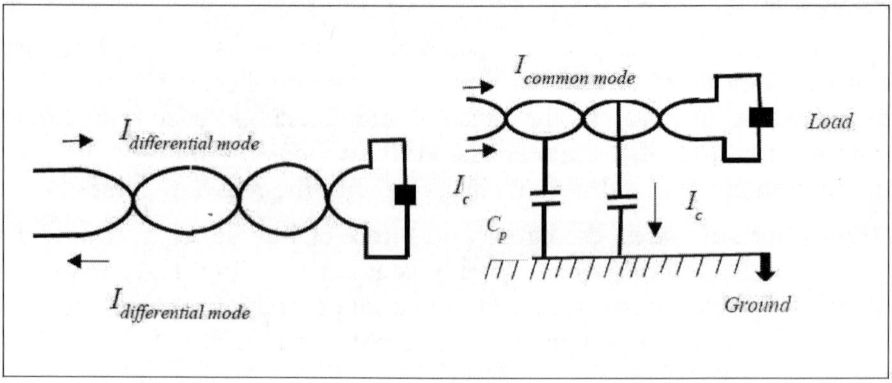

Figure 6.13 Showing the mechanism of mode conversion in unshielded twisted pair cabling

On the other hand, Figure 6.13 indicates that common-mode currents passing through the wires return to the virtual ground through the parasitic capacitors, C_p. The generated magnetic fields, in this case, are equal in magnitude and polarity and so do not cancel each other out [116] [117]. Hence, the generated EM fields outside the twist could cause the wires to behave more like unintentional radiators. Moreover, the radiated field is more when the return current loop is large. Thus, this work seeks to investigate if the nonuniformity in twist may result to asymmetry which can makes the cable behave more like an unintentional radiator.

6.9 The Design of the Test Head

The test head is an interface that provides a fixation method to establish connections between the CUT and the test instrument.

It must be noted here that standard test head devices are generally available in the open market for commercial solutions but are usually very expensive. However, these appropriate test heads are only for 4-pair terminations (16 terminal). As a result, it was decided to design and fabricate connecting devices for a single pair measurement with 4-terminals.

Figure 6.14 shows the test head that connects the ends of the CUT to the measuring balanced ports of the VNA. The test head, like the differential line, was designed using numerical modelling and fabricated in the Communications Lab of DMU. The figures below were used in the design specifications for the test head. The frequency range was extended to 550 MHz to cover the test frequency of the microstrip lines.

Design specifications

Sweep frequency	0 – 550 MHz
Trace length/width	30 mm/3.137 mm
Trace thickness	0.034 mm
Substrate thickness	1.6 mm
Material	FR4
Milling gap	0.5 mm
Dielectric constant	4.3
Loss tangent	0.025
Differential impedance	100 Ω
Metal conductivity	5.96e+007[s/m]

While one diagonal end of the test head was connected to the RF coax cable of the VNA through an SMA connector, the other end had a 2-way terminal block connector that connected the twisted pair to the microstrip line. With the use of the terminal block, it was much easier to test other pairs instead of maintaining a permanently soldered connection in the circuit. At both ends of the CUT, all unused wire pairs were terminated in the readily available pure 47 Ω (instead of 50 Ω) resistive load. It was however assumed that this difference would not make any considerable contribution to the imbalance in the circuit.

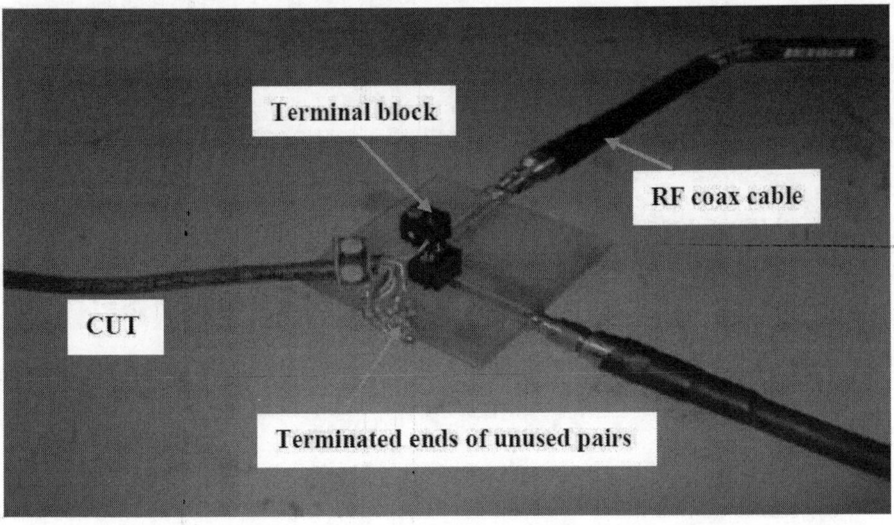

Figure 6.14 Showing the designed test head

Figure 6. 15 shows the setup used for the s-parameter testing of the Cat 6 cable together with the use of the test head.

Precautions while using the test head for measurements

The following extra precautions were observed during the measurement to ensure the good accuracy of the results:

- The test fixtures were placed at the same reference/measurement plane to avoid any cable movements and drifts during testing. This process was also done when testing the cable.
- The microstrip test head impedance was precisely 50 Ω at the design stage to match the impedance of the SMA connector
- To avoid unnecessary, untwist in terminations, only the gap of one twist was allowed between the twisted pair and the terminal block connector on the test head. This is to avoid creating any unnecessary loop current which can cause radiated noise
- Appropriate terminations (i.e. with matching impedance) were used to terminate all unused pair ends.
- Minimise the cable jacket removal.

Figure 6.15 Balanced 2-Port s-parameter testing of the 10m length of Cat 6 UTP network cable

6.10 Mixed Mode S-Parameter Tests for a CAT 6 UTP Cable (all meas. in Lin Mag)

The test methodology and setup has been described in chapter 3 section 10. A differential stimulus of 10 dBm was fed into the cable from the vector network analyser, and the responses were measured. Also, a 10-meter length of Cat 6 UTP cable was used.

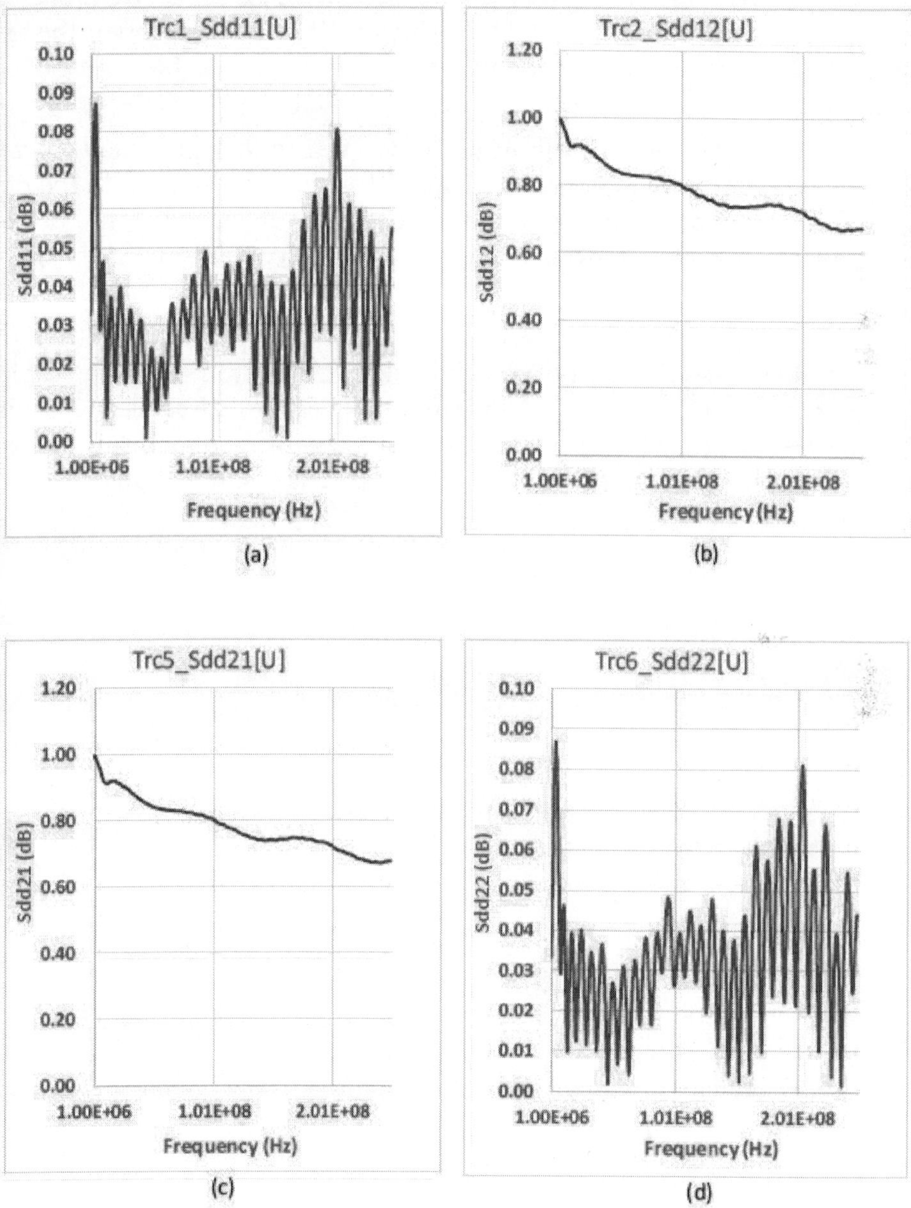

Figure 6.16 Shows the response plot of pure mode differential *(dd)* versus frequency of Cat6 UTP cable

Figure 6.16 shows the Lin Mag (dB) s-parameter plots for the Cat 6 UTP cable against frequency. The frequency range was between 1-250 MHz in line with the specification for Cat 6 UTP. The test revealed evidence of low-loss transmission to the differential stimulus. The differential return loss was between 0.08 dB to 0.05 dB within the range of test frequency 1 MH-250 MHz, for a 10 m Cat 6 UTP. This result was far less than the expected result (1.8 dB to 0.8 dB for an equivalent length of cable) and can be attributed to the test head not being de-embedded.

The observed periodic amplitudes of the return loss plot could be attributed to impedance mismatch resulting from approximations in the design of the test head. Another possible cause of the mismatch could be because of an incomplete twist at the terminal block contacts which is likely at the end of the twisted pair.

The cable also has about 0.68 dB differential insertion loss at 250 MHz. The decline in insertion loss is usually an indication of losses in the cable. Again, this is slightly off the test limit for a 10 m Cat 6 UTP cable and could have been affected by the test head. However, the differential insertion loss tended to start near 0 dB at low frequency which is an indication of correct port assignment.

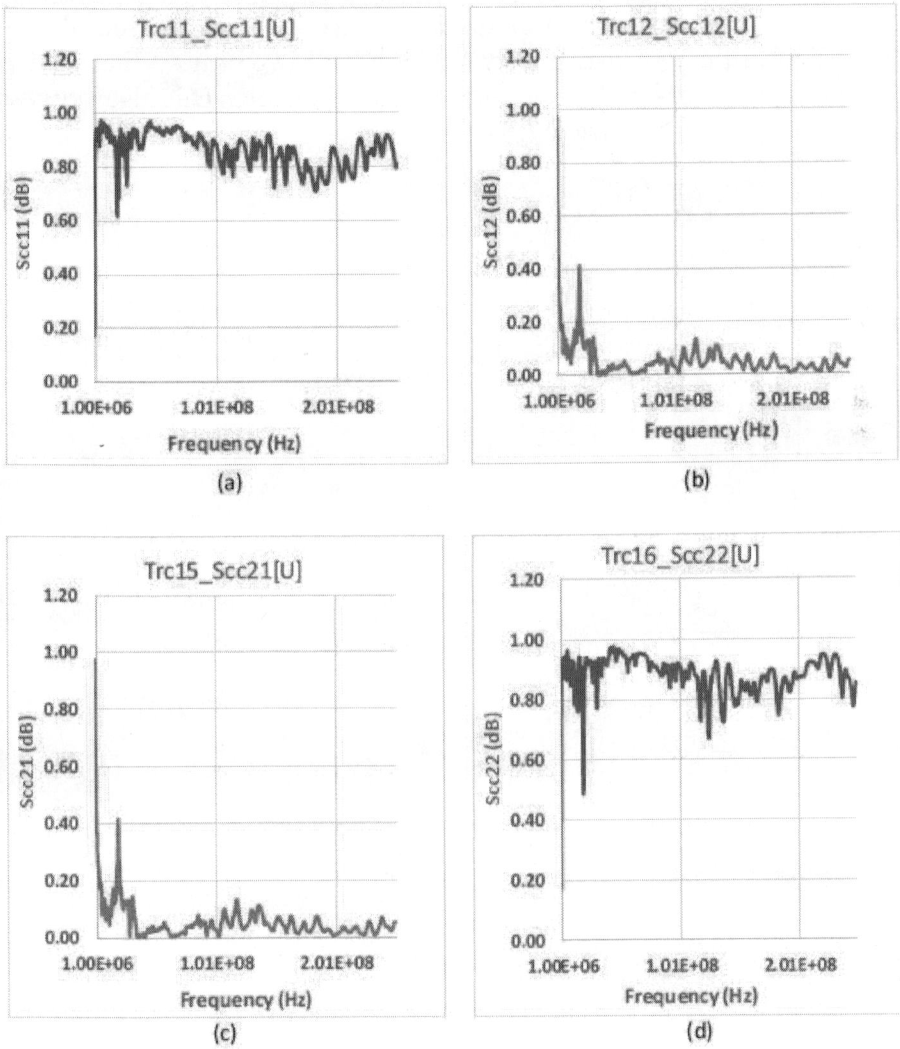

Figure 6.17 Showing the response plot of pure common mode (*cc*) versus frequency of Cat 6 UTP cable

The common-mode response plots in Figure 6.17 indicated that the cable is a good transmission line to the common-mode. This is because the response showed a relatively high level of common mode return loss and very low common mode insertion loss. However, the mode is not as well matched as compared with its differential mode counterpart. Scc_{11} and Scc_{22} represent the forward and the backward return loss in the pure common mode and showed the amount of signal reflected because of mismatch. The minor dissimilarities in the periodic wave of the common-mode return loss (a & d) tend to suggest the existence of a slight impedance mismatch. Nonetheless, a 25 Ω common mode impedance was chosen from the default setting of the test instrument. Again, it could be noticed that the two reflection parameters look very much undifferentiable. This also suggests that the ports are symmetrical.

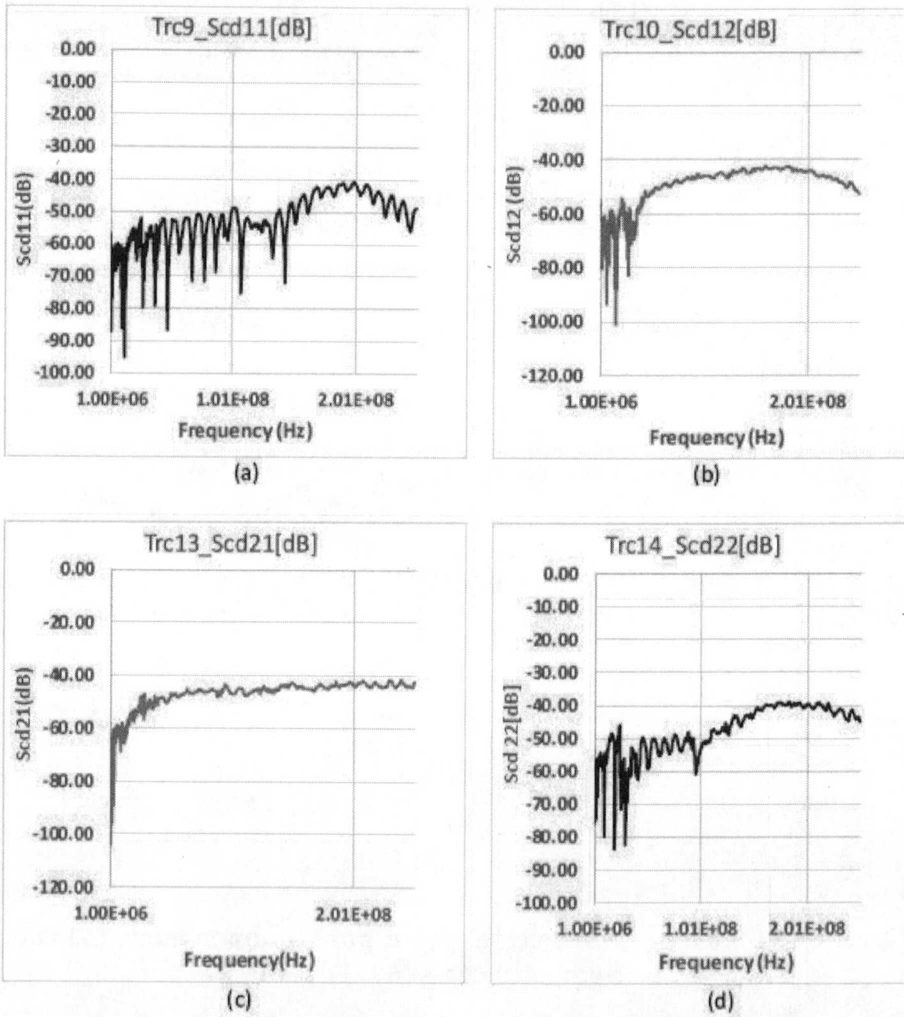

Figure 6.18 Showing the response plot of differential-to-common mode conversion (*cd*) versus frequency of Cat 6 UTP network cable.

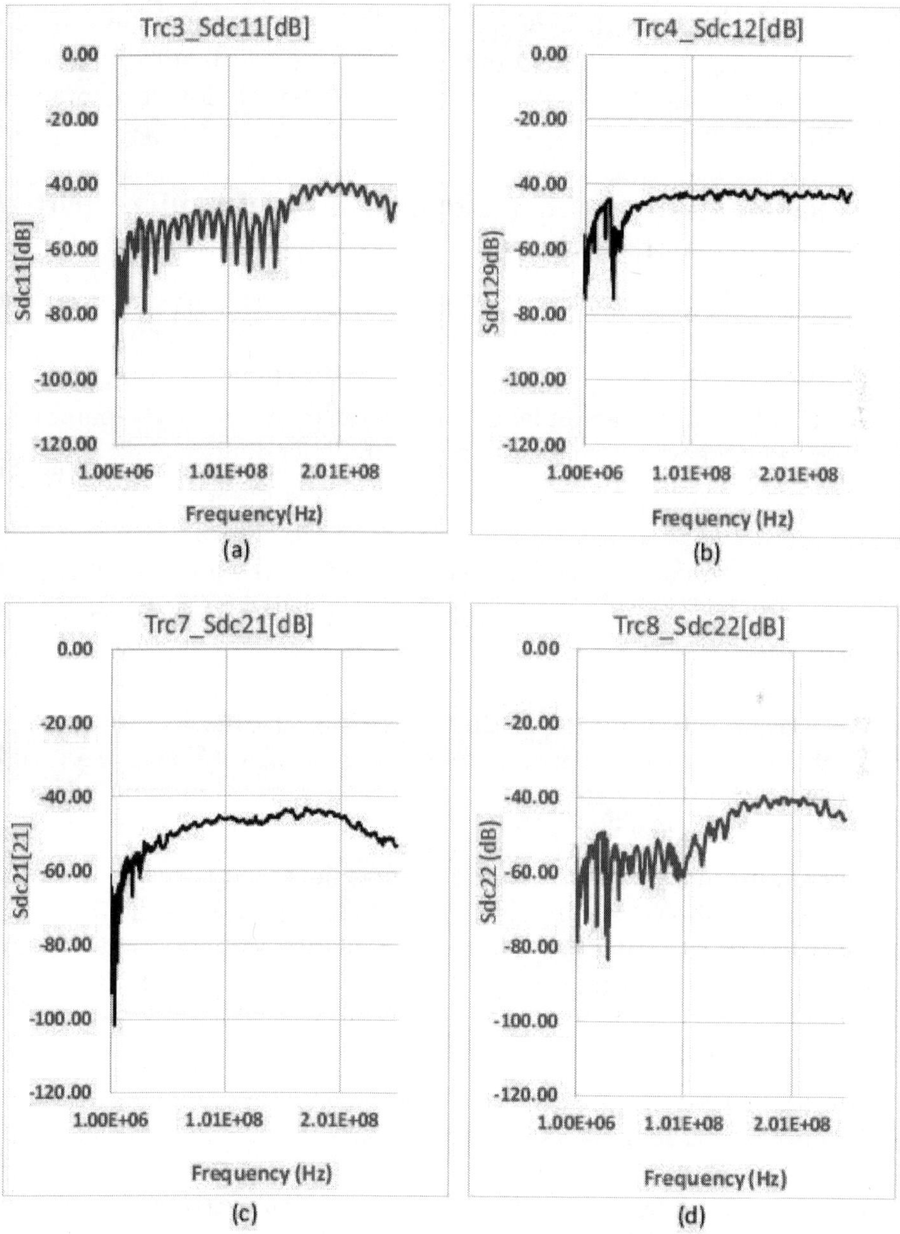

Figure 6.19 Showing the response plot of common-to-differential conversion (*dc*) versus frequency of Cat 6 UTP network cable

The mode conversion plots of Figures 6.18 & 6.19 show that both the return loss and the insertion loss parameters of the cable have their maximum values nearly within -40 dB. This can be seen in all the forward and reverse return and insertion loss plots in Figure 6.18 and Figure 6.19. This may well mean that the loss of power (reflection) due to mismatch (RL) and the attenuation (IL) of the communication cable is about 1% of its differential input. This also means that there is a tolerably low level of mode conversion in the cable.

6.11 Relating the mixed-mode analysis of the microstrip test structures with the Cat 6 UTP

To accurately compare the behaviour of the microstrip structures and the Cat 6 UTP was challenging because of the following reasons:

- The microstrip structures are only 100 mm in length, while the Cat 6 cable is 10 meters in length. It is worthy of note that s-parameter insertion and return losses are length dependent.
- The microstrip structures were designed and tested at higher frequencies (250-550 MHz), while the Cat 6 UTP has a functional frequency range of 1-250 MHz and was tested within that range.

Nevertheless, the plots of the microstrip line structure shown in Figures 6.6 and 6.7 showed that the symmetric line structure had an insertion loss of -40 dB (about 1%) in the cross conversion mode, while the asymmetric line showed a return loss -26 dB (about 5%). The measured Cat 6 network cable in its cross conversion mode in Figure 6.18 and Figure 6.19 also measured an insertion loss of -40dB (about 1%). This represents a measure of attenuation of the cable.

In the return loss parameters, the symmetric structure measured a differential return loss of -23 dB (about 7%) in Figure 6.4(a), while the asymmetric structure measured -15 dB to -12 dB (about 24%) across the test frequency as shown in Figure 6.9(a). The Cat 6 cable in Figures 6.18 and 6.19 measured a maximum return loss of -40dB (about 1%) in the cross conversion mode across the test frequency.

From the results in figures 6.18 (c) and figure 6.19 (c), it is evident that there is minor mode conversion in both Sdc_{21} and Scd_{21} (approximately -40 dB and -42 dB, respectively) for the cable which may be because of imperfections in manufacturing. However, even with a perfectly symmetrical cable, the proximity of other wires, whose position varies with length will add significantly to the potential cause of the imbalance and not just the cable structure itself.

In Figures 6.18 and 6.19, the Cat 6 UTP insertion loss plot (Lin Mag dB) in the mode conversion mode is well below -40 dB and tends to increase with frequency while the return loss is relatively low (within -40 dB) a about 200 MHz frequency. These results would seem to suggest that the CUT has approximately around 1% mode conversion of its stimulus signals. It could as well be that susceptibility of the CUT is about 1% since both parameters tend to be reciprocal. The table below summarises the characteristic behaviour of the insertion loss for the three tested structures.

Table 6.3 Characterising the Insertion loss behaviour of the tested structures.

Parameter/Quantity	Symmetric structure	Asymmetric structure	Cable structure
Mode conversion IL (S_{cd21} & S_{dc21})	-40 dB (1%)	-26 dB (5%)	-40 dB to -42 dB (1%-to-0.79%) (approxly. 1%)

It has been known that in the absence of mode conversion, a low insertion loss and a high return loss values in dB is more preferred. Although these values are reasonably tolerable (within experimental error), it shows that the CUT is not an ideally balanced transmission line with perfect symmetry, devoid of signal mode conversion.

Intuitively, the Cat 6 UTP share the attributes of both the symmetric and the asymmetric microstrip transmission line, particularly in the cross conversion mode since some amount of its differential input signal is lost to its environment. Hence, further investigation is needed into the non-ideal behaviour of the TWP as an asymmetric line. This is because from Figure 6.18, and Figure 6.19 both the insertion and the return loss values in the cross conversion mode tend to fall below -40 dB a little above 200 MHz to 250 MHz frequency.

In the next chapter further experiments will be carried out using the current probe and the 4-port VNA configured in 3-port to investigate Cat 6 UTP coupling attenuation. The aim is to show that a Cat 6 UTP can couple electromagnetic waves to its environment when stimulated with a differential signal. This radiated electromagnetic wave goes to show that there is mode conversion (differential-to-common mode) in a stimulated network cable.

Chapter Summary

This chapter has dealt with the practical usage of mixed-mode s-parameter concept in measuring and analysing RF differential devices. It summarises the trend to differential topologies. Various test fixtures were designed, and their mixed-mode s-parameters were measured to characterise their behaviours. Ideally, differential devices have the advantage of low-voltage requirements, immunity to noise and EM interference and have virtual grounds. They are generally symmetric. Non-ideal devices are not symmetric and therefore can be associated with signal conversion, common-to-differential and differential-to-common mode conversion. This knowledge was extended to the Cat 6 UTP, and it was found that the CUT showed evidence of non-symmetry, possibly as a result of nonuniformity in the wire pairs. Thus the Cat 6 UTP manifested evidence of mode conversion between the differential and common-mode signals. This shows that even though the category cable is generally regarded as a balanced line, it is not a perfect balance line.

For further investigation, a 1-single, 1-balanced connection of the CUT was made using a 3-port VNA. In this connection, the phase deviation of the common and differential responses at the balanced output port was examined. The CUT was then stimulated with a differential signal from the test instrument, and the current probe was used to measure the coupling attenuation. This is discussed in chapter seven.

CHAPTER 7

COUPLING ATTENUATION MEASUREMENT AND INVESTIGATING THE CONDUCTED DM DISTURBANCE OF THE TWP UNDER EXTERNALLY INJECTED NOISE

7.1 Coupling Attenuation

Definition: Coupling attenuation is described as the relationship between the power transmitted to the cable pair and the power coupled into its environment [118].

Coupling Attenuation = Ac = 10log (P_1/P_2) dB. The unit of coupling attenuation is decibel, dB.

An illustration of coupling attenuation using the current probe and a 3-port VNA can be seen in Figure 7.1 where P_1 and P_2 represent the transmitted and the received powers, respectively. The near end of the CUT was connected to the VNA through a test head, while the far end was terminated in the impedance of the CUT. All the unused pairs were as well terminated in the characteristic impedance of the cable.

In shielded and unshielded balanced pair cabling, coupling attenuation describes the overall effect against electromagnetic interference, EMI.

In this experiment, the current probe was used to clamp/surround a pair of twisted Cat 6 UTP in line with [117] and in the manner of [119] [120]. To determine coupling attenuation, a differential mode signal is required, and in this case, it was provided by the balanced input of VNA with the application of mixed-mode s-parameter.

Current Probe

The use of the current probe was an alternative method of testing the network cable for electromagnetic emission to its environment. Moreover, the technique/method had been used to test for RF immunity of cables structures, ICs and more extensive systems with cable harnesses. Like a current transformer, current probe produces changing electromagnetic fields when excited with an alternating current. The emitted fields can then couple to any system within the environment or induce CM noise voltage which becomes a source of interference as in the case of a data borne cable.

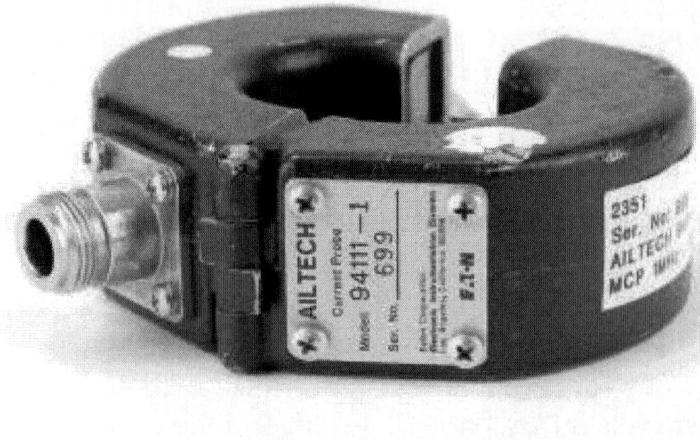

Figure 7.1 Shows the Current Probe

In the experiments that follow, the Cat 6 UTP was tested and compared with the Cat 5e UTP which was found to emit more fields than Cat 6 UTP. This result was widely expected since Cat 6 UTP has a better transmission performance than Cat 5e UTP. It is a commonly held view that the cause of the emitted electromagnetic fields could be due to imperfection/unbalance in the cable [117]. The scope of the experiment was limited to investigating the unbalance and its effect in twisted cabling. Although the concept of pair twisting has apparent advantages in noise cancellation, yet because of imbalance, the twisted pair cable cannot be regarded as an entirely perfect balanced transmission line.

The use of other methods like the direct power injection (DPI) [121] to test for cable EMI emission is also valid. In this method, the RF power is injected as RF current into the DUT supply and ground at the same time. Using this configuration, the DUT becomes DC-grounded through the cable harnesses and only referenced to ground through a weak capacitive connection. Thus, the RF power is injected as a common mode current into the cable. The mixed-mode translation from common-mode to differential-mode of the injected signal occurs as a result of cable asymmetry. In other words, for mode conversion to happen in a differential line, there must be a defect in the symmetry of the line. The local environmental noise is also a factor that contributes to mode conversion. The common to differential mode conversion of the RF signal is the disruption factor that affects the DUT, and that leads to EMC and Signal Integrity issues.

7.2 Modifying the VNA for 3-Port Measurement

In the previous experiments, the ZNB 8 VNA was used in its 4-port configuration to measure the mixed-mode s-parameters directly. In this section, the direct 4-port VNA is modified by terminating one of the instrument ports and using a pair of balanced ports as the stimulus port to inject a differential mode signal into the CUT. The setup is as shown in Figure.7.1 with the unused pairs (not shown) terminated in matched resistive loads at both ends and referenced to each other to form a virtual return.

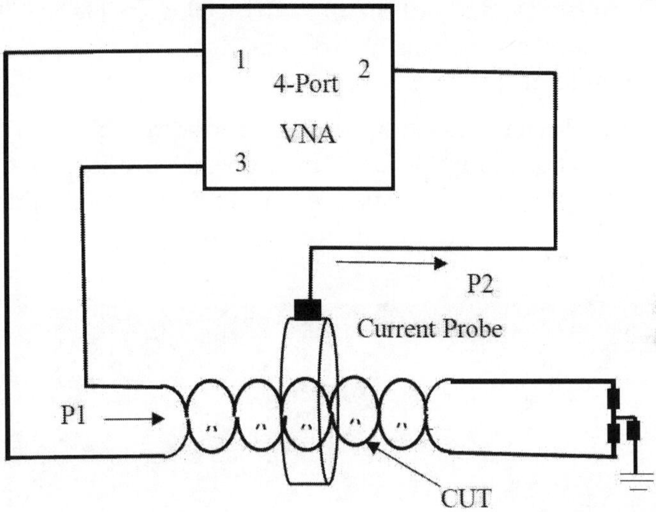

Figure 7.2 Showing sketch of the experiment setup

The same test head that was fabricated and used in chapter 6 was also adopted for the experiments in this chapter. Like in chapter 6, the test head was fitted with two SMA connectors to enable connection with the VNA using the instrument RF cable. The CUT was ideally driven by a differential source also from the VNA.

7.3 The Test Setup and Instrument Setting

As can be seen in Figure 7.2, both ports 1 and 3 of the test instrument were configured to transmit 10 dBm differential signal power into the CUT. The 10 dBm and above differential signal power levels were selected in order to inject a reasonable power level that would make a difference above the default power setting (-10 dBm), while within the power capability of the measuring device [122]. Extracts from [122] (Table 7.1) show that for a representative 10 m Cat 6, the impedance per meter (Ω/m) is approximately 0.85.

Table 7.1 Impedance per meter (Ω/m) for Cat 6 cable

AWG	Diameter	Ω/Km	Maximum current for power transmission
24	0.5 mm	85	0.577 amp

Hence, from P = I2 R = (0.577)2 * 0.85 = 0.2829 watts = 282.9 mW = 24.5 dBm. Therefore, 10 dBm differential power was selected to inject a reasonable power level that would make a difference above the default while working within the capacity of the measuring device. Hence, the choice of 10 dBm differential power was justified as the level of power that would not harm the cable under test.

Port 2 of the device was set as a single-ended receiver port to measure the radiated emission from the cable through the current probe. Hence, the 4-port VNA was placed in a 1 balanced, 1 single-ended mode yielding an overall 3-port network. Port 4 of the instrument was terminated in a 50 Ω impedance load.

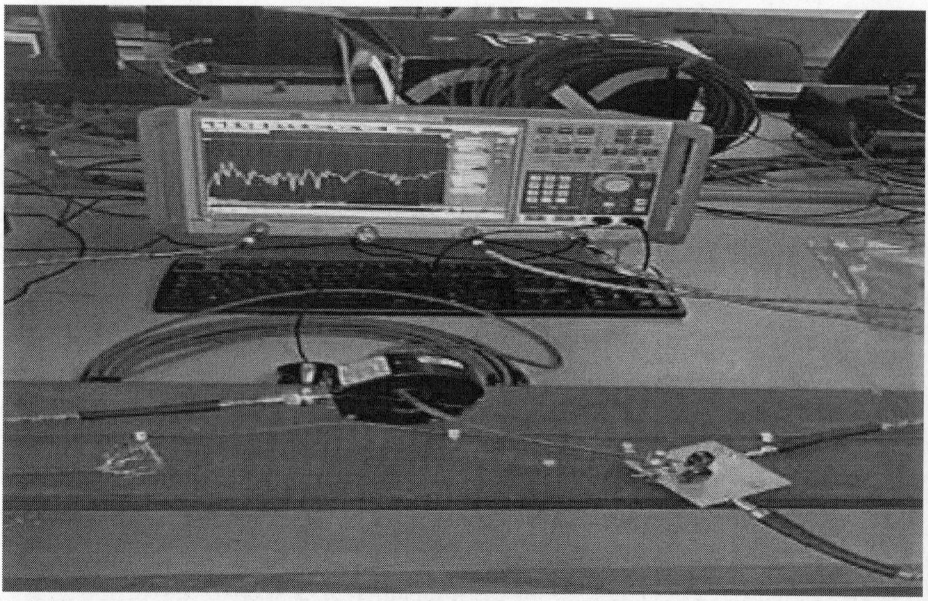

Figure 7.3 Showing the current probe test method for measuring coupling attenuation of the CUT (repeated for easy reference)

The instrument setting shown below was used for the current probe measurement for Cat 5e and Cat 6 cables. The variation in the instrument frequency setting was because of the frequency specifications of the cables used.

Instrument Setting

Sweep frequency	1 MHz – 250 MHz ; 1 MHz – 100 MHz
Power input	10 dBm
Meas. Bandwidth	100 KHz
Sweep point	1601

By selecting a bandwidth of 100 KHz, the instrument noise floor was reduced to around -120 dB. This was done to clearly separate all the measured quantity of interest from the noise of the instrument. However, it was necessary to include the environmental noise picked up by the device in the noise floor plot. To do this, the current probe was placed around the CUT with the cable disconnected from any input source. The noise floor plot with the environmental noise pick up is as shown in Figure 7.3.

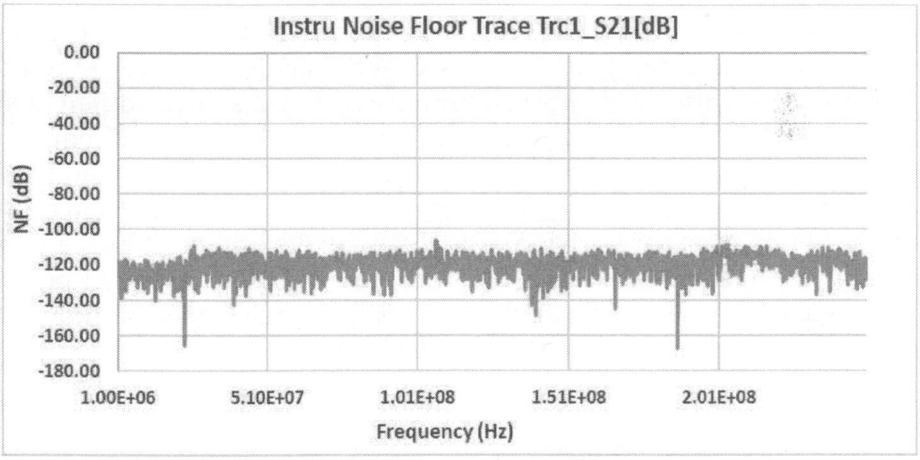

Figure 7.4 Instrument noise floor measurement

7.4 Three Port S-Parameter Measurement

A three-port device is categorised by a 3×3 scattering matrix as shown in equation (7.1).

$$\begin{bmatrix} b_1 \\ b_2 \\ b_3 \end{bmatrix} = \begin{bmatrix} S_{11} & S_{12} & S_{13} \\ S_{21} & S_{22} & S_{23} \\ S_{31} & S_{32} & S_{33} \end{bmatrix} \begin{bmatrix} a_1 \\ a_2 \\ a_3 \end{bmatrix} = B_{std} = S_{std.} A_{std} \qquad (7.1)$$

The nine basics of this matrix characterise the 3 reflection constants at each port and the 6 transmission constants between the 3 ports in same directions. In this work, a two-input, one-output network is studied. The features of the scattering matrix were measured in port 2 while using ports 1 and 3 as balanced source input port. The standard 3-port mixed-mode s-parameter solution is given in expression (7.2).

$$\left[\begin{array}{c|cc} Sdd_{11} & Sdc_{11} & Sds_{12} \\ \hline Scd_{11} & Sdc_{11} & Scs_{12} \\ Ssd_{21} & Ssc_{21} & Sss_{22} \end{array}\right] \qquad (7.2)$$

where S_{dd11} describes the differential stimulus at port 1 and response at port 1, S_{dc11} is common mode stimulus at port 1 and differential response at port 1, S_{ds12} is the single-ended stimulus at port 2 and the differential response at port 1, S_{cd11} is the differential stimulus at port 1 and common mode response at port 1, S_{dc11} is common mode stimulus at port 1 and differential response at port 1, S_{cs12} is single-ended stimulus at port 2 and common mode response at port 1, S_{sd21} is differential stimulus at port 1 and single-ended response at port 2, S_{sc21} is common mode stimulus at port 1 and single-ended response at port 2 and S_{ss22} is single-ended stimulus at port 2 and single-ended response at port 2 [123].

From the matrix of (7.2), the two columns and rows characterise the balanced mode, and the single matrix describes the single-ended mode. Information about the differential input at balanced port 1 and the single-ended response in port 2 of the experiment can be obtained by analysing the S_{sd21} parameter.

Test Assessment

Both Cat 6 and Cat 5e UTP cables were tested with the current probe located in three different positions on a 10-meter length of each cable. The results were plotted in negative dB along the y-axis as shown in Figure 7.4

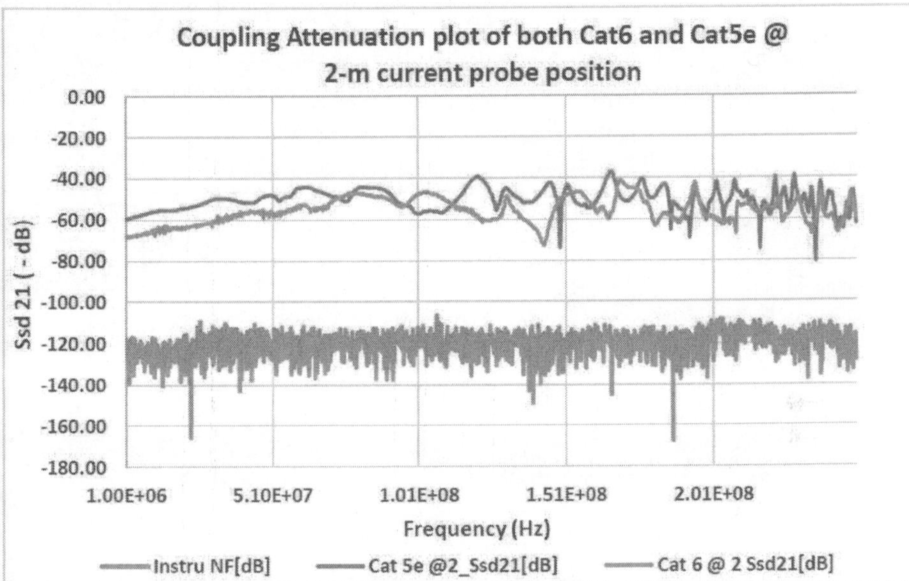

Figure 7.5 Showing measurement with current probe at 2-meter position on both cables

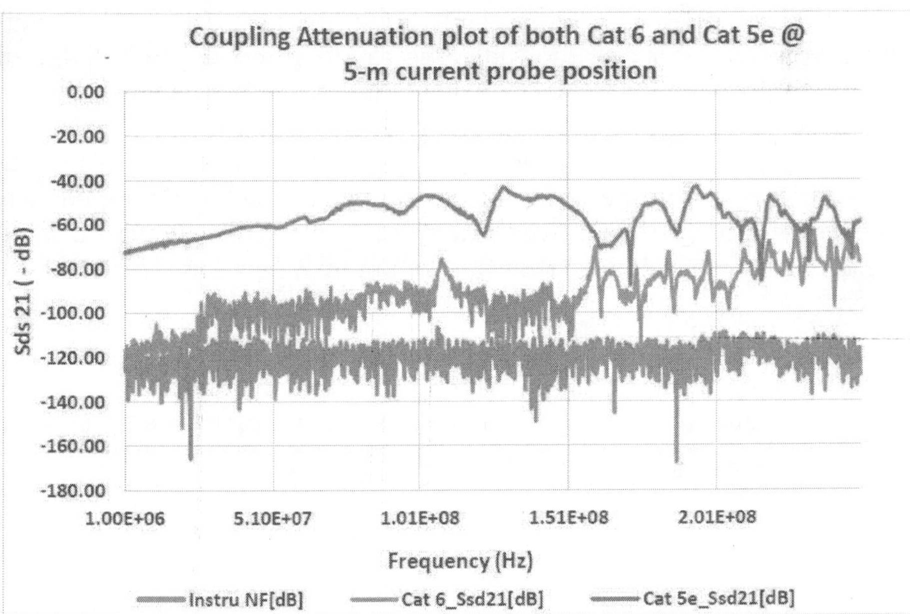

Figure 7.6 Showing measurement with current probe at 5-meter position on both cables

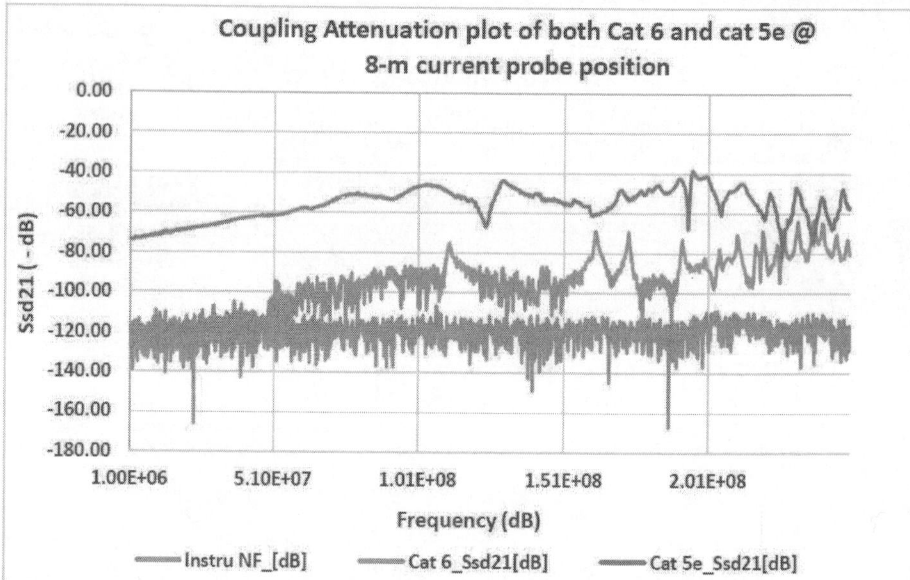

Figure 7.7 Showing measurement with current probe at 2-meter location on both cables

From Figures 7.4 – 7.6, it can generally be observed that as the current probe is moved along the cable, the common mode will be affected by wavelength. This is because, for the common mode, there will be an impedance mismatch at the far end of the cable and hence more reflections. This can further be explained using the concept of quarter wave impedance transformer with the line terminated in its characteristic impedance. As the current probe was moved towards the load end, $\lambda/4$ was affected and $Zo \neq ZL$, hence mismatch occurred and more reflections resulted at the load end.

Also granted that the differential-to-common mode conversion occurs along the length of the cable, the differential mode will be affected by attenuation, so that the translation will be most substantial at the near end.

For example, for a 10 m length of cable with a 5 m positioning of the current probe, the frequency at that wavelength can be calculated as

$$c = \lambda . f$$

$$f = {}^{3.10^8}/_5 = 60MHz$$

where;

$c = speedoflight$

$\lambda = wavelength$

$f = frequency$

From this frequency, constructive interference can be expected at a half wavelength, i.e., 30MHz. However, this is not the case as there are noticeable spikes at approximately that separation at higher frequencies – not quite at 30MHz. Nevertheless, the approximations are quite coarse.

As a result, it might be possible to treat the DM – CM as a distributed conversion equivalent, except for the fact that the DM and CM velocities are going to be a little different, the CM might be slightly higher with there being more air around the pair, which could lead to more complex interactions. Also, the fact that the capacitance, a key to DM – CM conversion (see later analysis in chapter 8.2 of this thesis to show that this is the case), leads to frequency dependence means that the transformation is more marked as the frequency rises. Up to 100 MHz for Cat5e and about 230 MHz for Cat 6, there is a monotonic rise in the conversion – suggesting capacitance is the key to the coupling: the fact that this is approximately 20 dB/decade indicates that an appropriate model should mostly be capacitive in nature, particularly at the lower frequencies. Hence, a correct model for mode conversion should be strongly capacitive.

For a 10 m length of cable and with a 8 m positioning of the current probe, similar trends occur which enables the same conclusion.

While this experiment may not be concerned with the radiation details of comparison between both cables, it has been used to demonstrate that a desired differential stimulus can convert to an undesired common mode quantity and be radiated out to the environment due to some unbalance in the cables.

In the next experiment, the stability of the mixed mode s-parameters of the Cat 6 UTP cable is investigated in a noisy environment. In chapters 5 and 6, s-parameter was used to describe the behaviour of a network or system as a function of frequency. The data/information on the network behaviour was accumulated within the four major quadrants matrices of a 4-port VNA, and its control was dependent on the symmetry of the line.

7.5 Investigating the conducted DM disturbance of the mixed-mode s-parameter under externally injected noise

In this experiment, a graduated power level of external noise (common mode) was generated from a 2-port VNA and fed through an RF connecting cable to the source point of a current probe. The CUT was configured in a balanced 2-port at ports 1 and 3, while ports 2 and 4 were the balanced output ports. By this configuration, all the 4x4 mixed-mode s-parameter measurements of the CUT were recorded.

From the literature in chapters 5 and 6, when a device converts some of its arriving common-mode signal (usually noise) at its input to differential mode on its output, the phenomenon reduces the systems immunity to noise.

The purpose of this experiment was to inject a progressed level of CM current through the current probe into the pair under test. This was to simulate a conducted DM disturbance [124] which was detected in the differential receiver ports 2 and 4 of the VNA. The current probe can also be used for CM monitoring or sensing performance, usually for frequencies well over 10 MHz. This can be useful in developing the conducted RF emission specification for items of electronics connected to the wiring harnesses.

Test Setup and Instrument Information

A sketch of the test setup was shown in Figure 7.7. The same current probe approach used in Figure 7.1 was adopted but with probe connected to an external common mode source in single mode. The 2 port VNA was being used as a non-coherent signal generator, thus ignoring the phase information (difference) between the two VNAs. The four terminals of the CUT were connected through a four-port test head to the measuring instrument.

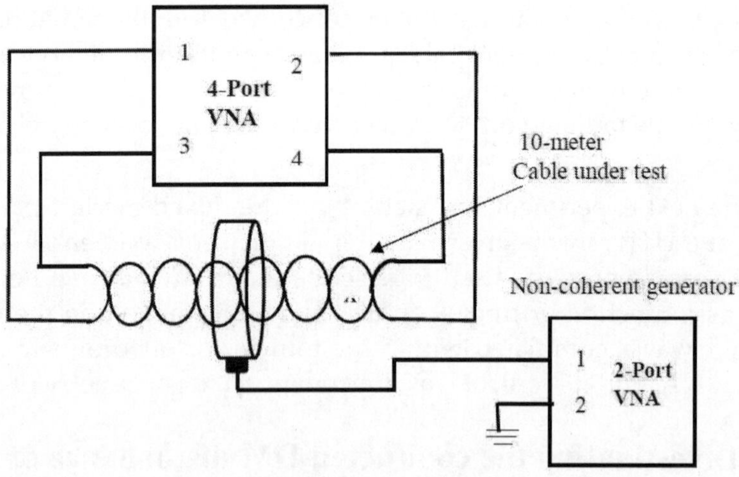

Figure 7.8 Setup for conducted DM disturbance of mixed mode s-parameter to externally injected noise power

The instrument information below was used for the experiment described in 7.5 and shown in Figure 7.7. All the data points were swept in both the forward and reverse directions (S21 & S12) for each sweep point. Since both, the source (2-port VNA) and the receiver (4-port VNA) have different frequency settings, the frequency offset mode of the receiver 4-port VNA was enabled to make frequency offset measurements. The current probe power was configured to vary from -10 dB (default setting of the test instrument) to +20 dB to simulate a varied noise environment around the cable under test.

Instrument Setting

The same instrument setting as in the coupling attenuation measurement was adopted for the 4-port VNA while the 2-port VNA has the following settings:

Sweep frequency	1-400 MHz
Power	-10 dBm to +20 dBm
Meas. Bandwidth	100 KHz
Sweep points	1601 (CW)

Aside providing for frequency offset in the sweep frequency between the source and the receiver VNAs, the source VNA provided variable power levels of the externally generated non-coherent noise signal.

Test Procedure

Firstly, a reference mixed-mode s-parameter measurement was measured with the CUT stimulated using a -10 dBm input power and without any noise power injected from the external source. The data file in equation (7.3) showed all the data for the 16 mixed-mode s-parameter matrix terms at the highest frequency of 250 MHz. This measurement was made at 2-meter length position on the 10-meter long data cable. Measurement at the 2 m location of the 10 m length of the cable was selected because of the explanation already given in the test assessment of 7.4 namely, that approximately the same trend of result was obtained even with 5 m, 8 m current probe positions.

The choice of 10 m length for the CUT did not represent any cable specification, but in a laboratory setting, 10 m was unvaryingly long enough to characterise a transmission line cable.

Again, data at 250 MHz frequency was used in this experiment to show results at the maximum frequency of test for Cat 6 UTP.

The s-parameter matrix equation of 7.3 (which was extracted from the *touchstone data file*) revealed a reasonable amount of data reciprocity and symmetry of the ports. This measurement represented the reference mixed-mode s-parameter measurement with no noise injection.

Secondly, the CUT was then stimulated with various levels of low noise power from -10 dBm to -20 dBm and from 10 dBm to 20 dBm representing higher noise power levels. Again, all the 16 mixed-mode s-parameter matrix terms at 250 MHz were recorded. Equations (7.4) to (7.9) showed all the data terms.

Nonetheless, the use of higher noise power levels was used to generate noisier operating environment while the lower noise power levels served for, the lower noise environments. This is because a higher input power into the current probe (by current transformer action), will generate higher alternating current into the probe which will, in turn, create a higher level of varying electromagnetic field (flux) intensity. Hence, more noise voltage will be induced into the CUT.

The scenario envisaged for this experiment was that of network cables running very close to noise generating components and systems, for example, fast switching components in a communication environment.

Therefore, the experiments seek to investigate how the induced noise voltages would affect the stability or otherwise of the mixed-mode s-parameters of the CUT especially in its cross-conversion mode when the cable is information bearing.

Reference Measurement (with no noise injected from the external source)

1. $[Sij]2_m \left| \begin{array}{l} \text{at 250 MHz} \\ \text{(X) = 0 where (X = injected noise)} \end{array} \right.$

$$\begin{array}{c|c} Sdd & Sdc \\ \hline Scd & Scc \end{array} = S_{ij}^{mm} =$$

$$\begin{array}{cc|cc} -6.66\angle{-7.18} & -9.73\angle{E1} & -7.27\angle{-7.87} & -9.14\angle{8.39E1} \\ -9.73\angle{-9.01E1} & -6.63\angle{-5.58} & -9.09\angle{8.33E1} & -7.07\angle{-1.06E1} \\ \hline -7.25\angle{-7.95} & -9.12\angle{8.34E1} & -6.63\angle{-7.35E1} & -9.80\angle{-8.96E1} \\ -9.09\angle{8.35E1} & -7.06\angle{-1.06E1} & -9.78\angle{-8.98E1} & -6.64\angle{-4.57E1} \end{array} \quad (7.3)$$

Next, equation (7.4) showed the data file for all the 16-mixed mode s-parameter matrix terms taken at 2-meter probe position with -10 dBm noise power input at 250 MHz.

2. $[Sij]2_m \left| \begin{array}{l} \text{at 250 MHz} \\ \text{(X) = -10 dBm where (X = injected noise power)} \end{array} \right.$

$$\begin{array}{c|c} Sdd & Sdc \\ \hline Scd & Scc \end{array} = S_{ij}^{mm} =$$

$$\left.\begin{array}{cc|cc} -7.69\angle{-3.76} & -8.94\angle 9.05E1 & -7.99\angle{-5.33} & -9.86\angle 8.01E1 \\ -8.95\angle{-9.07E1} & -8.07\angle{-1.19} & -9.84\angle 7.97E1 & -8.40\angle{-1.70E1} \\ \hline -7.97\angle{-5.55} & -9.82\angle 7.98E1 & -7.67\angle{-3.97E1} & -9.07\angle{-9.04E1} \\ -9.84\angle 7.97E1 & -8.39\angle{-1.71E1} & -9.08\angle{-9.05E1} & -8.08\angle{-1.19E1} \end{array}\right. \quad (7.4)$$

Next, equation (7.5) showed the data file for all the s-parameter terms for measurement taken at 2-meter current probe position with -15 dBm noise power input at 250 MHz.

3. $[Sij]2_m$ | at 250 MHz
(X) = -15 dBm where (X = injected noise power)

$$\begin{array}{c|c} Sdd & Sdc \\ \hline Scd & Scc \end{array} = S_{ij}^{mm} =$$

$$\left.\begin{array}{cc|cc} -7.69\angle{-3.89} & -8.97\angle 9.03E1 & -8.01\angle{-5.39} & -9.80\angle 7.99E1 \\ -8.98\angle{-9.06E1} & -8.07\angle{-1.26E1} & -9.79\angle 7.9E1 & -8.36\angle{-1.79E1} \\ \hline -7.97\angle{-5.54} & -9.78\angle 7.97E1 & -7.67\angle{-4.11E1} & -9.10\angle{-9.01E1} \\ -9.80\angle 7.96E1 & -8.38\angle{-1.79E1} & -9.10\angle{-9.02E1} & -8.08\angle{-1.28E1} \end{array}\right. \quad (7.5)$$

Equation (7.6) also showed the data file for the s-parameter terms for measurements taken at the 2-meter position with -20 dBm power at 250 MHz.

4. $[Sij]2_m$ | at 250 MHz
(X) = -20 dBm where (X = injected noise power)

$$\begin{array}{c|c} Sdd & Sdc \\ \hline Scd & Scc \end{array} = S_{ij}^{mm} =$$

$$\left.\begin{array}{cc|cc} -8.10\angle{-9.52} & -8.74\angle 8.86E1 & -8.16\angle{-1.29E1} & -9.95\angle 7.56E1 \\ -8.73\angle{-8.89E1} & -8.27\angle{-1.33E1} & -9.99\angle 7.48E1 & -8.45\angle{-1.56E1} \\ \hline -8.17\angle{-1.29E1} & -9.96\angle 7.47E1 & -8.05\angle{-9.82E1} & -8.66\angle{-8.91E1} \\ -9.96\angle 7.55E1 & -8.42\angle{-1.58E1} & -8.69\angle{-8.92E1} & -8.30\angle{-1.16E1} \end{array}\right. \quad (7.6)$$

Equations (7.4), (7.5) and (7.6) showed the data derived from measurements made in relatively less noise environment at -10 dBm, -15 dBm and -20 dBm power levels.

Similarly, measurements were made for increased power levels which were used to represent relatively noisier environment. Equation (7.7) thus showed the mixed-mode terms for the measurements taken at the 2-meter probe position with input power of 10 dBm at 250 MHz.

5. $[Sij]2_{m}$ | at 250 MHz
(X) = 10 dBm where (X = injected noise power)

$$\frac{Sdd \mid Sdc}{Scd \mid Scc} = S_{ij}^{mm} =$$

$$\left[\begin{array}{cc|cc} -7.77\angle -3.95 & -8.95\angle -9.02E1 & -8.02\angle -5.49E1 & -9.79\angle 8.00E1 \\ -8.95\angle -9.06E1 & -8.05\angle -1.21E1 & -9.80\angle 7.99E1 & -8.36\angle -1.76E1 \\ \hline -8.03\angle -5.71E1 & -9.76\angle 7.99E1 & -7.71\angle -4.22E1 & -9.07\angle -9.03E1 \\ -9.79\angle 7.96E1 & -8.35\angle -1.73E1 & -9.10\angle -9.03E1 & -8.02\angle -1.22E1 \end{array}\right] \quad (7.7)$$

Equation (7.8) again showed the mixed-mode s-parameter measurement for an increased power level of 15 dBm taken at the 2-meter test position when for 250 MHz.

6. $[Sij]2_{m}$ | at 250 MHz
(X) = 15 dBm where (X = injected noise power)

$$\frac{Sdd \mid Sdc}{Scd \mid Scc} = S_{ij}^{mm} =$$

$$\left[\begin{array}{cc|cc} -7.71\angle -401 & -9.00\angle -9.07E1 & -8.01\angle -5.59E1 & -9.79\angle 8.03E1 \\ -9.01\angle -9.06E1 & -8.03\angle -1.14E1 & -9.80\angle 8.00E1 & -8.36\angle -1.65E1 \\ \hline -7.98\angle -5.72E1 & -9.77\angle 8.00E1 & -7.68\angle -4.05E1 & -9.14\angle -9.04E1 \\ -9.78\angle 8.00E1 & -8.38\angle -1.65E1 & -9.11\angle -9.05E1 & -8.05\angle -1.14E1 \end{array}\right] \quad (7.8)$$

Finally, equation (7.9) showed the mixed-mode s-parameter for measurements made at the 2-meter mark with 20 dBm power injection at 250 MHz.

7. $[Sij]2_{m}$ | at 250 MHz
(X) = 20 dBm where (X = injected noise power)

$$\frac{Sdd \mid Sdc}{Scd \mid Scc} = S_{ij}^{mm} =$$

$$\left[\begin{array}{cc|cc} -7.71\angle -3.85 & -8.95\angle -9.05E1 & -8.00\angle -5.52E1 & -9.79\angle 8.02E1 \\ -8.98\angle -9.06E1 & -8.01\angle -1.11E1 & -9.79\angle 7.99E1 & -8.35\angle -1.63E1 \\ \hline -7.99\angle -5.52E1 & -9.76\angle 7.99E1 & -7.68\angle -3.92E1 & -9.09\angle -9.06E1 \\ -9.80\angle 7.99E1 & -8.33\angle -1.64E1 & -9.12\angle -9.06E1 & -8.02\angle -1.12E1 \end{array}\right] \quad (7.9)$$

Again, equations (7.7), (7.8) and (7.9) showed the data derived from measurements made in relatively noisier environments at +10 dBm, +15 dBm and +20 dBm power levels.

Looking at the matrix data terms so far presented for the different injected noise power levels, it was apparently challenging to observe any significant variations in the values of the data. Hence, it was difficult to predict any impact or effect of the injected common mode noise signal on the desired differential signal borne by the cable. Because of this, a graphical representation of the data was chosen.

From the literature in chapters 5 and 6, the matrix of the 16 mixed-mode s-parameter which was divided into four quadrants in pure differential mode, pure common mode, common-to-differential mode and differential-to-common modes were predominantly consisted of insertion loss and return loss. These were the two foremost quality benchmark parameters which influence cable performance.

To observe any effect of the injected common mode noise on the data cable, the *.CSV* reference measurement data in dB magnitude against frequency was plotted on a four-trace-to-one graph with related parameters for both the higher and the lower power levels. For example, for the case of reduced power levels, the reference forward insertion loss parameter, $Sdd_{21(ref\ at\ no\ injected\ noise\ power)}$, was plotted together with other forward insertion loss parameters for reduced power levels of -10 dBm, -15 dBm and -20 dBm, respectively. The same plot was repeated for increased probe power levels of +10 dBm, +15 dBm and +20dBm. Following this order, the mixed-mode s-parameter plots for the pure differential mode, pure common mode, common-to-differential and differential-to-common modes were made for both increases and decreases in current probe input power. These are shown in Figures 7.7 to 7.10.

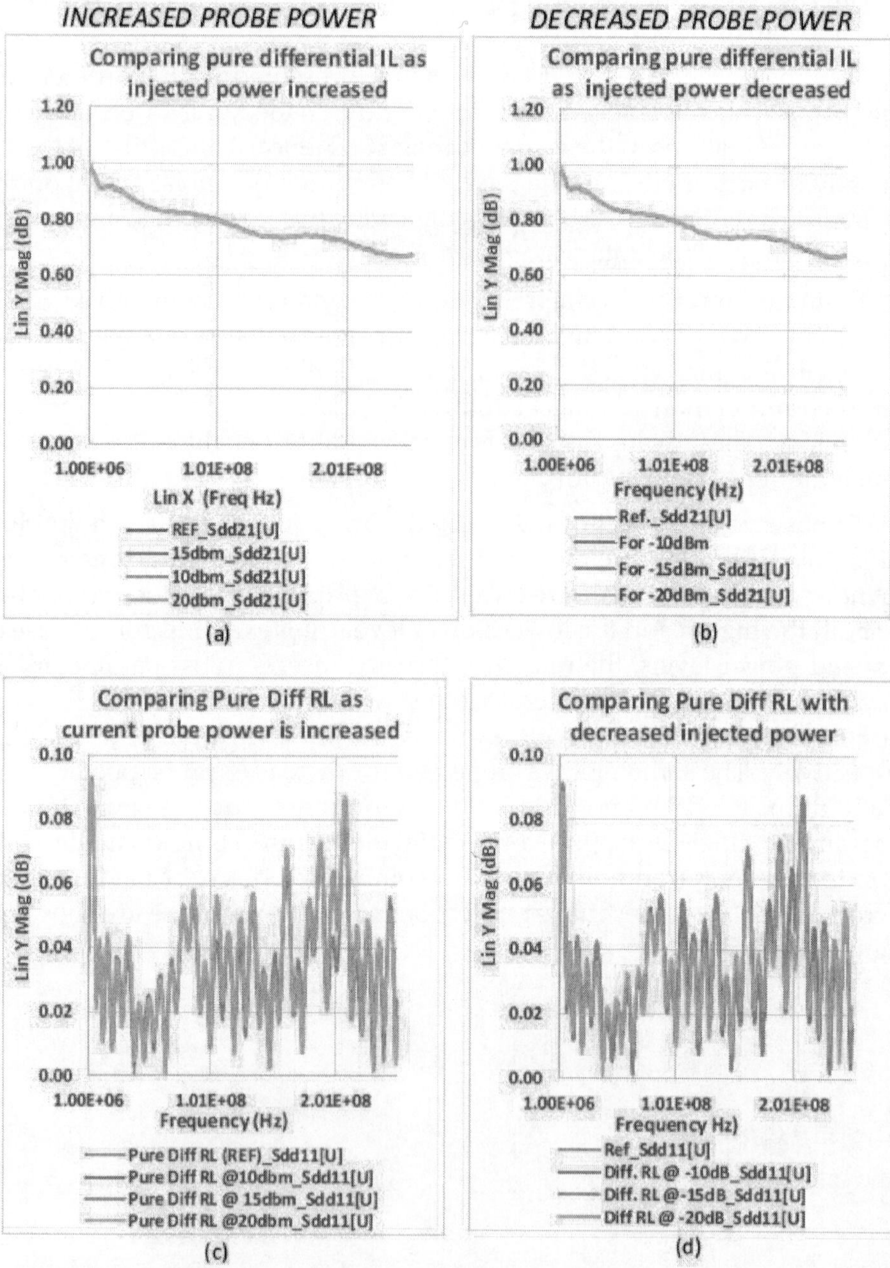

Figure 7.9 Showing consistent amplitude trends for differential mode measurements IL & RL at increased and reduced input probe power

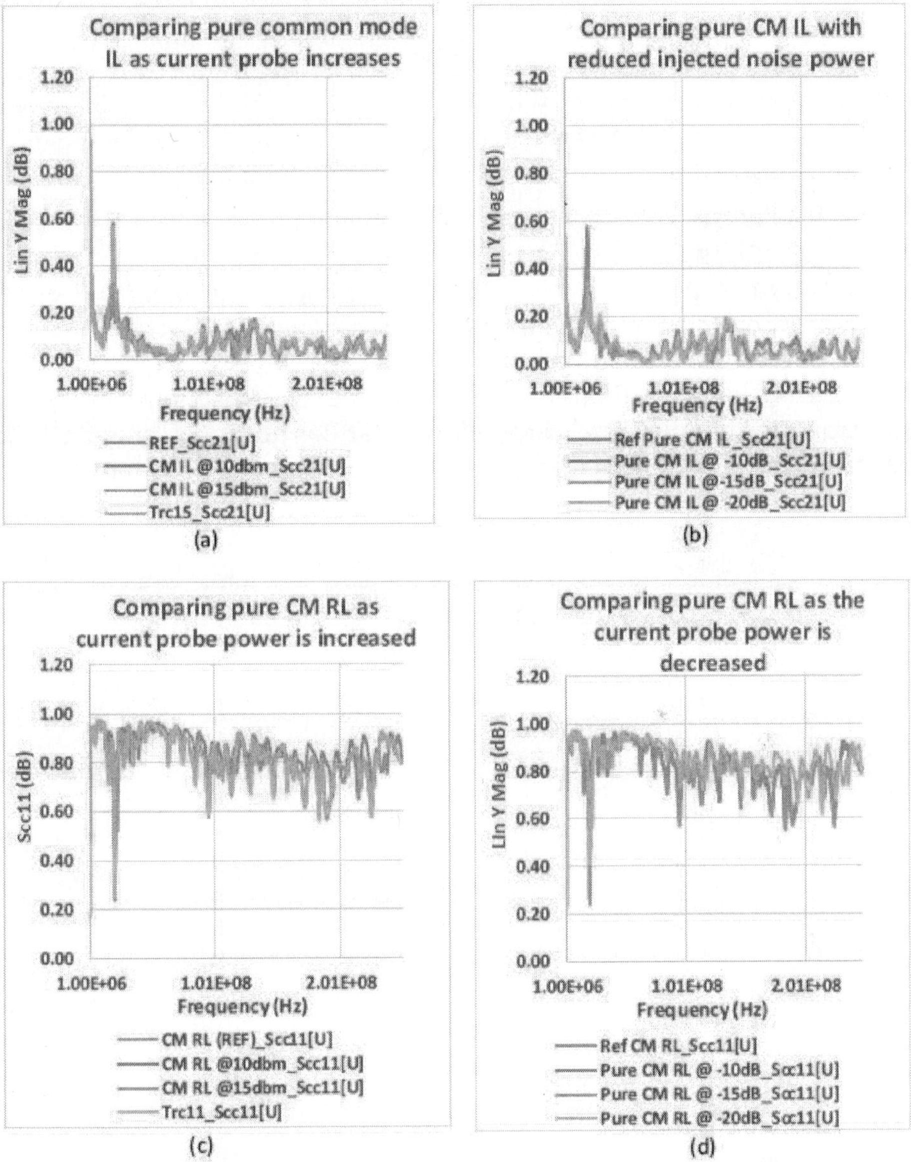

Figure 7.10 Showing consistent amplitude trends for common mode measurements for IL & RL at increased and reduced input probe power

It could be observed in Figure 7.8 that the differential mixed-mode insertion loss and the differential mixed-mode return loss parameters of the CUT were not affected by the changes in the injected noise power levels around the cable. However, in the common mode terms, Figure 7.9, there seemed to be little influence of the injected noise on the mixed-mode parameters, but the amplitude trends of the signals remained mostly the same. These tended to have the same character with Figures 6.16 and 6.17 as discussed in chapter 6 even when the current probe power was increased or decreased. However, in areas where there were slight disagreements in amplitude levels, the trend had remained nearly the same.

Ideally, Figures 7.7 and 7.8 showed relatively no significant mode conversion in both the pure differential and pure common mode configurations even when power in the current probe was either increased or reduced. The consistency in the mixed-mode differential insertion loss plot even with changes in the injected noise power seemed to suggest that the data cable is design for differential signalling. Besides, the figures also show that variations in noise levels around the CUT has no significant effects on the mixed-mode differential and mixed mode common-mode terms.

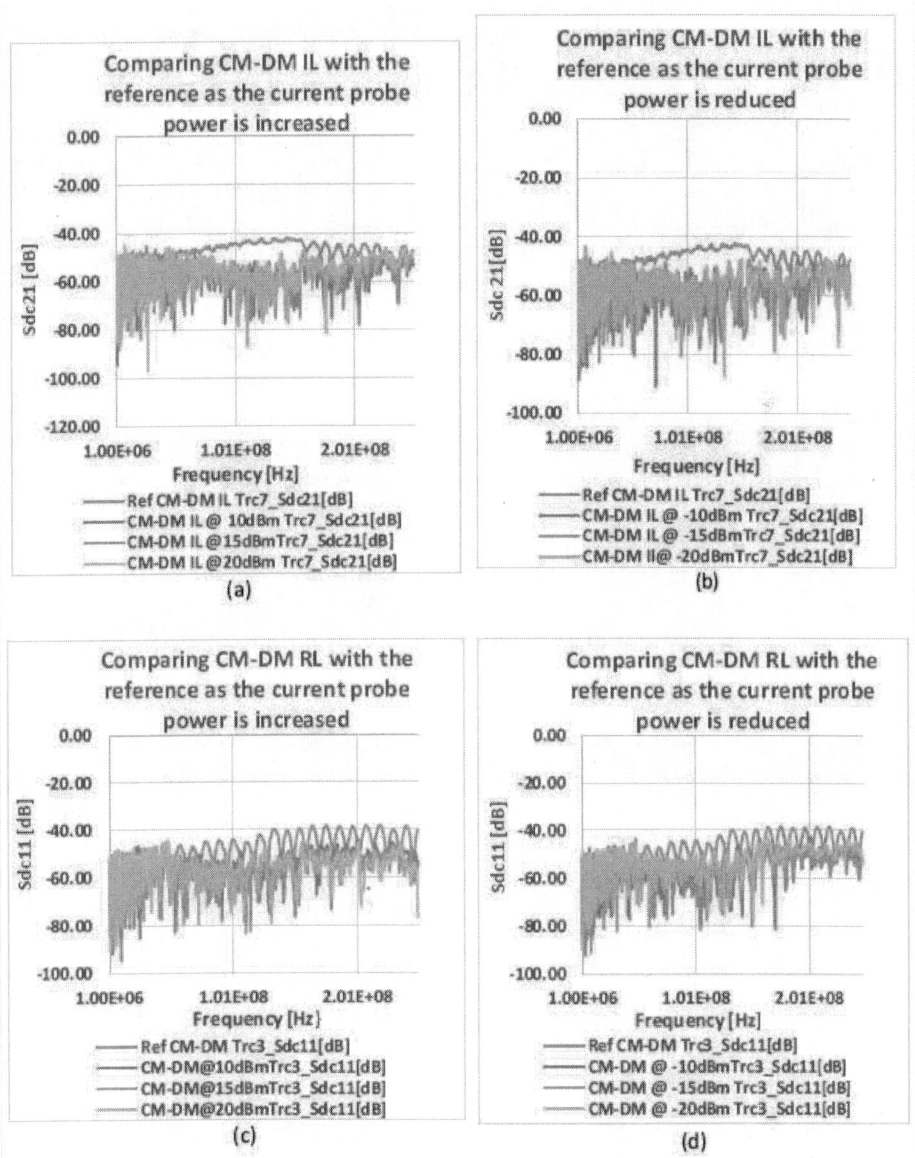

Figure 7.11 Showing disturbing amplitude variations for common-to-differential mode measurements (IL & RL) at increased and reduced input probe power

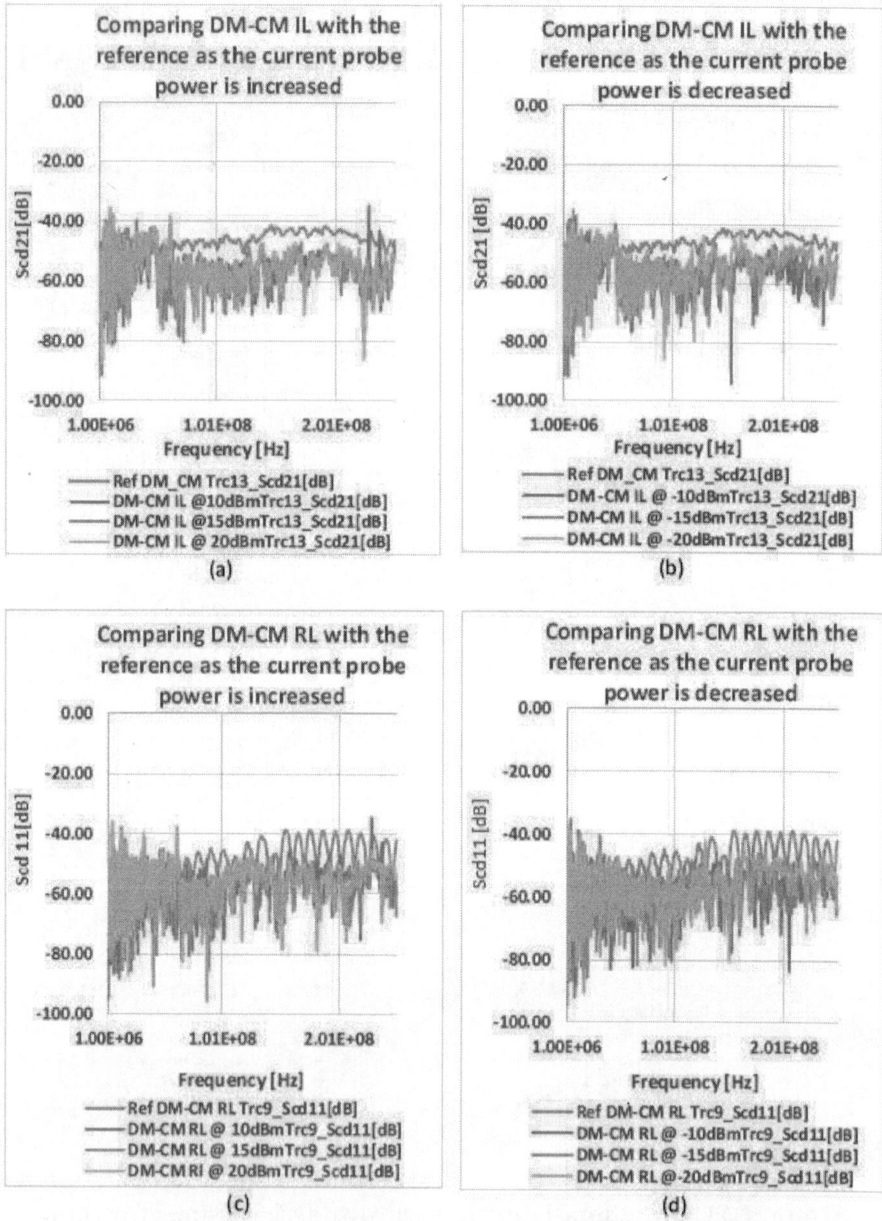

Figure 7.12 Showing disturbing amplitude variations for differential-to-common mode measurements (IL & RL) at increased and reduced input probe power

Referring to Figures 7.10 to 7.11, results showed a remarkable variation between the reference return loss and insertion loss parameters and the measured cross conversion return and insertion loss terms when the current probe power is either increased or decreased. These differences can be explained in part by the fact that the power in the current probe (increased or reduced) may have influenced the mode conversion. Hence, this effect was observed in both the RL and the IL terms.

However, a numerical analysis showing the return loss parameter in the common-to-differential and differential-to-common mode for the increased and reduced current probe power is shown in Table 7.2 below.

Table 7.2 Showing deviation of current probe power from the reference

Signal mode	Maximum Reference power in the current probe	Maximum at Increased current probe power	Maximum at Reduced current probe power	Deviation
S_{dc} Return loss	-41.4dB	-44.4dB	-45.1dB	3.0dB/3.7dB
S_{cd21} IL Loss	-41.9dB	-38.3dB	-44.6dB	3.6dB/2.7dB

It is noteworthy that the figures recorded in Table 7.2 were the maximum values of the return loss across the measurement frequency in the cross-conversion mode and showed how much power deviated from the reference when the circuit was stimulated with power-increased or reduced. It could be seen that the measured return loss varied/deviated by approximately 3dB from the reference in the common-to-differential. This showed that an increase/decrease in the injected common mode noise power has a remarkable effect on the differential mode. A possible explanation for this could be that an approximately 3dB deviation of the current probe power could produce a double conversion effect on the common-to-differential mode conversion when the current probe power (representing environmental noise) is increased. This is capable of affecting the BER of any data bearing network cable.

Figures 7.10 to 7.11 also showed that in all the measurements, these differences became pronounced as the frequency increased. However, between 1 MHz and up to 5 MHz, there were no apparent changes between the reference values and the values measured for both the RL and the IL values when the current probe power was either increased or decreased.

From the analysis provided above, it can be seen that the external electromagnetic noise (CM signal), presented by the current probe, can induce CM (noise) voltages and currents on the CUT and convert to differential mode signal (data borne by the cable) and make the CUT susceptible to external interference.

To further explain the effect of common-to-differential mode resulting from external noise injection, let us examine the mixed-mode matrix

$$\begin{array}{cc|cc} S_{dd11} & S_{dd12} & S_{dc11} & S_{dc12} \\ S_{dd21} & S_{dd22} & S_{dc21} & S_{dc22} \\ \hline S_{cd11} & S_{cd12} & S_{cc11} & S_{cc12} \\ S_{cd21} & S_{cd22} & S_{cc21} & S_{cc22} \end{array}$$

Referring to the literature of the mixed-mode matrix in chapter 5, the *DC* quadrant represents the common to differential mode conversion, and it is related to susceptibility to EMI.

With perfect symmetry of the pairs, there would be no mode conversion of the signals. But with line asymmetry which will result to imbalance, signal mode conversion will occur. Hence, further introduction of intentional twist nonuniformity as a means of checking cable crosstalk will introduce more asymmetry and signal mode conversion which will adversely affect the cable BER.

Chapter Summary

In summary, the experiments on coupling attenuation, (section 7.2 and 7.3) have been used to demonstrate that the differential signal (the desired signal) borne by a network cable can convert to common mode and be radiated out even with appropriate terminations at the ends. This could cause interference to adjacent circuitry in the environment. Likewise, experiments using the current probe injection method has been used to demonstrate that the same desired signal bearing cable can be susceptible especially to external noise.

Although the level of radiated EMI and susceptibility may be very very low, probably because of the use of spacers/separators in the CUT, the experiments and the test methods have shown their existence.

This then led to another line of further thinking in the research journey namely; whether manufacturing process could contribute to the observed mode conversion. To this end, the non-uniformity in the twist length of the CUT was studied.

It was hoped that this would have significant implications for system and cable manufacturers on the performance of network cables. The combination of outcomes may provide some support for the conceptual premise that introducing elements such as aluminium foils and sheets, filters, and other electronics, etc., could help enhance the performance of Ethernet cables instead of intentionally introducing twist nonuniformities.

CHAPTER 8

RESULTS AND ANALYSIS

In this chapter, the analysis of the phenomenon of mixed-mode conversion is provided in terms of lump circuit elements of the classic transmission line. A typical 10-meter length for one pair TWP was used. The reasons for choosing the 10-meter length of the Cat 6 UTP cable under test had been given and is re-emphasised hear for clarity, namely that: 10-meter is long enough to see effects develop. It is also a minimum length that one sees in standards generally, although it is not so long as to need to have attenuation effects fully accounted for in the first order analysis. The chapter also investigates and discusses imbalance due to cable twist nonuniformity that characterise the line length, possibly resulting from the manufacturing process.

The nonuniformity in the TWP is demonstrated as a lumped-parameter circuit to characterise an approximate representation of the cable imbalance and converted into the modal domain as in [125]. This enabled showing the mode conversion circuitry through lumped voltage and current sources controlled by the DM stimulus of the 4-port VNA.

It is worth noting that the analysis of the cable imbalance due to nonuniformity in pair twisting is a first step symbolic solution to identifying EM radiation and hence DM-to-CM mode conversion and vice versa that can occur in data cable. Thus, more research is needed to find out if it is possible to derive further mathematical representations depicting nonuniformity conditions that can lead to EMC emanations.

However, one of the primary ways of describing nonuniformity in transmission line was to approximate the line as a cascade of discrete line segments [126].

One major problem with this method is that the transmission line must be broken into many discrete segments for all the nonuniformities to be accounted for.

Another approach was based on characterisation, and it allows the conversion of the hyperbolic function relating to the partial differential equation of the nonuniform lines into a series of ordinary differential equation

[127]. However, this method is complicated and time-consuming.

In other previous works, mode conversion due to line termination imbalance [128] and circuit line trace asymmetry [129] have been investigated using the assumption of weak imbalance. By this assumption, it was possible to apply modal decomposition in the solution of the transmission line equations. Consequently, it was efficient to predict mode conversion due to nonuniformity and asymmetry in differential interconnects.

In TWP cabling, both wires of a single pair are twisted around each other to form a kind of helix with varying pair length as shown in Figure 8.1.

Figure 8.1 Examples of twist nonuniformities in TWP [130]

These varying degrees of twists make the TWP nonuniform, and as such, the wires in the twist could become unequal in length (non-symmetrical) particularly if the twist is strained or stretched out. The natural question then is whether cable twist nonuniformity plays any role in signal mode conversion observed in TWP cabling as noted in chapters 6 and 7.

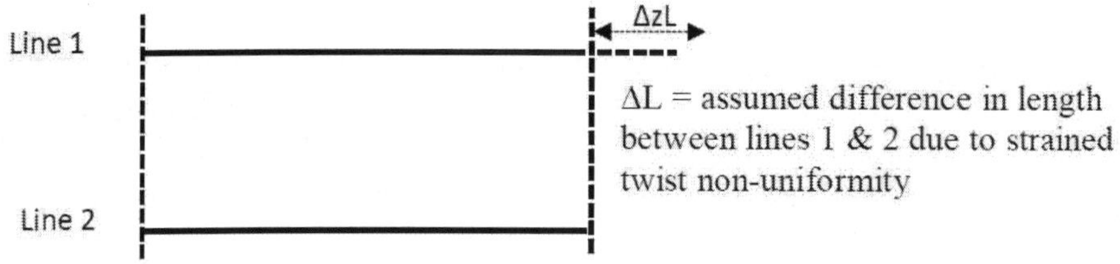

Figure 8.2 Showing sketch of assumed pair imbalance that could result from manufacturing process if the twist is strained

In the study of twist nonuniformity, it was assumed that if a given length of twisted pair had wires of lengths 1 and 2, and the twist was strained/unwound (made straight), there is the possibility that wire length 1 could be longer than wire length 2 by a tiny fraction of length ΔzL as demonstrated in Figure 8.2. This tendency could occur due to error in manufacturing process and is capable of the TWP imbalance because of the difference in length. This imbalance, therefore, could be assumed accountable for the mixed-mode conversions and its consequences as have been shown in previous chapters.

8.1 The Telegrapher's Equation

The use of per-unit-length parameter matrix shows that for a small length "z" of the twisted pair, R(z), L(z), G(z) and C(z) there will be a function of the extra length. From the generic per-unit-length equation for a multiconductor transmission line shown in Fig.8.3.

$$\frac{d}{dz}I(z,t) = -GV(z,t) - C\frac{d}{dt}V(z,t) \qquad (8.2)$$

where *R, L, G, C* represent resistance, inductance, conductance and capacitance of the line [125] [131].

The second order differential equation can be obtained by differentiating (8.1) with respect to z and (8.2) with respect to *t*. This yield

$$\frac{d^2}{dz^2}V(z,t) = -R\frac{d}{dz}I(z,t) - L\frac{d^2}{dzdt}I(z,t) \qquad (8.3)$$

$$\frac{d^2}{dzdt}I(z,t) = -G\frac{d}{dt}V(z,t) - C\frac{d^2}{dt^2}V(z,t) \quad [126]\,[130] \qquad (8.4)$$

Generally, the derivations with respect to z in (8.4) can only be possible if the lines are uniform. However, in the case being considered the lines are not. This is as a result of the cable twisting which makes one wire literally longer than the other (see Figure 8.2). To simplify this, it can be assumed that the line is a perfect conductor, i.e., R=0 and G=0. This leaves equations (8.3) and (8.4) as

$$\frac{d^2}{dz^2} V(z, t) = -L \frac{d^2}{dzdt} I(z,t) \quad (8.5)$$

$$\frac{d^2}{d_z d_t} I(z,t) = -C \frac{d^2}{dt} V(z,t) \text{ [126] [130]} \quad (8.6)$$

Multiplying equation (8.6) by *L*, yields

$$L \frac{d^2}{dzdt} I(z,t) = LC \frac{d^2}{dt^2} V(z,t)$$

Hence,

$$\frac{d^2}{dz^2} V(z,t) - LC \frac{d^2}{dt^2} V(z,t) = 0$$

Therefore,

$$\frac{d^2}{dz^2} V(z, t) = LC \frac{d^2}{dt} V(z,t) \quad (8.7)$$

$$= K \frac{d^2}{dt} V(z,t),$$

where $K = LC$.

If the circuit for the TWP is modelled by lumped-circuit network to represent the "difference in length" (in dash lines) ΔzL, we have

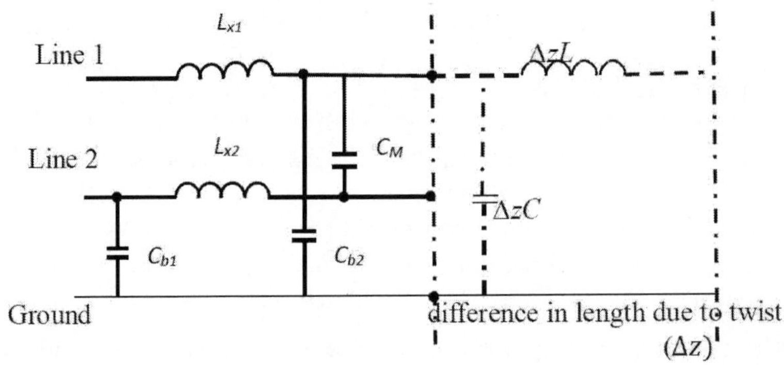

Figure 8.3 Lumped-circuit networks with *R* and *G* equal to zero

In this model, it had been assumed that both R and G are equal to zero and therefore had not been represented. L_{x1} and L_{x2} in the model represent the inductance in lines 1 and 2. C_{b1} and C_{b2} represent the capacitance between lines 2 and 1 respectively while C_M is the capacitance between both lines. However, ΔzL and ΔzC had been used to describe the inductance and capacitance due to the difference in length when the line is strained.

8.2 Analysis of Mode Conversion

Modifying the equivalent circuit of Figure 8.3 in the modal domain and introducing DM and CM currents and voltages following the transformation matrix of [132], a simplified equivalent model circuit for the capacitive and inductive sections are redrawn in Figure 8.4 (a) and (b).

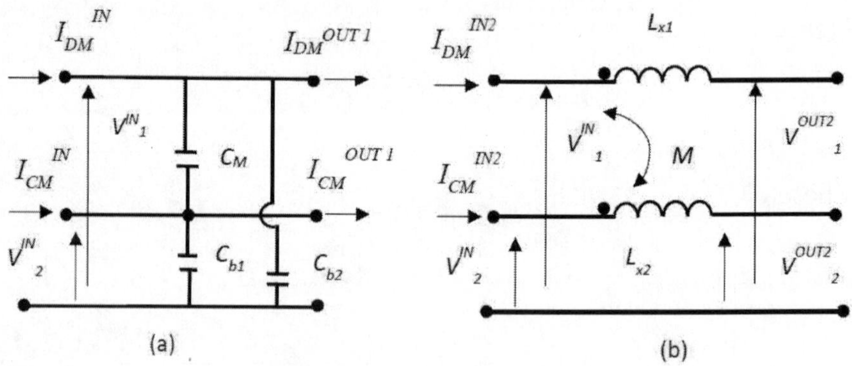

Figure 8.4 Equivalent modal circuits of the twisted wires showing (a) Capacitive section (b) Inductive section

This yields the modal current at the input and output of the capacitive section shown in Figure 8.4 as

$$\begin{Bmatrix} I_{DM}^{out1} \\ I_{CM}^{out1} \end{Bmatrix} = \begin{Bmatrix} I_{DM}^{IN} \\ I_{CM}^{IN} \end{Bmatrix} - j\omega \begin{Bmatrix} C_{DM} & \Delta C \\ \Delta C & C_{CM} \end{Bmatrix} * \begin{Bmatrix} V_{DM}^{IN} \\ V_{CM}^{IN} \end{Bmatrix} \quad (8.8), \text{ where}$$

$C_{DM}= C_M +(C_{b1} + C_{b2})/4$ and $C_{CM}= (C_{b1} + C_{b2})$ represents the differential mode and the common mode equivalent capacitance. $\Delta C=(C_{b2} - C_{b1})/2$ accounts for the unwanted mode conversion from DM to CM and vice versa due to the difference in wire length and it represents the per unit length capacitive matrix.

This is because of the difference in length between the two twisted wires.

This method which was initially used in [126] to account for length difference in a differential microstrip line within a bent region (as perturbation) was adopted in this analysis since both approaches are related and could be considered fit to be used to analyse the effects of such nonuniformities in a differential line.

Similarly, for the inductive circuit

$$\begin{Bmatrix} I_{DM}^{out1} \\ I_{CM}^{out1} \end{Bmatrix} = \begin{Bmatrix} I_{DM}^{IN} \\ I_{CM}^{IN} \end{Bmatrix} - j\omega \begin{Bmatrix} C_{DM} & \Delta C \\ \Delta C & C_{CM} \end{Bmatrix} * \begin{Bmatrix} V_{DM}^{IN} \\ V_{CM}^{IN} \end{Bmatrix} \quad (8.8), \text{ where}$$

$L_{DM} = L_{x1} + L_{x2} - 2M$ and $L_{CM} = (L_{x1} + L_{x2} + 2M)/4$ [126], represent the DM and CM equivalent inductances. $\Delta L = (L_{x1} - L_{x2})/2$ represents the inductance counterpart of the coefficient ΔC in equation (8.8) and accounts for the mode conversion. $V_1^{OUT2} = V_{DM}^{OUT2}$ DM voltage at the inductive circuit and $V_2^{OUT2} = V_{CM}^{OUT2}$ = CM voltage at the inductive circuit.

Furthermore, it was assumed that the difference in length between the two twist lengths is electrically short. Exciting the pair under test with DM source (i.e. considering that the pair under test was assumed to have been simultaneously stimulated by both DM and CM sources from the VNA source) makes for achieving an accurate prediction of the common mode in TCL measurement (CD_{11}) as to be seen in section 8.3.

In line with [126], if we consider DM-to-CM conversion and disregard all contributions due to CM quantities, it is possible to uncouple Figure 8.4 into DM and CM circuits as shown in Figure 8.5 (a) and (b) and sequentially resolve for V_{DM} and I_{DM} with false values for L_{x1}, L_{x2} and M. Also, if values are supposed for C_M, C_{b1} and C_{b2}, it is equally possible to have value for C_{DM}.

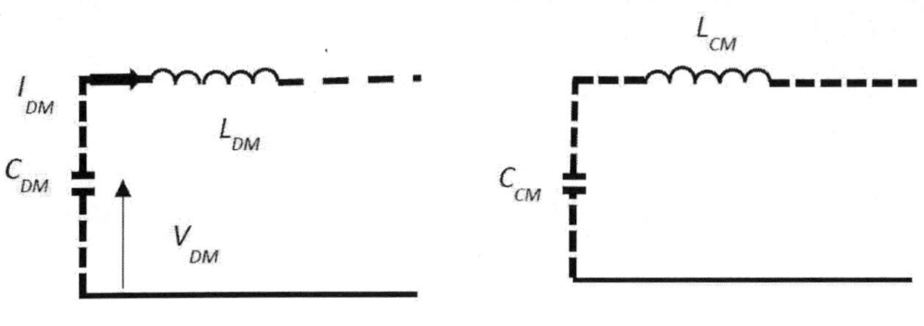

Hence, the circuits can be uncoupled as shown for both DM and CM circuits in Figure 8.5.

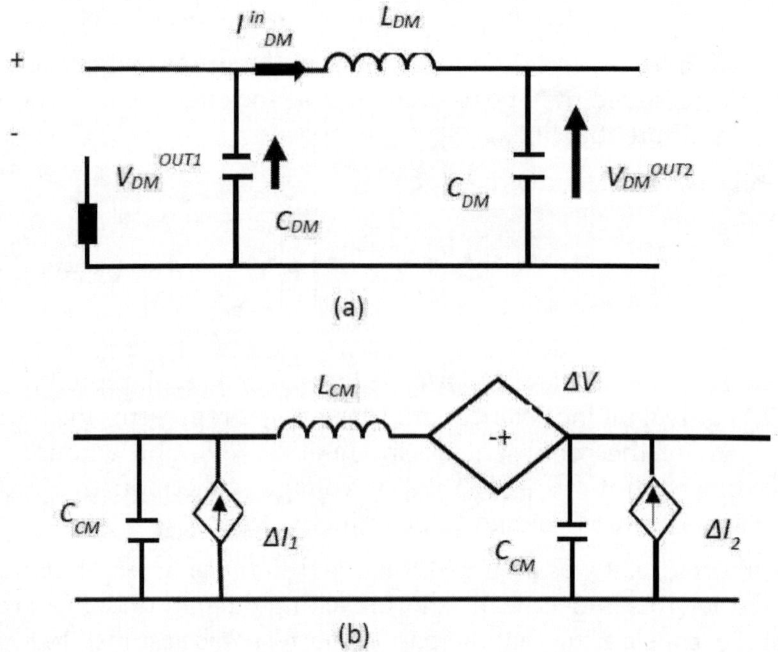

Figure 8.5 Approximate modal circuit for lump current and voltage sources

It is worth noting, however, that in the capacitive section (Figure 8.4 (a), the relationship between the modal voltages and currents are unchanged both at the input and the output, hence $\Delta I_{1,2}=j\omega\Delta CV^{1,2}{}_{DM}$. Here both scripts 1 and 2 are used to designate for differential input and output currents and voltages at the capacitive network. For example, if the following assumptions are made:

$$C_M = 9.97\ pF, C_{b1} = 24.12\ pF,\ C_{b2} = 140.84\ pF,$$

we can determine the value for C_{DM} from $C_{DM} = C_M + (C_{b1} + C_{b2}) / 4$.

$$= 9.78e^{-12} + \left\{ \frac{24.12e^{-12} + 140.84e^{-12}}{4} \right\}$$

$$= 5.102e^{-11}F$$

$$= 51.02\ pF$$

Also, from $\Delta C = \frac{C_{b1} - C_{b2}}{2}$, we can determine the value for ΔC which represents the p.u.l. capacitance matrix that accounts for unwanted conversion from differential-to-common mode. Hence

$$= \frac{140.84e^{-12} - 24.12e^{-12}}{2}$$

$$= 58.36 pF$$

From [125],

$$Z_{DM} = \frac{1}{\mu C_{DM}} = \frac{1}{3e^{8} * 51.02e^{-12}} = \frac{1}{0.0153} = 65.35\Omega .$$

Again from [125],

$$Z_{DM} = \sqrt{\frac{L_{DM}}{C_{DM}}}. \text{ Hence, } Z_{DM}^{2} = \frac{L_{DM}}{C_{DM}}.$$

Therefore. $L_{DM} = Z_{DM}^2 * C_{DM}$

$= (65.35)^2 * 51.02e^{-12}$

$= 2.178e^{-7}\, H$

Also, we can determine the differential mode voltage from $V_{DM} = \sqrt{L_{DM} * C_{DM}}$ to be equal to $\sqrt{2.178e^{-7} * 51.02e^{-12}} = \sqrt{1.111e^{-17}} = 3.33^{-9}V$. Therefore, V_{DM}= $3.33e^{-9}V$.

Hence,

$$I_{DM} = \frac{V_{DM}}{Z_{DM}} = \frac{3.33e^{-9}}{65.35} = 5.09e^{-11} A .$$

With similar assumptions, approximate values of the equivalent inductances can be derived, and the coefficient ΔL which accounts for the inductive equivalent of ΔC can also be estimated.

For instance, if L_{x1}= $0.072e^{-9}H$, L_{x2}= $1.813e^{-9}\, H$, $M = 0.069e\text{-}9\, H$, we can also determine values for L_{DM} as well as ΔL .

Hence, $\Delta L = (L_{x1}\, L_{x2})/\, 2 = 0.072^{-9} - 1.813e^{-9}/2 = 35.4e^{-9}\, H$.

As in [124] [126] [133], the DM voltages and currents associated with the length difference from the differential circuit are taken as input into the CM circuit where the DM-to-CM conversion is modelled like the lump current and voltage sources as shown in Figure 8.5 to give

$\Delta I_{1,2} = j\Delta C V^{a,c}{}_{DM}$ (8.10)

$\Delta V = j\omega L I^{b}{}_{DM}$ (8.11)

The differential modal currents and voltages on the line under analysis are associated with the electromagnetic fields resulting in mode conversion and are developed on the circuit elements of C_{DM} and L_{DM} in the region of the difference in length between the pairs where they serve as input into the CM circuit. The superscript $^{(a)}$ in equation 8.10 was used to represent input differential voltages into the decoupled capacitive network while $^{(c)}$ served for the output differential voltage at the decoupled inductive network.

8.3 Predicting LCL and TCL for the Network Cable

To better appreciate the mechanism of mode conversion in the TWP under analysis, the concept of longitudinal conversion loss (LCL) and transverse conversion loss (TCL) are employed [134] [135].

Using the 4-port VNA configured in balanced mode (see Figure 6.14), these parameters are defined to quantify LCL as CM-to-DM (i.e. S_{dc11}) and TCL as DM-to-CM (i.e. S_{cd11}), all with reference to port 1 of the VNA [136].

Longitudinal Conversion Loss, LCL

The longitudinal conversion loss parameter is a balanced measurement that describes the measure of unbalance in a cable. It represents the fraction of CM signal which is converted to DM and reveals how well a balanced cable is less susceptible to external noise. Also, LCL can be described as the proportion of differential mode (DM) signal introduced into a power circuit to the common mode (CM) signal which results from the power circuit unbalance [137]. The accuracy of the approximation modal circuit of Figure 8.5 is shown in the LCL plot for a pair of the TWP as shown in Figure 8.6.

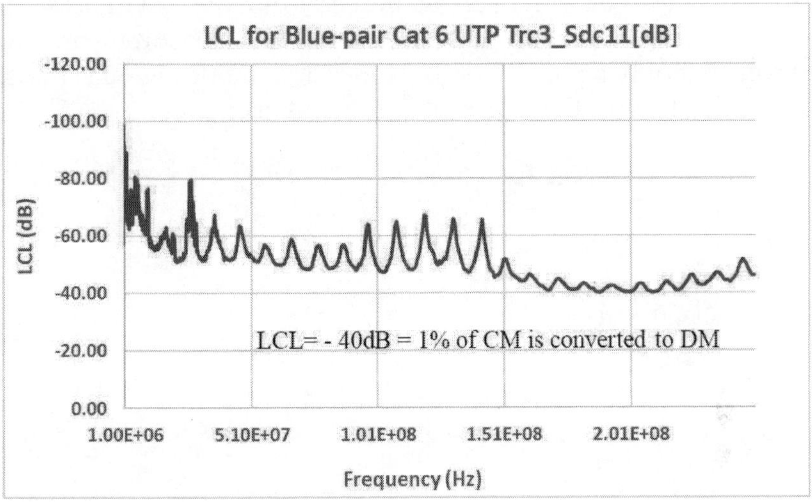

Figure 8.6 LCL Measurement for the blue pair of Cat 6 UTP Cable

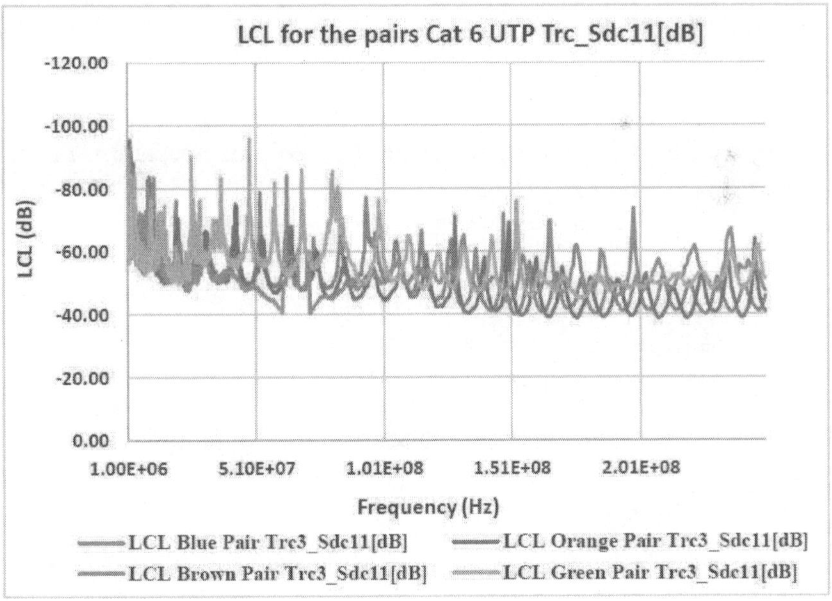

Figure 8.7 LCL Plot for all the 4-pairs of Cat 6 UTP

In Figure 8.7, the LCL s-parameter plot for all the 4-pairs is plotted against frequency and shows that LCL for the Cat 6 UTP under test is within -40 dB. This indicates that only about 1% of the CM is converted to DM signal.

Since measurements of LCL and TCL (transverse conversion loss) are "reciprocal due to symmetry", an s-parameter plot of the TCL as shown in Figure 8.8 confirms the robustness of the above test measurement. The TCL also proves that only about 1% of the differential mode signal is translated to common mode with the TCL plot within -40 dB.

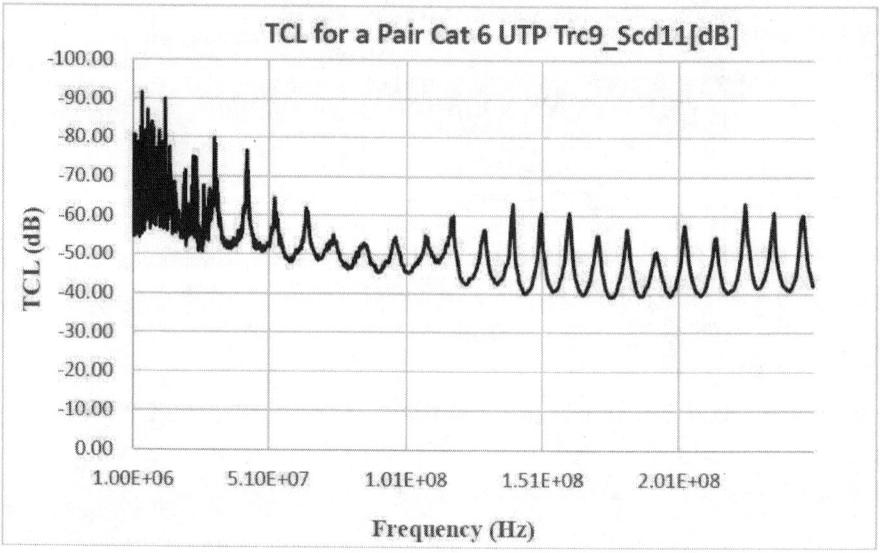

Figure 8.8 TCL plot for the blue twisted pair of Cat 6 UTP

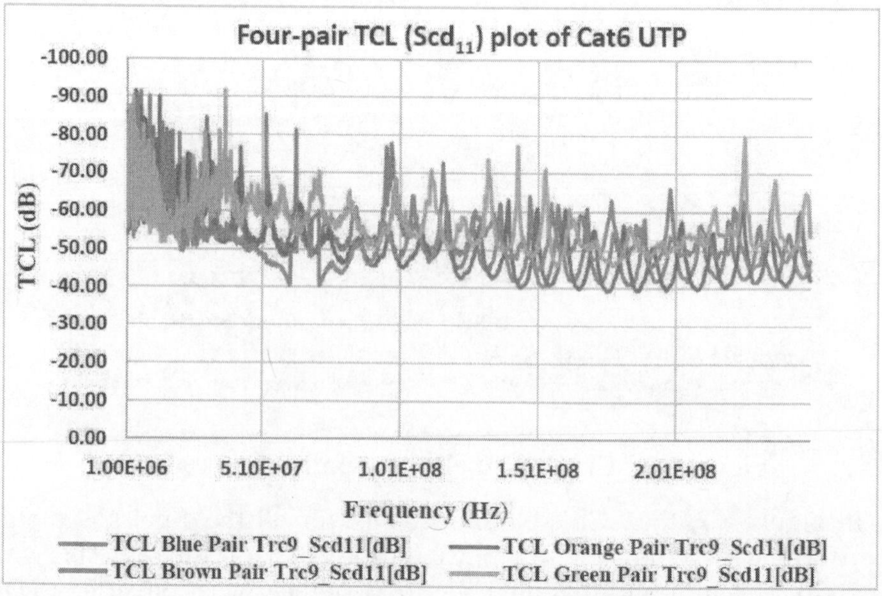

Figure 8.9 TCL for all the 4-Pairs of Cat 6 UTP

This assessment also agrees with that in section 6.10 where the response plot of differential-to-common mode conversion (S_{cd11}) and common-to-differential conversion (S_{dc11}) were made. Both plots show that approximately between -40 dB to -42 dB (1% to 0.79%) of differential signal are converted to common mode signal by the Cat 6 UTP cable under test and vice versa. Although this proportion of conversion may be regarded as being quite small, it is big enough to cause crosstalk among pairs and between pairs in twisted cabling. This can also be noticed in the values of the differential currents and voltages responsible for the differential-to-common mode conversion as seen in section 8.2.

As shown in Figure 8.10 an approximate graph of the longitudinal conversion loss LCL parameter is obtained from the table of estimated values for Sdc_{11} as shown in Table 8.1.

Table 8.1 Showing approximate value of Sdc_{11}

Frequency (MHz	20	30	70	140	150	170	180	200 - 250
Sdc_{11} (dB)	-55	-51	-48	-47	-46	-42	-40	-40

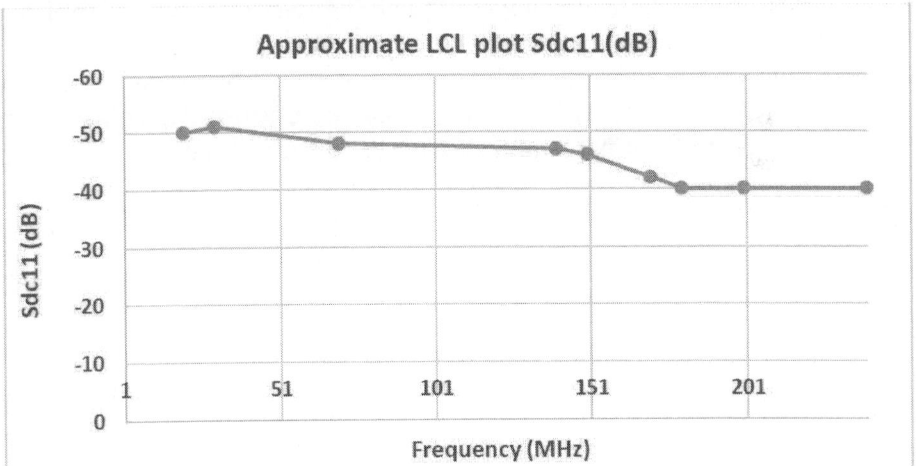

Figure 8.10 Approximate plot of LCL

The graph shows that the LCL remains almost steady around -40 dB beyond 200MHz.

Again from [138] the factor of unbalance (nonuniformity) *h* for the two twisted pair cables can be estimated from

$$h = \frac{C_{b2}}{C_{b2} + C_{b1}}$$

Chapter Summary

In summary, it has been demonstrated that nonuniformity in cable twisting means that a small CM interference (which the cable may have picked up by induction) could be converted by the cable imbalances into unwanted differential mode signal. This would likely add up with the noise of the circuit but would still maintain the original nature of the differential mode signal, thus making it indifferentiable by the circuit terminating electronics.

From the analysis, it has been shown that an infinitesimal amount of differential currents and voltages arising from well-assumed circuit element values can cause substantial cross mode signal conversion well able to cause interferences in adjacent circuits. Although this remains to be substantially verified through simulation, the result could serve as a guide to cable manufacturers in the design process to reduce/eliminate crosstalk and other consequences of mode conversion in UTP network cables, e.g. introducing electronics between and among wire pairs in a cable.

The test results have also brought to the fore the challenges of intentional twist non-uniformity as a technique to manage crosstalk in cables. It has been demonstrated using the Cat 6 network cable, that a network cable with no twist non-uniformity, was capable of -40dB (approximately 1%) signal mode conversion. Hence, with twist nonuniformity, which introduces some form of imbalance on the cable, the percentage of signal conversion can be expected to rise. Therefore, intentionally introducing twist nonuniformity as a means of minimising cable crosstalk would degrade the cable's transmission performance.

CHAPTER 9

CONCLUSION AND FUTURE WORK

In this chapter, the conclusion of the research study and the suggestions for future work are presented. The initial purpose of the research was to investigate, the characteristics of noise coupling to network cable particularly in a noisy environment. The principle of mixed mode s-parameter conversion was adopted to explain the performance of the cable without twist nonuniformity.

9.1 Summary & Conclusion

Twisted cabling has continued to attract immense interest especially in wired-IoT and Power over Ethernet (PoE), yet they also provoke concerns about the generation of electromagnetic interference EMI to other neighbouring circuitry. Because of this, this study has investigated the mode conversion parameters in an unshielded, balanced twisted-pair Cat 6 cable with a view to investigating its support for mode conversion, being a balanced transmission line. The hypothesis was based on unbalances caused by the nonuniformity in the pair twist.

The study has also shown that data cables can become susceptible especially under very noisy condition thus leading to data corruption. Experiments performed in the mode-stirred reverberation chamber showed how sensitive two most popular data cables can perform when subjected to a noisy environment irrespective of the cable length and orientation.

In chapter 7, both balanced and the unbalanced test fixtures were fabricated and tested to show that balanced (symmetric) structures do not support mode conversion. The unbalanced (asymmetric) structure was also seen to support mode conversion due to impedance anomalies. The tests from these structures reveal that noise can couple to the adjacent transmission line as a result of asymmetry in the transmission line. The second significant finding was that due to transmission line asymmetry, differential-to-common mode and common-to-differential issues arise which could result in EM radiation from the asymmetrical differential-paired lines and susceptibility matters. These findings have significant implications for the manufacturing of systems and data cables. Although nonuniformities in twist rates of cables cannot be entirely avoided, reducing the it to the barest minimum can help minimize cross-mode conversion and crosstalk issues in TWPs. Further experiments using the s-parameter mixed-mode analysis and a 4-port VNA showed the desired differential data borne by the cable can convert to common-mode signal and cause EM radiation to adjacent circuitry. Also, the sensitivity of the mode conversion was verified under different injected current probe power levels. It was also found that the pure differential and common-mode conversion terms were insensitive to any power level change. The cross-conversion terms were however found to be sensitive to the changes in the injected power. This was attributed to the imbalance in the wires of the cable pair which resulted to nonuniformity.

The study went further to develop a numeric solution to assist developers of differential systems and cable manufacturers in controlling nonuniformities during design. It is worth emphasizing here that this attempt is a first step symbolic solution to identifying EM radiation and hence show differential-to-common mode conversion and vice versa that can occur in a simulated data cable.

The experiments in chapter 7 of this work have shown that intentional twist nonuniformity of network cables is not an answer to reducing or minimising cable crosstalk. They have also demonstrated that twist nonuniformity introduces imbalances which are responsible for interferences and cable susceptibility issues.

However, more research is required to establish if it is possible to develop solid mathematical conditions under which cable twist uniformity can lead to Signal Integrity and Electromagnetic Compatibility issues.

The findings of these investigations complement those of earlier studies and contributes additional evidence that suggests that the degree of susceptibility and indeed radiation from the twisted pair is tolerably low. Although this study focuses generally on noise coupling, the findings may well have a bearing on the cable and RF component manufacturing industries on ensuring symmetry in their designs and hardware.

9.2 Future Work

This work has generated some outline results with regard to cross conversion mode of signals in TWP cabling which could give rise to EMC and signal integrity issues. This is particularly of interest in information bearing cables. However, there are still some clear next step for this work before it can formally be used for discussion as a recommended test method.

First, there is need to confirm the tests results using simulation technique (ADS Circuit Model Simulation as used in [113] 116). Secondly, the results of simulation will need to confirm the measurement/practical approach used in modelling the twist nonuniformity.

Having completed the modelled circuits that could be used to explain the predicted EMI from a non-uniform TWP with time domain input signal, it was agreed between the supervisory team and myself to halt the work at this stage. It was further decided that work will be continued by the next generation of PhD student in the department who might be interested in working on the topic.

The twisted pair was connected to the 4-Port measuring instrument through a test fixture and the RF coax cable, and the calibration plane was taken from the end of the RF network cable as can be seen below.

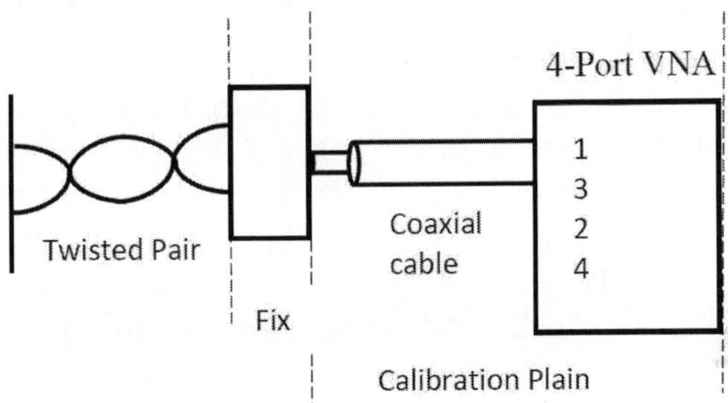

Figure 9.1 Calibration plan

Further research work is required to include the extension of calibration plain to the end of the test fixture. It is hoped that this will de-embed the microstrip line in the test head of any impedance anomalies so that the actual mixed-mode s-parameters measurement will exclusively involve the twisted pairs only. This will yield a more accurate characterization of noise on the cable whether the noise is injected or environmentally couple.

REFERENCES

[1] "What is The Internet of Things?"- Government Technology. [Online]. Available: *http://www.govtech.com/fs/what -is-the-Internet-of-Things.html.Assessed,* Assessed, October 22, 2017.

[2] *http://computer.howstuffworks.com/ethernet3.htm* [Online]. Available: Assessed, February 2018.

[3] H. A. Munir, H. A., Saad, A., Junid, S.A.A.S., Zaidi, A.M.A., Yusoff, M.Z., (2012), *Fundamental study and analysis of CAT5e cable for NEXT and ELFEXT,* IEEE 4th International Conference on Intelligent and Advanced Systems (ICIAS), DOI: 10.1109/ICIAS.2012.6306190, Kuala Lumpur, Malaysia.

[4] Watanabe, Y., Uchida, T., Sasaki, Y., Oka, N., Ohashi, H., (2014), Study on *Grounding Condition of Shield Sheath in Shielded Twisted Pair Cable,* IEEE International Symposium on EMC, Tokyo (EMC'14/Tokyo), INSPEC Accession Number: 14837757, pp 753 – 756.

[5] Grassi, F., Pignari, S. A., Wolf, J., (2010), *Assessment of CAN performance for Powerline Communications in dc differential buses,* IEEE International Conference on Microwave, Communications, Antennas and Electronics Systems (COMCAS), Tel Aviv, Israel DOI: 10.1109/COMCAS.2009.5385959, INSPEC Accession Number: 11085963

[6] COMMSCOPE White Paper: *Single balanced twisted-pair cabling infrastructure for IoT and M2M connectivity.* [Online] Available: https://www.commscope.com/Blog/Single-Pair-Ethernet-Will-Connect-IoT-Devices. Assessed March 2018.

[7] Tarasov, D., (2017), *On increase of immunity to EMI in high-performance analog system with differential signal line,* 6th IEEE Mediterranean Conference on Embedded Computing (MECO), DOI: 10.1109/MECO.2017.7977174, INSPEC Accession Number: 17040406, Bar, Montenegro.

[8] Pignari, S. A., Spadaccini, G., (2011), *Influence of twist-pitch non-uniformity on the radiated immunity of twisted-wire pairs,* in Proc.30th URSI Gen. Assembly Sci. Symp., Istanbul, Turkey, pp 1-4.

[9] Pignari, S. A., Spadaccini, G., (2011), *Plane-Wave Coupling to a Twist-*

ed-Wire Pair Above Ground, IEEE Transactions on EMC, Vol. 53, No. 2, pp 508 – 523.

[10] Cao, Y., Wen, J., Hong, H., Liu, J., (2015), *A Compact Branch-Line Coupler with Arbitrary Power Division and Multi Frequencies Suppression,* Communication 16th IEEE International Conference on Communication Technology (ICCT), DOI: 10.1109/ICCT.2015.7399861, INSPEC Accession Number: 15774637, Hangzhou, China, pp 376 – 379.

[11] Kraemer, M., Ercoli, M., Dragomirescu, D., (2010), *A wideband single-balanced down-mixer for the 60GHz band in 65nm CMOS,* IEEE Asia-Pacific Microwave Conference Proceeding (APMC), Yokohama, Japan, Accession No 11863028, pp 1849-1852.

[12] Sturm, J., Popuri, S., Xiang, X., (2014), *CMOS noise cancellation balun LNA with a tunable bandpass from 4.6GHz to 5.8GHz,* IEEE International Conference on Electronics, Circuits and Systems (ICECS), pp 84-87.

[13] Fan, W., Lu, A. L. L., Lok, W. B. K. (2003), *Mixed-mode s-parameter characterisation of differential structures,* 5th IEEE Conference (EPTC) on Electronics Packaging Technology, DOI: 10.1109/EPTC.2003.1271579, INSPEC Accession Number: 7915050, Singapore, Singapore, pp 533-537.

[14] Tabesh, M., Arbabian, A., Niknejad, A., (2011), *60GHz Low-loss compact phase shifter using a transformer-based hybrid in 65nm CMOS,* IEEE Conference on custom integrated circuits (CICC), San Jose, CA, USA, DOI: 10.1109/CICC.2011.6055324.

[15] Wu, Y., Yoa, L., Wang, W., Liu, Y., (2015), *A wide-band 180-degree phase shifter using a pair of coupled-line studs,* IEEE Inter Symposium on Antennas and Propagation & USNC/URSI National Radio Science Meeting, Vancouver, BC, Canada, DOI:10.1109/APS.2015.7304506, pp 240-241.

[16] Andee, Y., Prouvee, J., Graux, F., Danneville, F., (2014), *A fast and functional technique for the noise figure measurement of differential amplifiers,* IEEE Conference on PhD. Research in Microelectronics and Electronics (PRIME), Grenoble, France, DOI:10.1109/PRIME.2014.6872691.

[17] Dressel, W., Maggold, T., Vietzorreck, L., (2001), *Time Domain characterisation of multichip module elements,* IEEE Conference on Microwave Symposium Digest, Phoenix, USA, DOI:1109/MWSYM.2001.967068, pp 1033-1036.

[18] Letavin, D. A., (2017), *Miniature branch-line coupler structure analysis*, IEEE Inter-Conference on young specialists on Micro/Nanotechnologies & Electronic Devices (EDM), DOI:1109/EDM.2017.7981717, pp 99-101.

[19] Sandler, S. M., (2016), *Extending the usable range of the 2-port shunt through impedance measurement*, IEEE MTT-S Latin America Microwave Conference (LAMC),Puerto Vallarta, Mexico, DOI:10.1109/LAMC.2016.7851286, pp 1-3.

[20] McNamara J., *The Complete, Unofficial TEMPEST Information page*. [Online]. Available: *Online, http://www.askimo.com/~joelm/tempest.html.* Assessed 25/02/2017.

[21] Mathews, J. N., (Dec 2017), Side-channel attacks: even in a crypto-ideal world is data truly secure. [Online]. Available: www.cs.tufts.edu/comp/116/archive/fall2017/mathews.pdf Assessed April 2018.

[22] Specification NSA No. 94-106, *National Security Agency Specification for Shielded Enclosures*, 24 October 1994 (http://cryptome.info/0001/nsa-94-106.htm - Available Online, Accessed February 2017).

[23] Standard, "SDIP 29: Facility Design Criteria and Installation of Equipment for the Processing of Classified Information," 2014.

[24] Solak, V., Efendioglu, H. S., Colak, B., Garip, M., (2017), *Analysis and simulation of cable crosstalk*, IEEE IV International Electromagnetic Compatibility Conference (EMC Turkiye), DOI: 10.1109/EMCT.2017.8090354, INSPEC Accession Number: 17334903, Ankara, Turkey, pp 1-4.

[25] Zhao, H., Li, G., Wang, N., Zheng, S., Yu, L., (2012), Journal of Computers, No.9, pp.2240–2247.

[26] Wen, T., Wen, T., Chen, T., (2013), *Special Issue: Advances in Computational Intelligence*, Journal of Computers, No.2, pp.308–312.

[27] EIA/TIA 568.2, Balanced twisted-pair telecommunications cabling and components standards, Aug 2009

[28] What is the Difference Between a Network Cable and an Ethernet Cable?". [Online]. Available: *https://www.techwalla.com/articles/what-is-the-difference-between-a-network-cable-and-an-Ethernet-cable* Assessed Wed 22 Oct 2017.

[29] IEEE Standards 802.3u Part 2 Fast Ethernet

[30] IEEE Standards 802.3z Part 3 Gigabit Ethernet

[31] TIA/EIA-568-B.1 (Revision of TIA/EIA-568.A), Building Telecom-

munication Cabling Standard for Telecom Industries Association and Electronic Industries Alliance, Section 5.5 backbone Cabling Distance, May 2001.

[32] Sarma, M., Sarma, S. K., (2013), *Quantitative Performance Analysis and Critical Parameter Evaluation of UTP Cables,* UKSim 15, IEEE International Conference on Computer Modelling and Simulation, DIO 10.1109/UKSim 2013.93, pp 491-494

[33] ANSI/TIA – 568.1 – D, Commercial Building Telecommunication Infrastructure Standards, revised D Sept. 2015.

[34] IEEE Std. 802.3bz 2.5GBASE-T and 5GBASE-T

[35] Cabling Maintenance and Installation, TestPro 100 validates copper links for 2.5G, 5G, 10G, and 90W PoE, [Online]. Available: http://www.cablinginstall.com/articles/2018/02/aem-testpro-100-5g-10-90w-Poe-tester.html, Assessed, March 2018.

[36] URSI, *URSI resolution on criminal activities using electromagnetic tools,* Minutes of the XXVIth General Assembly of the URSI, 1999.

[37] Electromagnetic compatibility (EMC) Part 2-13: *Environment High power electromagnetic (HPEM) environments Radiated and conducted.* IEC Standard 61000-2-13, 2005.

[38] Sabath, F., Garbe, H., (2015), *Assessing the likelihood of various intentional electromagnetic environments the initial step of an IEMI risk analysis,* IEEE Inter. Symposium on Electromagnetic Compatibility (EMC), No. 15455294, DOI: 10.1109/ISEMC.2015.7256319, pp. 1083-1088.

[39] G. Lugrin et al., *Overview of IEMI Conducted and Radiated Sources: Characteristics and Trends,* Electromagnetic Compatibility (EMC EUROPE), 2012 International Symposium on, 2013.

[40] Sabath, F., (2011), *What can be learned from documented Intentional Electromagnetic Interference (IEMI) attacks,* General Assembly and Scientific Symposium, 2011 XXXth URSI, Vol., No., pp.1,4, 13-20 Aug. 2011.

[41] Radasky, W, A., Hoad, R., (2015), *Status and Progress of IEC SC 77C High-Power Electromagnetics Publications in 2015,* IEEE International Symposium on EMC, DOI: 10.1109/ISEMC.2015.7256330, pp. 1141 – 1146.

[42] Radasky, W. A., Caruso, M., (2013), *HPEM protection of commercial facilities,* IEEE International Symposium on Electromagnetic Compatibility, No. 6670525, pp. 829-833.

[43] Karcoon, H., Parr, S., Dickmann, S., Rambousky, R., (2015), *Shielding Effectiveness of Screened Rooms with Line Feed-Throughs - a Semi-Analytical Approach,* IEEE Inter. Symposium on Electromagnetic Compatibility (EMC), No. 15455367, DOI: 10.1109/ISEMC.2015.7256178, pp. 312 316.

[44] Savage, E., Radasky, W., (2013), *IEMI evaluation of network protectors,* IEEE International Symposium on Electromagnetic Compatibility, DOI: - 10.1109/ISEMC.2013.6670447, pp. 407 – 410.

[45] Klouda, J. C., (1998 April), *EMC Testing Part 1 test procedure requirements,* In Proceedings of the 44th Annual technical meeting of Inst. Of Environment Science, Phoenix USA, ISSN 0073-9227, pp. 313-315.

[46] BS EN 61000-4-21:2011 *Electromagnetic Compatibility (EMC) Part 4-21: Testing and measurement techniques –Reverberation chamber test methods, 31 Jul 2011.*

[47] Zhu, S., Zhu, Y., (2013), *Stirrer Swing Experiment in Reverberation Chamber,* 5th IEEE Int. Symposium on Microwave, Antenna Propagation and EMC Technology for Wireless Communication, MAPE 6689920, Chengdu China, pp. 642-645.

[48] Rajamani, V., Freyer, G. J., (2015 Aug), *Feasibility Study of Multi-frequency test in a single rotation of mode-stirred reverberation chamber,* IEEE Int. Symposium on EMC, Vol 2015-Sept, No. 7256345, pp.1228-1231.

[49] Rhee, E., Lee, J. H., (2013 Apr.), *Electric Field Uniformity characteristics of a Reverberation Chamber with component QRD,* 2nd Int. Conference on Applied Materials & Electronic Engineering, AMEE, Hong Kong China, Vol. 684, pp. 518-521.

[50] Carter, N. J., (1999), Mode Stirred Chambers, Available http://ourworld.compuserv.com/homepage/Nigeel_Carter/modestir.htm. Assessed March 2018.

[51] Zhang, F., Guizhen, L., Jiang, R., (2010), *Field Uniformity Measurement of a Small Reverberation Chamber,* IEEE Symposium on EMC Application of Electromagnetism & Student Innovation Competition Awards, (AEM2C), pp. 221-225.

[52] Coates, A. R., *Electromagnetic compatibility testing of communication cables, PhD Thesis,* Faculty of Technology, De Montfort University, Leicester, UK, 2004.

[53] Tim Williams, *EMC for product designers, 4th Edition,* Elsevier publisher, M.A.USA, pp340-353, 2007.

[54] Crawford, M. L., Koepke, G.H. (1986), Design, Evaluation and Use of Reverberation chamber for performing electromagnetic susceptibility/vulnerability measurements, NBS Technical Note 1092, US Department of Commerce/Natural Bureau of standards, 1986.

[55] Garcia-Fernandez, M. A., Decroze, C., Carsenat, D., (2014), *Antenna radiation pattern measurements in reverberation chamber using Doppler analysis,* IEEE Conference on Antenna Measurement and Application (CAMA), DIO: 10.1109/CAMA.2014.7003320, pp. 1-4.

[56] Wang, S., Wu, Z., Wei, G., Cui, Y., Fan, L., (2013), *A new method of estimating reverberation chamber Q-factor with experimental validation,* (PIER letter, Progress in Electromagnetic Research letter), Vol. 36, pp. 103-112 [Online]. Available: www.jpier.org/PIER/pier.php. Assessed 30/03/2017.

[57] Kumpuniemi, T., Tuovinen, T., Hamalainen, M., Vuohtoniemi, R., Linatti, J., (2013), *Measurement-based on-body path loss modelling for UWB WBAN communication,* Int. Symposium on Medical Information & Communication Technology, ISMICT, Tokyo-Japan, pp. 233-237.

[58] John Crisp, Introduction to Copper Cabling: Applications for Telecommunications, Data Communications and Networking 1st Edition 2002, Newnes Publishers, pp

[59] Uribe-leal, A., Munoz-Sancen, M. N., Garcia-Ruiz, I., (2014), *Extended Characterization of an open-area Antenna Calibration Test site,* 29th Conference on Precision Electromagnetic Measurements, CPEM 2014, Rio de Janerio, Brazil, Aug 2014, No. 6898327, pp198-199.

[60] Magdowski, M., Vick, R., (2013), *Simulation of the stochastic electromagnetic field coupling to an unshielded twisted pair of wires,* in International Symposium on Electromagnetic Compatibility, IEEE, Ed., Vol. 1, Denver, CO, USA, pp. 33 – 37.

[61] Bdour, T., Reineix, A., Guiffaut, C., (2014), *Statistical investigation of a field coupling to random twisted pair using Design of Experiment,* International Symposium on Electromagnetic Compatibility, DOI: 10.1109/EMCEurope.2014.6930988, pp. 665 – 669.

[62] Vogt-Ardatjew, R., Leferink, F., (2015), *Experimental plane wave and random field coupling to uniform and non-uniform transmission lines,* IEEE International Symposium on Electromagnetic Compatibility, No. 7256260, pp. 767-772.

[63] Zhang, H., Xiang Zhao, X., Luo, Q., Yan, L., Liu, C., Huang, K., (2012), *An Alternative Semi-analytical/Analytical Solution to Field-*

to-Wire Coupling in an Electrically Large Cavity, IEEE Transactions on Electromagnetic Compatibility, Vol. 54, Issue 5, No. 13038153, pp.1153 - 1160.

[64] Kovalevsky, L., Langley, R.S., Besnier, P., Sol, J., (2015), *Experimental validation of the Statistical Energy Analysis for coupled reverberant rooms,* IEEE International Symposium on Electromagnetic Compatibility, No. 7256221, pp. 546-551.

[65] Höijer, M., Kroon, L., (2013), *Field Statistics in Nested Reverberation Chambers,* IEEE Transactions on Electromagnetic Compatibility, Vol. 55, Issue 6, DOI: 10.1109/TEMC.2013.2249510, pp. 1328 – 1330.

[66] Salhi, M. A., Şen, S., Çakır, S., (2016), *3D/2D radiation pattern measurement of different GSM phones for EMC applications,* 2016 International Symposium on Electromagnetic Compatibility - EMC Europe, No. 16449418 DOI: 10.1109/EMCEurope.2016.7739219, pp. 695 – 700.

[67] Lee, C-H., Yao, C-Y., Li, H-C., Lin, D-B., (2016), *Radiation from a PCB trace with broadband harmonic frequency signals,* 2016 Progress in Electromagnetic Research Symposium (PIERS), DOI: 10.1109/PIERS.2016.7734686, pp. 1476 – 1479.

[68] Menssen, B., Hamann, D., Garbe, H., (2015), *Extension of the emission measurements for alternative test methods above 1 GHz for unintentional electromagnetic radiators,* International Symposium on EMC, No. 15455537, DOI: 10.1109/ISEMC.2015.7256203, pp. 444 - 449.

[69] Hurtig, T., Adelöw, L., Akyuz, M., Elfsberg, M., Larsson, A., Nyholm, S. E., (2015), *Destructive high-power microwave testing of simple electronic circuit in reverberation chamber,* IEEE International Symposium on Electromagnetic Compatibility (EMC), DOI: 10.1109/ISEMC.2015.7256328, pp. 1133 – 1135.

[70] Bockelman, D. E., Eisenstadt, W. R., (1995), *Combined Differential and Common-Mode Scattering Parameters: Theory and Simulation,* IEEE Transactions on Microwave theory and techniques, Vol 43, No. 7, pp. 1530-1539.

[71] Ferrero, A., Pirola, M., (2006), *Generalised mixed-mode s-parameters,* IEEE Tran. on Microwave Theory and Techniques, Vol. 54, no. 1, pp. 458–463.

[72] Cooman, A., Vandersteen, G., (2015), *Wideband Distortion Contribution Analysis of analogue circuits with differential signalling,* International Conference on Synthesis, Modelling, Analysis and Simulation Methods and Applications to Circuit Design (SMACD), DOI: 10.1109/SMACD.2015.7301674, pp. 1 – 4.

[73] Vulfin, V., Shavit, R., (2015), *Constitutive parameters extraction for thin two-dimensional cylinders based on scattering field measurements,* IET Journals & Magazines of Microwaves, Antennas & Propagation, Vol. 9, Issue 6, DOI: 10.1049/iet-map.2013.0714, pp. 585 – 592.

[74] Potéreau, M., Curutchet, A., D'Esposito, R., De Matos, M., Fregonese, S., Zimmer, T., (2016), *A test structure set for on-wafer 3D-TRL calibration,* International Conference on Microelectronic Test Structures (ICMTS), DOI: 10.1109/ICMTS.2016.7476182, pp. 96 – 99.

[75] Bockelman, D. E., (1997), *Pure-Mode Network Analyser for On-Wafer Measurement of Mixed-mode S-Parameters of Differential Circuits,* IEEE Transaction on Microwave and Techniques, Vol. 45, No. 7, pp. 1071-1077.

[76] Hall, S. H., Hall, G. W., MaCall, J. A., (2000), *High-Speed Digital Systems Design,* John Wiley & Sons Inc., USA, pp. 53-63.

[77] Tesche, F. M., Plane wave coupling to cables, in Handbook of Electromagnetic Compatibility, San Diego, CA, Academic Press 1995, Ch. 4, pp 67-115.

[78] Stolle, R., (2002), Electromagnetic coupling of twisted pair cable, IEEE Journal Sel. Areas Comm., Vol. 20, No 5, pp 883-892.

[79] Armenta, R. B., Sarris, C. D., (2007), Modelling the terminal response of a bundle of twisted-wire pairs excited by a plane wave, IEEE Trans. on EMC, Vol 49, No 4, pp 901-913.

[80] Xiao, F., Murano, K., Kami, Y., (2016), Prediction of electromagnetic radiation from coupled differential microstrip pairs due to skew and imbalance, 7th Asian Pacific Symposium on EMC, Vol. No. pp 683-686.

[81] Grassi, F., Yang, Y., Wu, X., Spadacini, G., (2015), On mode conversion in geometrically unbalanced differential lines and its analogy with crosstalk, IEEE Trans on EMC, Vol 57, No 2, pp 283-291.

[82] Kenny, R.., Reeves, S., Ford, K., Grosh,J. W., Stutzman, S., Anderson, R., Wiekhorst, D., Johnston, F., Cable utilising varying lay length mechanism to minimise alien crosstalk, U.S. Patent Application 2005/0279528 A1, Dec 22, 2006

[83] Hopkinson, W., Hayes, T., Antonijevic, B., Master, C., Beames, R., Wyer, E., Black, R., Method and apparatus for forming cable media, U.S. Patent Application. 2006/0059883 A1, Mar 23, 2006.

[84] Stutzman, S., Wiekhorst, D., Johnston, F. W., Juengst, S., Multi-pair cable with varying lay lengths, U.S. Patent 7550676B 2, Jun 23, 2009.

[85] Huynh, A., Hakanssan, P., Gong, S., (2007), *Mixed-mode S-parameter Conversion of Networks with Coupled Differential Signals*, Proceedings of the 37th European Microwave Conference, pp. 238-241.

[86] Rajamani, V., Bunting, C. F., West, J.C., (2012), Stirred-Mode Operation of Reverberation Chambers for EMC Testing, IEEE Transactions on Instrumentation and Measurement, Vol. 61, Issue 10, DOI: 10.1109/TIM.2012.2196398, pp 2759 – 2764.

[87] Gagliardi, L., Micheli, D., Gardoni, G., Moglie, F. Primiani, V. M., (2015), *Coupling Between Multipath Environment Through a large Aperture*, IEEE Antenna, and Wireless Propagation Letters, Vol. 14, No. 7057544, pp. 1463-1466.

[88] Hollander, F., Probability Theory: *The Coupling Method,* Mathematical Institute, Leiden University, The Netherlands, [Online] Available http://websites.math.leidenuniv.nl/probability/lecturenotes/CouplingLectures.pdf.

[89] Max Integrated, Understanding Common-mode signal. Available. [Online] https://www.maximintegrated.com/en/app-notes/index.mvp/id/2045 Assessed April 2018.

[90] Gradoni, G., Antonson, T. M., Anlage, S. M., Ott, E., (2014*), Random coupling models for the interconnected wireless environment,* IEEE Inter. Symposium on EMC, DOI: 1109/ISEMC.2014.6899076, pp 792-797.

[91] Hugh, G. S., Kang, V. Duffy, A. P., *Reverberation chamber testing of noise coupling to category cabling,* in the Proceeding of 62nd IWCS, Rhodes Island, 2011.

[92] Alistair, D., Hugh, G. S., Alyse, R. G., Choon-see Lee, Hodge, K.G., (2006), *Cable coupling measurement in a reverberation chamber,* in the proceeding of 56th IWCS, Rhodes Island.

[93] Chunqing, X., (2013), *Research of balanced network measurement based on vector network analyser,* IEEE Conference on Electronic Measurement & Instruments ICEMI, pp 361-365

[94] Huynh, A., Karlsson, M., Gong, S., *Mixed-mode s-parameters and conversion techniques,* [Online]. Available: www.intechopen.com . Assessed Feb 2018

[95] Samamori, T., (2014), *S-Parameter method and its application for antenna measurements,* IEICE Trans. on Comm., Vol. E97-B, No. 10, pp. 2011-2021.

[96] Vulfin, V., Shavit, R., (2015), *Constitutive parameters extraction for thin two-dimensional cylinders based on scattering field measurements,*

IET Journals & Magazines of Microwaves, Antennas & Propagation, Vol. 9, Issue 6, DOI: 10.1049/iet-map.2013.0714, pp. 585 – 592.

[97] Liu, D., Guan, T., Liu, X., (2015), *Investigating scattering parameters measurements for 50GHz high-speed Printed Circuit Boards (PCBs),* 85th IEEE Conference on Microwave Measurement (ARFTG), No. 15307837, DOI: 10.1109/ARFTG.2015.7162907.

[98] Rohde & Schwarz, (2014). *R&S®ZVA / R&S®ZVB / R&S ® ZNB Vector Network Analysers Operating Manual.* [Online]. Available: http://www.rohde-schwarz.com/en/manual/r-s-zva-r-s-zvb-r-s-zvtoperating-manual-manuals-gb 1_7870 1-2 9013 .html.Assessed 17/09/2017.

[99] Rohde & Schwartz GmbH & Co. KE (DE), Rohde- [Online]. Available: schwartze.com/us/home_48230.html. Assessed, 17/09/2017.

[100] Vulfin, V., Shavit, R., (2015), *Constitutive parameters extraction for thin two-dimensional cylinders based on scattering field measurements,* IET Journals & Magazines of Microwaves, Antennas & Propagation, Vol. 9, Issue 6, DOI: 10.1049/iet-map.2013.0714, pp. 585 – 592.

[101] How to convert 2-Port s-parameters to 4-port s-parameters [Online}. Available: http://ieee802.org.3/bladesg/public/channel_adhoc/boyd_01_0504,pdf. Online. Assessed Aug 31,2017.

[102] Anritsu Application Note, "Three and four port S-parameter measurements," (May 2002.), 11410-00279, Anritsu, Morgan Hill, CA, USA.

[103] Huynh, A., Hakanssan, P., Gong, S., (2007), *Mixed-mode S-parameter Conversion of Networks with Coupled Differential Signals,* Proceedings of the 37th European Microwave Conference, pp. 238-241.

[104] Zhang, N., Kim, K., Lee, H., Nah, W., (2017), *Theory, Simulation and Experiment on Extended Mixed-mode S-parameter in Three-Conductors,* IEEE Transactions on Electromagnetic Compatibility, Vol. 59, Issue 6, DOI: 10.1109/TEMC:2017.2665582, pp. 1932-1939.

[105] Huang, S., (2015), *Technique to improve the accuracy of mixed-mode S-parameters derived from single-ended results and application to shorter test coupon design,* 2015 IEEE Symposium on Electromagnetic Compatibility and Signal Integrity, DOI: 10.1109/EMCSI.2015.7107700, pp 283 – 288.

[106] Fernández, I; Finke, J (2015), Transitivity of reciprocal networks, IEEE Conference on Decision and Control (CDC), December 15-18, Osaka, Japan, pp.1625 – 1630.

[107] IEEE Standards 8802-3-2014 (E) – (2014 1st Ed.), ISO/IEC/IEEE International Standard for Ethernet, pp:1 – 3754.

[108] Shiue, G-H, Shiu, J-H, Tsai, Y-C., Hsu, C-M., (2012), *Analysis of Common-Mode Noise for Weakly Coupled Differential Serpentine Delay Microstrip Line in High-Speed Digital Circuits*, IEEE Transactions on Electromagnetic Compatibility, Vol.54, Issue 3, DOI: 10.1109/TEMC.2011.2173765, pp. 655 – 666.

[109] Shiue, G-H., Shiu, J-H., Tsai, Y-C., Hsu, C-M., (2011), *Analysis of Common mode noise for weakly coupled differential serpentine delay microstrip line in the high-speed digital circuit*, IEEE Transactions on Electromagnetic Compatibility, Vol. 54, Issue 3, DIO: 10.1109/TEMC.2011.2173765.

[110] Grochowski, A., Bhattacharya, D., Viswanathan, T. R., Laker, K., (1997), *Integrated circuit testing for quality assurance in manufacturing: history, current status, and future trends*, IEEE Transactions on Circuits and Systems II: Analog and Digital Signal Processing, Volume 44, Issue: 8, pp 610 – 633.

[111] Lauder, O. M., Marshall, R. C., (2014), *Measurement method, uncertainty and cable balance-with implications for the CDNE-M*, IEEE International Symposium on EMC, Tokyo, No. 14847499, ISBN 978-4-8855-2287-1, pp. 251-254.

[112] Wang, K., Chang, C.-H., Onabajo, M., (2014), *A fully-differential CMOS low-pass notch filter for biosignal measurement devices with high interference rejection*, IEEE 57th International Midwest Symposium on Circuits and Systems, MWSCAS 2014; College Station Hilton Conference Centre College Station; United States, Category number CFP14MID-PRT; Code 114803, DOI: 10.1109/MWSCAS.2014.6908596, pp 1041-1044.

[113] Koledintseva, M., Vincent, T., (2 016), *Comparison of mixed-mode S-parameters in weak and strong coupled differential pairs*, IEEE International Symposium on EMC, No. 16336556, DOI: 10.1109/ISEMC.2016.7571718, pp. 95-97.

[114] Chunquing, X., (2013), *Research of balanced network measurement based on vector network analyser*, IEEE conference on electronic measurement and instruments, Vol. 1, DOI: 10.1109/ICEMI.2013.6743078, pp. 361-365.

[115] Hagmann, J. H., Dickmann, S., (2012), *Determination of common mode currents with generalized mixed-mode parameters*, IEEE International Symposium on EMC (EMC Europe), INSPEC Accession Number:

13225782, DOI: 10.1109/EMCEurope.2012.6396888, Rome, Italy.

[116] Doshi, K., Khristi, Y., Kedia, S., Pradhan, S., (2010), *Time-varying magnetic field coupled noise reduction in low-voltage measurement in superconductors,* IEEE Trans. on Instrumentation and Measurement, Vol. 60, Issue 3, DOI: 10.1109/TIM.2010.2064392, pp 990-995.

[117] Baltag, O., Rosu, G., Rau, M. C., (2017), *Magnetic field of parallel and twisted wire pairs,* 2017 10th Inter. Symposium on Advanced Topics in Electrical Engineering (ATEE), pp 324 – 329.

[118] TIA-1005 (Revision A), May 2012, *Telecommunications Infrastructure Standard for Industrial Premises* Addendum 1-M12-8 X-Coding connector

[119] IEC 62153-4-5: *Metallic communication cables test methods - Part 4-5: Electromagnetic compatibility (EMC)* - Coupling or screening attenuation - Absorbing clamp method.

[120] Hähner, T, Mund, B., (2013), *Balunless Measurement of Coupling Attenuation of Balanced Cables & Components,* Wire and Cable Technology International, Vol. 41, Issue 4, pp 104-107.

[121] Pfeiler, C., Mund, B., (2015), *Balunless measurement of coupling attenuation of screened balanced cables up to 2GHz,* Proceedings of the 64th IWCS Conference, Oct 6th - 8th 2015, Hyatt Regency Atlanta, pp 509 - 518.

[122] www.cablesondemand.com Available Online . assessed April 2018.

[123] IEC 62132-4: *Integrated Circuit-Measurement of Electromagnetic Immunity,* part 4, Direct Power Injection.

[124] Armstrong, K., Williams, T., (2002), EMC Testing Part 5 - Conducted Immunity, EMC Compliance Journal. [Online] Available, www.compliance-club.com.

[125] Duc, L. L., Nan, W., (2014), *Selection of specific s-parameters in multiport measurement for the renormalization technique using 4-port VNA,* Journal of International Council of Electrical Engineers, Vol 3.3, DIO:10.5370/JICEE, 2013.3.3.205, pp 205 – 209.

[126] Wu, X., Grassi, F., Pignari, S. A., Manfredi, P., Ginste, D. V., (2017), *Circuit interpretation and perturbative analysis of DM -to – CM conversion due to bend discontinuities,* IEEE Electrical Design of Advanced Packaging and Systems Symposium (EDAPS), Haining, Hangzhou, China, DOI: 10.1109/EDAPS.2017.8276966, ISSN: 2151-1233, pp 1-3.

[127] Frankel, S., *Multiconductor Transmission line Analysis,* Artech House, Dedham, MA, 1977.

[128] Orhanovic, N., Wanh, P., Tripathi, V. K., (1993), *Time domain simulation of uniorm and nonuniform multiconductor lossy lines by the method of characteristics*, IEEE Trans. on Computer-Aided Design Integrated circuit systems, Vol. 12, No 6, pp 900-904.

[129] Grassi, F., Yang, Y., Wu, X., Spadacini, G., Pignari, A. S., (2015), *On mode conversion in geometrically unbalanced differential lines and its analogy with crosstalk*, IEEE Trans. on EMC, Vol 57, No 2, pp 283-291.

[130] Grassi, F., Spadacini, G., Pignari, A. S., (2013), *The concept of weak imbalance and its role in the emissions and immunity of differential lines*, IEEE Trans. on EMC, Vol.55, No. 6, pp 1346-1349.

[131] Clayton, R. P., 2008, Analysis of Multiconductor Transmission lines, John Wiley & Sons, Inc 2n Ed.,Hoboken, NJ 07030

[132] Spadaccini, G., Pignari, S. A., (2013), *Numerical Assessment of Radiated Susceptibility of Twisted-Wire Pairs with Random Nonuniform Twisting*, IEEE Transactions on Electromagnetic Compatibility, Vol. 55, No. 5, pp 956-964.

[133] Tripathi, V. K., (1975), *Asymmetric coupled transmission lines in an inhomogeneous medium*, IEEE Trans. Microwave Theory Tech., Vol 23, No. 9, pp734 – 739.

[134] Xiao, F., Murano, K., Kami, Y., (2016), *Prediction of the electromagnetic radiation from coupled differential microstrip pairs due to skew and imbalance*, in Proc. Asia-Pacific Int. Symp. Electromagn. Compatibility, Shenzhen, China, pp 683-686.

[135] Gazda, C., Ginste, D. V., Rogier, H., Wu R.-B., Zutter, De D., (2010), *A wideband common-mode suppression filter for bend discontinuities in differential signalling using tightly coupled microstrips*, IEEE Trans. Adv. Packaging, Vol. 33 No. 4, pp 969 – 978.

[136] ITU-T Rec. G117, (2013), *Transmission aspects of unbalance about earth*, Geneva, Switzerland.

[137] Grassi, F., Pignari, A. S., (2013), *Immunity to conducted noise of data transmission along DC power lines involving twisted-wire pairs above ground*, IEEE Trans. on EMC, Vol.55, No1, pp 195-207.

[138] "atlc2-Arbitrary Transmission Line calculation" [Online]. Available: http://www.hdtvprimer.com/KQ6QV/atlc2.html. Assessed February 2018.

INDEX